Jacques Ranci
Contempora

Also available from Continuum

Althusser's Lesson, Jacques Rancière

Chronicles, Jacques Rancière

Dissensus, Jacques Rancière

The Politics of Aesthetics, Jacques Rancière

Mallarmé, Jacques Rancière

Jacques Rancière: An Introduction, Joseph J. Tanke

Jacques Rancière: Education, Truth, Emancipation,
edited by Gert Biesta and Charles Bingham

Reading Rancière, edited by Paul Bowman and Richard Stamp

Jacques Rancière and the Contemporary Scene

The Philosophy of Radical Equality

Edited by
Jean-Philippe Deranty and Alison Ross

continuum

Continuum International Publishing Group

The Tower Building   80 Maiden Lane
11 York Road   Suite 704
London SE1 7NX   New York NY 10038

www.continuumbooks.com

British Library Cataloguing-in-Publication Data
A catalogue record for this book is available from the British Library.

ISBN: HB: 978-1-4411-3361-8
        PB: 978-1-4411-1409-9

Library of Congress Cataloging-in-Publication Data
Jacques Rancière and the contemporary scene : the philosophy of radical
equality / [edited by] Jean-Philippe Deranty and Alison Ross.
   p. cm.
Includes bibliographical references (p.   ).
ISBN 978-1-4411-3361-8 (hardcover) – ISBN 978-1-4411-1409-9 (pbk.) –
ISBN 978-1-4411-2771-6 (ebook (epub)) – ISBN 978-1-4411-5297-8 (ebook
(pdf)) 1. Rancière, Jacques. I. Deranty, Jean-Philippe.
II. Ross, Alison, 1968- III. Title.
B2430.R274J33 2012
194–dc23   2011031386

Typeset by Deanta Global Publishing Services, Chennai, India
Printed and bound in India

Contents

Acknowledgements

The editors would like to thank Mark Howard for his assistance in the preparation of the final manuscript. This project has also benefited from the 2010 workshop on 'Jacques Rancière and the Philosophy of Radical Equality' held in conjunction with the Research Unit in European Philosophy at Monash University. This workshop had the support of the Australian Research Council Discovery Project scheme (Persuasive Force: The role of aesthetic experience in moral persuasion). We are especially grateful to Jacques Rancière for his involvement in this collection.

J-P. D and A. R.

Contributors

J. M. BERNSTEIN is University Distinguished Professor of Philosophy at the New School for Social Research. He works primarily in the areas of aesthetics and the philosophy of art, ethics, critical theory and German Idealism. Among his books are: *The Philosophy of the Novel* (Minneapolis, 1984); *The Fate of Art: Aesthetic Alienation from Kant to Derrida and Adorno* (Oxford, 1992); *Adorno: Disenchantment and Ethics* (New York, 2001); *Against Voluptuous Bodies: Late Modernism and the Meaning of Painting* (Stanford, 2006); he edited and wrote the introduction for *Classic and Romantic German Aesthetics* (New York, 2003). He is presently at work on book provisionally entitled: *Torture and Dignity: Reflections on Moral Injury.*

JEAN-PHILIPPE DERANTY is Associate Professor of Philosophy at Macquarie University, Sydney. He has written extensively on contemporary French and German philosophy. His recent publications include the edited volume *Jacques Rancière. Key Concepts* (Acumen, 2010).

TODD MAY is Class of 1941 Memorial Professor of the Humanities at Clemson University. He is the author of ten books of philosophy, including *The Political Philosophy of Poststructuralist Anarchism and Gilles Deleuze: An Introduction.* Two of his recent books are concerned with the political thought of Jacques Rancière: *The Political Thought of Jacques Rancière: Creating Equality,* and *Contemporary Movements and the Thought of Jacques Rancière: Equality in Action.* He has just finished a manuscript on the political role of friendship in the contemporary period.

DMITRI NIKULIN is Professor of Philosophy at the New School for Social Research in New York. He is the author of the books *Metaphysik und Ethik: Theoretische und praktische Philosophie in Antike und Neuzeit.* (C. H. Beck, 1996); *Matter, Imagination and Geometry: Ontology, Natural Philosophy and Mathematics in Plotinus, Proclus and Descartes.* (Ashgate, 2002); *On Dialogue.* (Lexington, 2006) and *Dialectic and Dialogue.* (Stanford University Press, 2010).

PAUL PATTON is Professor of Philosophy at The University of New South Wales in Sydney, Australia. His publications deal with aspects of French poststructuralist philosophy, Nietzsche and a variety of topics in contemporary political philosophy. He is the author of *Deleuze and the Political* (Routledge, 2000) and *Deleuzian Concepts: Philosophy, Colonization, Politics* (Stanford, 2010).

CAROLINE PELLETIER is a lecturer at the Institute of Education, University of London. Her research is concerned with new media, social and cultural theory, and subjectivity. Recent publications include essays on Rancière in *Psychodynamic Practice*, the *International Journal of Research and Method in Education*; and *Discourse: studies in the cultural politics of education*.

JACQUES RANCIÈRE is Emeritus Professor of Philosophy at Paris 8 University. He is the author of numerous books covering a wide range of topics, from the history of the labour movement, to education, politics, historiography, literature, the visual arts and film. All of his books have been translated into English. His most recent publication in French is *Les Ecarts du cinéma* (La Fabrique, 2011).

EMMANUEL RENAULT teaches Philosophy at the École Normale Supérieure de Lyon and is the director of Actuel Marx. His book publications include *Marx et l'idée de critique* (PUF, 1995); *Hegel, La naturalisation de la dialectique* (Vrin, 2001); *Où en est la théorie critique?* (La Découverte, 2003); *Mépris social. Ethique et politique de la reconnaissance* (Editions du Passant, 2nd ed., 2004); *L'Expérience de l'injustice. Reconnaissance et clinique de l'injustice* (La Découverte, 2004) and *Souffrance sociale* (La Découverte, 2008).

ALISON ROSS is a member of the Research Unit in European Philosophy, Monash University, Australia. She is the author of *The Aesthetic Paths of Philosophy: Aesthetic Presentation in Kant, Heidegger, Lacoue-Labarthe and Nancy* (Stanford University Press, 2007). Her current project deals with the role of aesthetic elements in moral persuasion.

ANDREW SCHAAP teaches politics at the University of Exeter. He is the author of *Political Reconciliation* (Routledge 2005) and editor of *Law and Agonistic Politics* (Ashgate 2009) and (with Danielle Celermajer & Vrasidas Karalis) *Power, Judgment and Political Evil: In Conversation With Hannah Arendt*. His current research investigates the history and politics of the Aboriginal Embassy in Canberra, Australia. He is also writing a book called *Human*

Rights and the Political, which examines how Hannah Arendt's notion of the 'right to have rights' has been taken up in continental philosophy.

LISA TRAHAIR is senior lecturer in the School of English, Media and Performing Arts at the University of New South Wales. She is author of *The Comedy of Philosophy: Sense and Nonsense in Early Cinematic Slapstick* (SUNY, 2007) and is currently working on an ARC funded project entitled 'Film as Philosophy: What is Cinematic Thinking?' with Dr Robert Sinnerbrink (Macquarie University) and Dr Gregory Flaxman (University of North Carolina). Her contribution to this volume was made possible by this funding.

Chapter 1

Jacques Rancière and the Contemporary Scene: The Evidence of Equality and the Practice of Writing

Jean-Philippe Deranty and Alison Ross

One of the most fascinating features of Rancière's thinking is the contribution that is made to the articulation of his views by the style of his writing and the tone of his voice. Indeed, as the essays in this collection demonstrate – each grappling in its own way with the difficulty of doing justice, both in exposition and in criticism, to his fluid arguments and delayed conclusions – it is, in fact, impossible to dissociate the conceptual tenor of Rancière's claims from the context and manner in which they are articulated. This intrinsic performative dimension of Rancière's philosophical writing applies especially to the guiding axiom of his thinking, the axiom of equality. Equality for Rancière cannot be demonstrated through induction or deduction; it can only be verified locally and problematically in practice. Such practical verification of equality, which for Rancière constitutes the core definition of politics, involves a series of moves and displacements within existing discourses, since politics for him aims fundamentally at challenging a given 'sharing/dividing (*partage*) of the sensible'.[1] This core discursive dimension of the verification of equality, however, has ripple effects in the different universes of established thought, which prop up, through reasons and explanations, the existing discourses of society. In other words, the practical verification of equality aims to achieve 'real life' effects, but in all necessity is also waged in discourse and in thought, and thus necessarily enrols the theorist in its process.

This conjunction of a practical verification of equality in action, in discourse and in thought is most eminently represented in the now-famous historical figure, reawakened by Rancière, of the nineteenth-century revolutionary pedagogue Joseph Jacotot. Jacotot's idea of the 'equality of intelligences', as retold by Rancière, does not amount to a puzzling, counter-factual idea. Rather, equality exists as the very condition of intelligence. This is because 'intelligence' is not measured by 'comparing knowledge with its object' but is rather 'the power to make oneself understood through another's verification'.[2] As Jacotot/Rancière claim:

> There are no madmen except those who insist on inequality and domination, those who want to be right. Reason begins when discourses organized with the goal of being right cease, begins where equality is recognized: not an equality decreed by law or force, not a passively received equality, but an equality in act, verified, at each step by those marchers who, *in their constant attention to themselves and in their endless revolving around the truth, find the right sentences to make themselves understood by others.*[3]

Here we find articulated together a theory of revolutionary practice that challenges simultaneously social attitudes, ways of using speech and the theories that accompany these attitudes and forms of speech. In particular, this passage stresses the work on the self that the practice of equality in the act of communication requires. It is difficult not to take such a passage as an implicit description by Rancière of his own method. Accordingly, the acts of speaking and writing are moral and political acts because they display 'the intention to communicate', to recognize 'the other as an intellectual subject capable of understanding what another intellectual subject wants to say to him'.[4]

The immediate problem that arises, however, and the great irony, is that the exhortation to 'find the right sentences to make [oneself] understood by others'[5] and to recognize the moral dimension of what it is that 'an intellectual subject' wants to say to another such subject,[6] skirts over the difficulty that the reader often faces in isolating 'Rancière's' position. What is it that Rancière wants to say, in among the words he uses for his presentation of the views of others? If equality is to be verified in action and in thought by finding the right sentences to make oneself understood by others, how come so many of Rancière's texts appear so abstruse and, indeed, as Badiou once nastily remarked, so afraid of drawing conclusions?[7] Why and how does Rancière entrust his difficult writing with the task of the verification of equality? How can we relate Rancière's precise practice of writing with his quest for the verification of equality?

Of course, Rancière's writings do not avoid categorical statements, but when these occur they tend to have a specific form. Some of his polemical treatments of the doxa of the contemporary theoretical scene, such as the 'hatred of democracy' or the understanding of 'ethics' as an infinite call to an anonymous other, would be some such examples. However, by his own admission the choice of style and tone in his other works intends a challenge to the 'distribution of roles', which, he says, 'concerns the status of my own assertions as well. I have tried to offer them as *probable* assertions, to avoid a certain affirmative, categorical style which I know is elsewhere encouraged in philosophy, but which I have never been able to assimilate.'[8] How do you effectively communicate a presupposition like 'equality' when this latter is specifically understood to work against the presumption of incapacity? When he discusses Jacotot, Rancière cites this probabilistic style and qualifies the axiom of equality in a voice that merges his position with Jacotot's own: 'It is true that we don't know that men are equal. We are saying that they *might* be. This is our opinion, and we are trying, along with those who think as we do, to verify it.'[9] A style in which the emphasis falls on what is probable is one way of communicating the presupposition of equality, but there are many others, not least the voice that one adopts on political questions and topics. Does this style of writing support an idea that is a mere fiction? How do we measure the precise hold of equality, as Rancière understands the term, outside the specific voices that sustain it in his writing? Where and how does one look for evidence to verify the axiom of equality? Are the words of these particular voices sufficient? How should these words be written about so they do justice to these voices' claims?

One answer comes by way of a prestigious reference, as when Rancière states in an interview that: 'If, among the thinkers of my generation, there was one I was quite close to at one point, it was Foucault'. He continues: 'Something of Foucault's archaeological project – the will to think the conditions of possibility of such and such a form of statement or such and such an object's constitution – has stuck with me.'[10] This gesture of acknowledgement is significant for a number of reasons. Foucault, of course, also eschewed the demand for 'solutions' and 'programmes' of political action and understood such demands to be paternalistic. In particular, this link to the Foucault of 'archaeology' may be used to show how Rancière's presupposition in favour of equality, a presupposition that, as the comments on Jacotot (cited above) indicate, is confirmed in acts of communication, is guided by 'evidence' rather than mere speculative warrant, in the sense that it is only exercised in specific cases and contexts of interaction. Foucault's 'method' provides an exemplary model of how to accompany – through work within the realms of thought and writing – the work performed by individuals and groups in social life to challenge existing definitions and boundaries.

Therefore, the first feature of the practice of writing that is adequate to the verification of equality is that it be steeped in historiography.

Rancière's reference to Foucault shows most eminently that it is not his insistence on 'equality' *per se* that marks out Rancière's unusual place in the contemporary philosophical scene, but rather the distinctive manner in which he approaches the topics of his research. For this approach, the status of 'knowledge' is broadly understood. Hence *The Names of History* treats the redeployment of certain techniques and conceptions of literary meaning for the establishment of historical claims. This approach allows Rancière to identify and analyse the system of preconceptions and procedures of authentication that makes features of ordinary life discernible as facts relevant for historical 'knowledge'. Or, to take a more recent example, the modern constitution of a new sense of 'aesthetic value' is analysed from the perspective of the conceptual presuppositions that potentially admit any and all kinds of artefacts and experience into the 'aesthetic regime'. In this case, what is within the 'aesthetic regime of the arts' is potentially anything; but despite this apparent ubiquity, certain identifiable protocols and preconceptions work to determine how mundane things qualify to become aesthetically significant.

However, the verification of equality occurs not just through the historiographical problematizing of taken-for-granted knowledge claims and disciplinary boundaries. Other key features of Rancière's writing are also particularly noteworthy and help to dissolve the two apparent paradoxes noted above; namely, the obscurity and wilful inconclusiveness of his praxeological egalitarianism.

As Rancière tells us in this volume, the key obstacle to equality is identity, and it is this obstacle that he has consistently sought to undermine throughout his work.[11] Political struggles seek to undo the knots, which, by tying together ways of being, ways of doing and ways of speaking, construct frames of domination and marginalization. In parallel ways, theoretical work aims to undo the identitarian and substantializing logics at play in modes of discourse, forms of expression and schemes of thought. We might say that this is Rancière's own version of understanding the nexus of knowledge and power. This task has not just a deconstructive, critical dimension, but also a constructive one; and deconstruction and reconstruction are themselves performed in a subjective and an objective mode. That is, political actors and the politically committed theorist engage in critique and construction, both as their agents – directly confronting various hurdles and oppositions – and as observers of these practices and their oppositions. At the theoretical level, critique and construction occur through a politics of reading and a politics of writing.[12]

On the deconstructive side, Rancière's practice of writing seeks, as we saw above, to first of all denaturalize social categories through historiographical contextualization. Rancière's deconstructive work is also typically performed at the direct logical level, in identifying and highlighting the *non sequitur* hidden in many taken-for-granted arguments. As Badiou correctly remarks, one of Rancière's favourite gestures is to undermine the master's self-assurance.[13] Indeed, in many cases, notably in the paradigmatic figure of Jacotot, and also through all the forgotten figures of proletarian writers, like Gauny, the gesture of proving the master wrong is performed from the perspective of 'those who have no part', in merging the theorist's own discourse with their voices. In this respect, Rancière's well-studied use of free indirect style thus serves a double purpose: to rearticulate the repressed logical revolts of the dominated; and/or, to modestly borrow from them their valuable objections and alternative solutions. Rereading the 'archives of the proletarian dream' (*The Nights of Labour's* subtitle) is thus simultaneously a subjective and objective way of revolting at the level of the logos. Entomological historiographical research, reconstruction of the poetics and logics of proletarian discourse, and critical analysis of the hidden premises of the social and human sciences, are only different sides of the same critical work.

On the constructive side, Rancière's practice of writing reaches a deeper level, one that must be called ontological. The fact that knowledge and power, the discourse and the practices of social domination, are intertwined in a tight nexus means that one cannot rearrange the stage after its background hierarchical mechanisms have been debunked without reassembling together material and ideal elements. Indeed, in the rejection of material practices of exclusion and their accompanying discourses and thoughts, it is also taken-for-granted ontological divisions that are challenged: the passive and the active; subject and object; nature and spirit; the material and the symbolic. How does this affect the practice of writing? Rancière's models here are the great modernist poets and novelists (Baudelaire, Mallarmé, Rimbaud, Flaubert, Proust), who all searched, each under a different guise, for a new language that would overcome the gap between the symbolic, the material and the natural. Rimbaud in particular seems to present a model for Rancière:

The point is not to read but to write. Rimbaud does not read the theories of his century; he writes the century that brings them together. And writing a century, whatever the erudite might say, does not require a great number of preparatory studies, but rather and more simply an attentive gaze able to make some writings intersect that ordinarily feature on different shelves of a library.[14]

A few pages later he asserts that: 'Rimbaud writes his century. He determines (*fixe*) its codes and emblems. He establishes its coordinates and traces between them all possible liaisons within the same space. He makes it obvious and, in the same instant, illegible.'[15]

We want to suggest that this description of Rimbaud's poetic practice could very well be Rancière's secret confession of his ideal methodology. Indeed, it would be easy to show that Rancière's literary and film criticism, as well as his political writings, follows a programme of this kind.[16] The paradox of a verification of equality that remains obscure and inconclusive would thereby be resolved or, at the very least, be explicable from the perspective of its stated motivations and desired effects: the obscurity might be understood as the apparent complexity that results when our habitual frames of reference and modes of perception are challenged and new constellations and relations between things, between words, and between words and things, are suggested. Similarly, inconclusiveness may be simply a product of old, misguided expectations, when we face an unknown space that has been opened for new forms of practice. More generally, the poetic rationale for Rancière's deliberate evasion of the magnetic pull of consensus lies in this model of the careful perusal of forms in such a way that the contingent taxonomies of existing forms of order are distilled and disrupted without new ones taking their place.

Questions remain, however, regarding the salience of such a 'methodology' for tackling the substantial challenges involved in providing an insightful treatment of the hierarchical composition and lines of prevailing social order and sketching out possible responses to these. Moreover, the prospects and 'results' of this 'methodology' in art criticism have also provoked querulous responses.[17] As we have seen, Rancière's practice of writing intends to diminish the apparent gap between aesthetic questions and the forms and problems of politics. It is a corollary of Rancière's poetic approach that he identifies a wider field of sources as being relevant for the critical understanding of the functioning of social order than is generally the case in political theory. Indeed his most recent discussions of visual art and film deliberately hook these fields up with questions at the core of the political order of the community. In our view, the breadth of sources that Rancière's writing covers, together with its distinctive voice and methodology, make the critical assessment of his relation to various figures and topics within the conventionally distinct fields he writes on a central task in the emerging debate over his work.

This collection has as its primary aim the critical evaluation of Rancière's singular work in several of its most prominent fields of engagement. The order of the essays starts with studies of the poetic logic of his method and works back to the analysis of its original contexts of political reflection. The first four essays treat works of Rancière's in which the poetic dimension of his writing is in the foreground: there are two essays on film, followed by critical treatments of Rancière's advocacy for the poetic dimension of historical writing and his idiosyncratic revisions of modern aesthetic theory. The fifth essay treats the topic of Rancière's work in education, a topic of signal importance in classical and modern treatments of politics, and the next five follow on from this to focus especially on Rancière's significant interlocutors (such as Arendt and Marx) as well as themes (work and anarchism) and problems (such as his revision of what political theory means) in his writing on politics. The collection concludes with Rancière's reflections on the main topics and issues that have shaped his work, from the early political writing to the later focus on aesthetics.

The opening essay by J. M. Bernstein is an incisive treatment of the democratic and popular dimension of cinema. Bernstein examines the political status of film as 'democratic' in light of the dimensions that accrue to this term in Rancière's categories of the 'aesthetic regime' and the 'film fable'. However, this essay has much broader significance than an analysis of Rancière's thinking in the field of cinema. Bernstein queries the habituated approach to the arts and especially the disdain for popularity that blocked from view the ways that film fulfiled the status of an engaging stimulus and occasion for the practice of criticism. He inflects this practice specifically in relation to the unique conditions movies provide for probing the intelligibility of one's life and circumstances. Films do this on account of their singular capacity to provide compelling presentations of the prosaic and the ordinary without the awkwardness of theatrical artifice. Bernstein's essay draws attention to some of the salient consequences of this hypothesis – chief among them are the implications of the fact that, in his words, 'Movies are modern in the way that no other art form is because, in virtue of the manner in which the image function is tethered to its object world, they are more fully anchored in their time than other modern art forms.'

Lisa Trahair also takes up the topic of Rancière's writing on cinema, but her essay focuses specifically on the particular conceptual machinery (such as, the sentence image and symbolic montage) that organizes Rancière's analyses of Godard's *Histoire(s) du cinéma*. This essay grapples with the subtlety of Rancière's critically motivated account of Godard and the shifts in emphasis and focus that the differently located frames of the sentence-image and symbolic montage enable. The focus of her essay falls on whether the sequence of ideas (or the practice of thinking) generated out of Godard's film can be adequately accessed and analysed through Rancière's conceptual terminology.

Rancière has often pointed out the way that the meaning of prosaic things or elevated art forms are themselves written, in the broad sense of the liaisons that words conjugate between things and the meanings that these conjugations impart, even, if not especially, in the so-called 'visual arts'. One prominent example in his recent work in aesthetics is the moralizing function of Godard's voice-over in his *Histoire(s)*.[18] The next two essays move beyond the case studies of the visual arts to focus on the meanings that Rancière intends for his writing to impart, respectively, to the writing of history and the writing of the history of aesthetics.

Dmitri Nikulin examines the complex question of the allocation of intelligible meaning to previously inaudible voices in modern historical writing. His essay asks whether one should look at the ways in which proper names are kept and accounted for *in* history, rather than at the names *of* history, as Rancière's *The Names of History* suggests. Structured as a critical reflection and evaluation of Rancière's understanding of the exigencies of history writing, Nikulin illuminates the workings of history with 'restricted' narratives by looking both at recent Eurocentric historiography as well as the ways in which history constitutes itself when it does not yet understand itself as a highly reflective historical enterprise, as it is practised in the works of Hecataeus, Herodotus and Tacitus.

Next, Alison Ross's essay argues that what separates Rancière from the Romantic attempt to find political significance in aesthetic experience, is the priority he gives to the meaning of 'words' over the meaning of 'things'. Her essay thus looks at the conceptual logic that guides his treatment of topics such as Michelet's revision of history writing or the ontology of Deleuze. She argues that despite his frequent positive references to Kant and Schiller, it is Rancière's occasional references to Hegel's aesthetics that provide important insights into the motives and consequences of his critical revision of Romanticism. Her essay focuses specifically on the ways in which Rancière uses the motif of the story to attach a series of political expectations to his distinctive recasting of the practice of finding aesthetic significance in everyday things in thinkers like Walter Benjamin.

At the mid-point in this volume, Caroline Pelletier's essay treats the key moment on which the progression of Rancière's work hinges, namely, the figure of Jacotot and his method of 'universal teaching'. Pelletier rereads Rancière's free-indirect recount of Jacotot's method from the perspective of contemporary education theory. She thereby provides a particularly telling illustration of the 'untimeliness' of Rancière's performative essays in egalitarian interventions. As she shows, 'universal teaching is not a pedagogic model to be followed through, and debates about education have evolved since *The Ignorant Schoolmaster* was first published'. Indeed, *The Ignorant Schoolmaster* was never intended as a tract to correct or replace other models. At the same time, however, this perpetually untimely piece of writing radically challenges the coordinates of educational thinking. In Pelletier's words, it 'makes a case for a different problematic; a different justification for education. One which starts from the "illusion" of equality [...] experiments with ways of demonstrating this, [and] opens up again the possibility of seeing teaching/learning as a hopeful endeavour, concerned not with knowing the world, but with creating it anew.'

Following Pelletier's assessment of the place of Rancière's Jacotian arguments in educational research, the stage is then set for the essays dealing with the formation, significance and impact of Rancière's political thought. The essays by Todd May and Paul Patton help us to get a better understanding of its place within the scene of contemporary political thought by locating it in relation to the traditions of anarchism, post-structuralism and liberalism.

Todd May's essay begins by establishing the premise we have encountered several times now, according to which equality is demonstrated simultaneously in action and in the performative practices of writing and reading. As he writes: 'Rancière's texts are often short and suggestive. This, one might argue, is in keeping with the requirements of his thought. It seems to imply the equal intelligence of his readers. His writings do not tease us with obscure references or jargon, and neither do they explain themselves exhaustively. This invites the reader to engage with his texts; but this invitation is one not only to read but also to think and to work.' In his response to this invitation, May carefully constructs his understanding of the exact import of key Rancièrian declarations regarding the identity of politics and democracy and the assumption of radical equality. For May, these core Rancièrean theses have to be seen as new ways to articulate a modern conception of anarchism. Rancière, he argues, has to be taken at his word when Rancière writes that 'democracy means ... anarchic "government," one based on nothing other than the absence of every title to govern'; and this, in turn, means 'to act alongside others in a common creation of governing that stems from a common presupposition of equality'.

Paul Patton's essay takes a more critical perspective than either Pelletier's or May's endorsement of the utopian approach in political theory and education found in Rancière's writing. For Patton, Rancière promotes a series of utopian theses that depend on the cogency of his revision of what political theory means. It is the frailty of the terms of this revision that occupy Patton's attention. He takes a comparative approach to show that the types of questions and problems that are important in the liberal tradition of political philosophy, and which concern substantive issues such as access to resources and ways of achieving the redistribution of such goods, are generally disparaged in favour of the radical commitments held by the grouping commonly called 'post-structuralist', and in which he includes work by Deleuze and Guattari, Derrida and Foucault. In Patton's view, this tradition leaves to one side the awkward question of how to make concrete changes, and also, how to defend the value of particular political projects. Ultimately, Patton questions whether Rancière's writing is able to justify his idiosyncratic redefinitions of politics and democracy when those redefinitions are deprived of the normative structure that gives terms such as these their bite in the work of left egalitarian liberals such as Rawls. Rancière's writing on political topics, he concludes, 'resembles the just-so stories of postmodern social reality that Baudrillard candidly described as "theory-fictions". Just as Rancière is right to refuse the label of political philosophy for his stipulative redefinitions of politics and democracy so we should refuse to accept such analyses as political sociology.'

The next set of essays focus on Rancière's complex relationship with two constitutive reference points for the contemporary scene: one, Hannah Arendt, a key figure for those who seek to pursue political theory outside the mainstream framework of political liberalism; the other, Karl Marx, the overwhelming reference in radical politics in France at the time when Rancière was beginning to find his own voice. These studies face the specific difficulty of accurately gauging the full implications of Rancière's performative mode of positing the axiom of equality, and the latter's destabilizing effects in established discourse. In relation to such dominant references as Arendt and Marx, this amounts to the difficult task of precisely describing the subtle (and in the case of Marx, substantial evolution in the) interplays of borrowings and displacements, of simultaneous implicit homage and outright rejection that characterize Rancière's mode of relating to key conceptual figures.

In his chapter 'Hannah Arendt and the Philosophical Repression of Politics', Andrew Schaap reconstructs Rancière's complex relationship to Arendt's theory of political praxis. The difficulty here is that, as others have argued, several of the most salient features of Rancière's political thinking, for instance, his suspicion of political philosophy, the opposition he sets up between political subjectivation and social identity, or the aesthetic dimensions of political action, could easily be said to have their origin in, or at least bear a strong family resemblance, with Arendtian arguments. However, Schaap demonstrates that even if he appears to borrow key Arendtian concepts, by unmooring them from their phenomenological and ontological foundations, Rancière substantially transforms them. As a result, what political praxis unveils is not a world as seen through a plurality of perspectives, but the constitutive dissensus at the heart of the community. And the equality at the heart of the dissensus is not the shared quality of select individuals destined for the life of action, but the disruptive force of a universal axiom that anyone can claim.

In his study on 'The Many Marx of Jacques Rancière', Emmanuel Renault carefully follows the many twists and turns in the constantly evolving thread of Rancière's difficult relationships with Marx. This is an important topic to tackle because Rancière references very few authors in any substantial or repeated way throughout his writings. Marx is the striking exception to that rule. This exception makes good sense in the context of Rancière's understanding of emancipation as intellectual emancipation, and his thesis of the equality of intelligences. One clear implication Rancière drew from these key axioms was that the texts and actions of the 'oppressed' should not be used in a manner that would make of them the passive material in which an intelligibility developed elsewhere would somehow be embodied. As a result, rather than covering them up with interpretive tools from the social sciences or the conceptual machinery of classical philosophy, the texts and actions of 'the people' should be quoted and explained for themselves. *The Nights of Labour* is the most striking exemplification of this method of wilful inversion of the intellectual hierarchy, since in the 400 pages dedicated to the 'archive of the proletarian dream', not a single historical or sociological reference in labour movement studies is mentioned, nor any classical philosopher, while the writings of the carpenter Gauny or the seamstresses Désirée Véret and Jeanne Deroin are examined as carefully as the words of Plato or Aristotle would be by academics and scholars. Marx, however, was, for a while at least, an exception, as Rancière believed that he, of all the theorists, developed his conceptual work not outside, above or against the discourses and actions of the oppressed, but in direct response to them.[19]

Very schematically, the trajectory of Rancière's attitude to Marx, as Renault retraces it, goes from fairly dogmatic acceptance in the years preceding and immediately following May 1968, to a vision of Marx's oeuvre as being rife with unresolved tensions (and as being exemplary and useful for that very reason), to the ranking of Marx as a typical 'philosopher', needing his 'poor' the better to exclude them from the realm of meaningful thought and serious action. Renault bemoans the fact that Rancière's unparalleled knowledge of Marx's oeuvre and of Marxist scholarship, which were demonstrated in his early writings, gradually gave way to a fairly reductive criticism, culminating in *The Philosopher and his Poor* – a psychological and sociological attack at odds with Rancière's own anti-sociologism. However, Renault's criticism, by remaining internal to Rancière's work, also uncovers a more productive dimension. The great interest in rereading Rancière's early texts, notably *Althusser's Lesson* and the first articles in *Révoltes logiques* is that they make us realize to what extent Rancière found in Marx the very insights he would later develop against Marx and that would form the staple of his original stance, like the idea of intellectual emancipation, or the need for theory to position itself in a direct dialogue with the oppressed. Looking at the contemporary scene, the lesson to be drawn from this, according to Renault, could be called 'Rancière's Lesson'; namely, that much of what one has learnt about oppression and emancipation might well have been learnt reading Marx, and that it might be useful to remind oneself of it.

In his study of the changing status of the work reference in Rancière's writings, Jean-Philippe Deranty highlights an evolution comparable to the evolution of Rancière's relationship to Marx. That is, while work and the worker were paradigmatic categories in Rancière's thinking and writing early on – particularly in the period leading up to *The Nights of Labour* – it can be shown that their gradual disappearance is in fact only a surface phenomenon, and work and the worker continue to play significant, if underlying, conceptual roles in the later writings. Even Rancière's aesthetic reflection, which could appear to represent a caesura in his work, has its roots in the 'workerist' writings of the previous period. In view of the contemporary scene, this might be another one of the key lessons to be learnt from Rancière's rich body of work; namely, that much of what is said and written today about creation and emancipation might have been discovered before in reflecting on the topics of work and labour.

The final essay in the volume is a new piece by Jacques Rancière: 'Work, Identity, Subject'. The piece sets out a response to Deranty's characterization of his thinking around the 'work' reference, and from here it builds up a retrospective view of what motivated the signal shifts in his thinking, subtly challenging the orthodox accounts of the frameworks in which his key ideas took shape. For instance, he claims to have been decisively influenced by the theatrical metaphor of standing apart from the role-playing of social being, and by the radical ontology of freedom in Sartre's early *Being and Nothingness*. Thus, Rancière re-presents the terms of his early critique of the shaping function claims to identity exerted over political thinking so that the prestigious reference to Marx is replaced by the reference to Sartre's early existential tract. Moreover, he allows that *The Nights of Labour* – his now classic text – references its title to a more literally theatrical reference: Shakespeare's *Twelfth Night*. This revision of his early writing in relation to what is now a largely unfashionable philosophy and the English canon of Shakespearean theatre leads into Rancière's presentation of his aesthetic turn as a way of resolving the problems that he found difficult to negotiate with other resources. Indeed, we see in his most recent work a positive take on thinkers like Schiller, Kant and Hegel, each of whom articulates something important about the leisure time that the aesthetic attitude presupposes. His essay reiterates this stance. As Deranty and Renault each show, themes like leisure time may be cited to show the resilience of Marx's vocabulary in the late work. However, as Rancière insists, in a typical gesture of ironic displacement, it also puts in play a new way of looking at the aesthetic settings of his approach to politics, less as critical takes on the 'masters' of modern philosophical aesthetics than as a generalization of their perspective – one that puts into question set ontological boundaries and leaps into non-aesthetic fields, in particular (and most famously, though not exclusively), politics. It is interesting to consider in what respects the mechanics of such generalization implies a specific kind of normative claim, one that is different to the mode of argumentation in mainstream liberal political philosophy: after all, the requirement of a general access to leisure time as the condition for the freeing experience of aesthetic judgment is a version of Kant's early democratic thesis, which Kant had used against the privileges of the expert, that everyone has the capacity for aesthetic taste and intellectual maturity. The big difference with Kant of course, and the latter's Enlightenment predecessors and Romantic heirs, is that Rancière believes that democratic action and a corresponding practice of reading and writing can always demonstrate this thesis here and now.

Chapter 2

Movies as the Great Democratic Art Form of the Modern World (Notes on Rancière)

J. M. Bernstein

Might it be the case that for identifiable stretches of its history – say, between 1939 and 1963, through the 1970s (the movie brat era), and sporadically before and after – movies have been the great democratic art form about which theorists and critics have dreamed of but always despaired? Could it be that movies were in fact the Holy Grail that progressive thought fantasized: an art form that was both popular and political at the same time, where the orienting political thought was democratic and egalitarian? Perhaps because movies did not look like the art form of their dreams – it did not look like the great works of modern and modernist fiction, drama, painting, poetry, dance or music – because, like democracy itself, movies are conflicted and contradictory, not always imbued with the politically and morally appropriate sentiments – as if any serious art form ever was – they were devalued, even despised. There would be a terrible irony if it turns out that the very art form that has routinely been condemned as failing to even be an art form – as opposed to being a sleek form of mass entertainment designed to distract, the bread and circuses of bourgeois culture – should, unnoticed by all those for whom this was a burning issue, turn out to have been all along the only truly democratic art form of the twentieth century, standing to that century's uprising of democracy as tragedy had to the uprising of Greek democracy.

This thesis would have some plausibility if it could be shown that movies did in fact fulfil the desiderata that a progressive conception of art stipulates for an art form that could bear the weight of our connection to and conviction in the world – or rehearse compellingly the absence of such connection and conviction, the inscape of our despair – in the way claimed for the exemplary achievements of modernism while escaping modernism's fetishized self-consciousness and anti-representational formality. Although Jacques Rancière nowhere makes the strong claim for movies that I am proposing, his way of connecting art and politics, on the one hand, and his manner of connecting movies to the aesthetic regime of art that he takes to be the progressive feature of modern art, on the other hand, provide for the possibility that movies are the achievement of what the other art of the aesthetic regime only promise. A version of that thought is the thesis of this essay.

What, most visibly, made movies unrecognizable as the promised democratic art form is their attachment to what are argued to be outmoded, illusion-producing narrative forms, together with their easy accessibility, which is always interpreted as making them a mass art rather than a popular one, a base rather than a democratic art form. If movies are the great democratic art form of the modern world – taking up the baton from the eighteenth-century novel – their practice will entail the overcoming of the division between high and popular art, the latter notion a term of abuse for those discomforted by the rough and tumble of democratic art.

There is a surprising convergence among sophisticated theories of film that a successful general account of movies requires two axes, which, not altogether arbitrarily, I will denominate as 'image' and 'narrative'. Of course, much of the real debate in the field is precisely how to configure the two axes, and what the relation between them is. I will begin with an elaboration of a dual axis theory that is derived from Jean-Luc Godard's modernist practice, thus providing an exemplary version of a sophisticated theory that is nonetheless motivated by a thesis directly opposed to the democratic thesis: Hollywood movies are paradigmatic episodes of ideological illusion. After opening a space for questioning, I provide an increasingly refined articulation of Rancière's conception of the aesthetic regime of art in the following sections, on the basis of which I claim that the two axes of modern art – narrative and image – deserve to be regarded, *pace* Rancière, as having equal validity and authority. I then play out this thesis in terms of Rancière's own film theory, before concluding with a bare bones elaboration of the democratic hypothesis.

1 Montage, Photography, Narrative, Image etc.

In his historical account of the necessity for a dual axis theory of cinema, V. F. Perkins (in a work that, I believe, remains the best introduction to film theory available) contends that in its earliest manifestations, film theory became established 'as the embodiment of twin mystiques, one of the *image* and the other of *montage*'.[1] The mystique of montage follows the trajectory of modernist formalism; if representative form possesses value, it is as form and not as presentation: 'The representative element in a work of art may or may not be harmful': argued Clive Bell in his standard work *Art*, 'always,' he continues, 'it is irrelevant.'[2] Montage, from this point of view, was to film what pigment, flatness and the delimiting of the flatness of the canvas were to modernist painting. On its own, the image is dead, meaningless, like a mere word outside the sentences in which it can be used; only the connecting of one image with another through editing gives to images life and meaning. Montage, the argument assumes, is the making explicit of the dependence of image-meaning on the contextual ordering provided by editing. This seems naïve and exorbitant in its denial that individual images possess content that is not wholly relational in character. Individual images possess semantic value on their own, constraining how other images can be meaningful in relation to them, even if the character and pervasiveness of those constraints is knowable only a posteriori. Furthermore, images on their own may bespeak a context that they do not directly show. All these concessions are necessary if the simplest photograph is to be acknowledged as possessing some intrinsic intelligibility, and why, a forteriori, the image pole of movies is routinely regarded as exemplifying movies' dependence on the photographic image.

Conversely, the mystique of the image emerges from the conception of a movie as a visual medium that has its basis in the still image, the photographic image. The camera is a recording instrument before it is anything else; its function is to record reality, providing a record of whatever is placed in front of it. Because it is tethered to what it records, the camera cannot create an enclosed or aesthetically self-sufficient world in the way that a sonnet or painting can create such a world. As Perkins underlines, the camera 'does not always *add* significantly to what it records, but its ability to select, mould, heighten, or comment on events is a consequence of its ability to record them'.[3] Because it is the record of an earlier encounter, the image pole of a movie is always ready to ruin its claim to aesthetic self-sufficiency and independence, to have causal history interrupt narrative construction. Of course, to isolate the recording function effectively, it denies the narrative and dramatic aspects of cinema.

However, I do not wish to continue with Perkins' level-headed call for a 'synthesis' (his word) of image and montage, but rather with something more fervid and polemical: Peter Wollen's defence of avant-garde cinema in 'Godard and counter cinema: *vent d'est*'.[4] Wollen opens his essay with a table comparing the seven deadly sins of cinema in opposition to the seven cardinal virtues. I have provided each column with a categorical and a descriptive name.[5]

Identity	*Difference*
(Representing the World)	*(Writing in Images)*
Narrative transitivity	Narrative intransitivity
Identification	Estrangement
Transparency	Foregrounding
Single diegesis	Multiple diegesis
Closure	Aperture
Pleasure	Unpleasure
Fiction	Reality

Since montage was associated with modernist reflexivity, it was natural with the montage-versus-image schema to assume that the image represented the force of reaction. That assumption is turned on its head when montage, as the principle of connectivity, is translated into narrative closure, where closure or homogeneity or static unity is taken as the driving impetus of Hollywood cinema.[6] Godard's post-1968 program was intended to be an inversion of the ideals of Hollywood's cinematic practice. In part, at least, this revision is driven by a structuralist or formalist understanding of narrative as a movement that begins with a state of equilibrium into which a disturbance is introduced – a body is found dead, a gunman comes into town, a new, perhaps, an eligible man appears at a party – that continues until a new equilibrium sufficiently responsive to the original disturbance is found (the killer is found and punished; the nice hero stands up and saves the town; the lovers marry).[7] Once narrative is understood as a pretence of difficulty whose primary function is to vindicate the equilibrium of its closure as one fully responsive to the rupture in the claims of society represented by the initial disturbance, and thus responsive in a more general way to our ideas of justice or happiness or necessity, of what we require as social beings in way of response to what threatens the integrity of our life together, then the rest of the schema follows. The satisfactions of narrative are those of social reassurance: we have acknowledged the threat and found a way to continue, since continue we must; the status quo triumphs, yet again. The assumption here is that the narrative function, a priori so to speak, excludes (represses, conceals, silences, abjects, devalues, disavows) everything that is not functional for the movement from the initial to the concluding equilibrium. Assume now that a state of equilibrium is always either a fiction (the way a frictionless surface is a fiction) or a state of human mortification dressed as satisfaction or satiation, then the movement from original to final equilibrium is a movement from one ideality to another ideality (one dead state to another). The conclusion then becomes irresistible that classic cinematic narratives are fictions, where being a fiction is equivalent to being: a mystification, ideology, lie, deception, illusion, representation – death.[8]

As Wollen is aware, there is a hyperbolic character to the Godardian schema: the virtue/vice structure asks to be taken as absolute, yet while some of the virtues would indeed replace their corresponding vice (multiple diegesis drives out simple diegesis), other virtues are internal correlatives of their corresponding vice: foregrounding is relative to transparency, the idea of everything being foregrounded incoherent – writing in images still requires images with which to write; dissatisfaction must become the bearer of its own form of satisfaction – as tragedy does – if the provocation is to matter; and there can only be quotation and intertextuality if there is a text to be quoted from and a text that quotes. As Wollen notes, Godard belongs in the modern tradition that is 'suspicious of the power of the arts – and the cinema above all – to "capture" its audience without apparently making it think'.[9] The Godardian schema is in this respect hardly innocent, the proposing of one view of the truth of cinema in opposition to another; his counter-cinema means to be a way of destroying cinema, at least as anything remotely continuous with what cinema has been for the past 80 years. Since his dual axis analytic, while more or less continuous with the twin mystiques of image and montage, aims at destruction rather than synthesis, some clarification of Godard's schema is urgent.

There are two interlocking structures driving Godard's project. Wollen nails these twin structures elegantly:

> Especially since May 1968, the attack on fiction has been given a political rationale (fiction = mystification = bourgeois ideology) but, at the beginning, it is much more closely connected with Godard's fascination (Cartesian, rather than Marxist) with the misleading and dissembling nature of appearances, the impossibility of reading an essence from a phenomenal surface, of seeing a soul through and within a body or telling a lie from a truth.[10]

While scepticism about the arts can seem like art's own shadow, there is an especial fierceness in Godard's critique since the spontaneous charge of the photographic image from which the moving image derives is towards transparency, discretely removing itself from the appearing of the object it reveals to become a record of what appeared; and it is the authority of the cinematic image that is then transferred onto the cinematic narrative that makes the latter appear as reliable and authoritative as the images delivering it (above and beyond the authority achieved through narrative order itself). If the basis of the authority of every other art is its material removal from its worldly objects, forcing upon it an internality or reflexivity or autonomy (call it literarity or painterliness, or musicality), then each artwork's very appearing bespeaks its detachment from the world, its unreality, its potential for emptiness. Hence for traditional arts, the philosophically freighted question is always: how might something that is necessarily structurally detached from experience and the world, which neither explains the world the way science does nor normatively reorders it the way morality does, matter to human self-understanding? The traditional arts bear their emptiness on their sleeve, making their seductions so transparent as to make one wonder what the sceptic is worried about.

Cinema is otherwise: it solves the traditional problem of the arts – how works can acquire attachment to world and experience – effortlessly. It is that effortlessness – 'Reproducing the world is the only thing film does automatically,'[11] as Stanley Cavell has it – that makes movies seem to be simultaneously the fullest satisfaction of the desire to recover the world, reproduce it, and an unforgivable deception, making every other sceptical denial of art appear lame in comparison. With movies, the more natural sceptical question is: how could anything so causally bound to the world rise to the level of art?[12] Put that question aside. Godard's cinephilia cannot bear the weight of his Cartesian anxieties about surfaces and appearances any more than it can bear his Marxist scepticism about ideal wholes and the satisfactions they arouse in the midst of a corrupt, unjust world. Although looking uncannily like a reversion to modernist self-consciousness, Godard's counter cinema can more rightly be diagnosed as (a sceptical) cinephobia. But this is equally to say that at stake in providing a dual axial account of movies is the relation between modern and modernist art as it gets played out in cinema.

What makes Godard's virtues suspect is that rather than being mechanisms that might aid cinema in entrenching itself in its sources of authority, the devices and formalities Godard deploys (as listed by Wollen) are intended to be, precisely, inversions – brute negations of the vices they correct. But this makes Wollen's apparently innocent use of the language of virtue and vice strangely apt: the virtues are not, effectively, cinematic structures, but rather defences against the threat of epistemic, emotional, moral, and political deception – sin – as if every desire satisfied and belief affirmed were a further step into darkness, into the quagmire of ideological delusion.

Behind this moralized schematism of cinematic experience lies, as my titling of the competing columns suggests, a crude structure of identity and difference. Each virtue Wollen lists arrives as a mechanism for ruining and rupturing affirmations of identity: unity, closure, transparency, empathy and so on. The virtues of difference – heterogeneity, gaps and interruptions, emotional distance, medium reflexivity, open-endedness, quotation and parody, displeasure – receive all their force and authority from the identity they purportedly undo. Those differences need those forms of identity to matter, and nothing in the argument or the practice makes compelling that they could matter on their own. If, however, these virtues are not spontaneous structures but possess just the force of a corrective, salutary reminders of something we may have forgotten, then what is the force of what they contest? It looks like sin is more original than virtue on this account, and hence that *all* of film's authority derives from the vices that Godard's virtues work to sceptically undermine. It is this that makes the placement of 'reality' on the side of writing in images fraught; transparency belongs to the logic of the photographic image, a logic that tracks the relation between image and world. In order for 'reality' to belong to difference – in a manner in which in accordance with the very idea of a writing in images, it should not – it must be presupposed that narrative closure turns the transparency of the image from a mark of the real into an illusion, a fiction. Only then could the destruction of narrative unity yield 'reality' (via what amounts to a second-order transparency).

Although he does not fully unravel his claim, Wollen does insist that there are 'various confusions' in Godard's strategy 'which blunt its edges and even, at times, tend to nullify it – mainly, these concern his confusion over the series of terms: fiction/mystification/ideology/lies/deception/illusion/representation'.[13] On any reasonable analysis these terms are not interchangeable. What prima facie plausibility can be gathered for their being equated will have to derive from the smooth mechanics of narrative coherence; there the notions of unity, homogeneity, exclusion, identification, empathy, transparency and the rest fold into one another in ways that could make a narratively satisfying result a deception in some of the ways that Godard is wont to worry about. But this entails that even as a sceptical project, Godard is presupposing that movies must possess a diegetic level, a narrative dimension that, however interrupted, pluralized and obfuscated, remains intrinsic to the possibility of a certain kind of cinema.

It is this that makes it plausible to argue that the structural axes of movies are *image* (in its photographic sense) and *narrative*, because these two elements are the competing forms of *authority* out of which the authority of movies is built. For reasons I shall come to, montage needs to be seen as a species of narrative – namely, one in which the activity of narrating supervenes on the material narrated – rather than narrative being a species of montage. Without the narrative function, montage would lose the connection between time and action it presupposes. But saying that only makes montage a component of writing in images, and a typical Godard critical virtue, leaving in place his sceptical cinephobia in which artistic and critical advance – the whole transition from movies as representing the world to movies as writing in images, from classical Hollywood cinema to cinematic modernism – does not secure movies more firmly in the resources of the medium, but rather depends on alienating movies from the only sources of authority they possess; a gesture that makes even the landmarks of cinematic modernism all but unintelligible.

2 The Aesthetic Regime of Art

In calling the dominant material a priori of modern art an 'aesthetic regime', Rancière intends a provocation, dismissing the usual suspects – modernism, postmodernism, avant-garde – with an explicit gesture back to Kant and Schiller. Part of the motivation for the gesture is to reconnect art and politics. Rancière operates with a weak and strong conception of politics. Politics in its strong sense is the creation by a previously socially excluded, silenced and invisible group of a dissensus; a contestation over what sensibly appears, hence a redistribution of what sensibly appears through a making visible of the previously invisible – both, who was previously unseen and unheard, and what cares and interests, what things were previously not part of the appearance of the world because they were discounted. Social counting (what matters, is valued, taken as demanding consideration) and social visibility (what sensibly appears and so can be seen and heard) are here taken as brusquely aligned. On this notion of the political, those who have been previously without voice, because assumed not deserving or needing it, give voice to their exclusion, denying in practice the inequality that the original exclusion presupposed. The original distribution of the sensible, with its exclusions and inequalities, Rancière refers to as a 'police' order. Political dissensus rises up against police consensus.

The effort of creating a dissensus itself presupposes that political space is constituted through a partition of the sensible, of the visible and the sayable, into what is seen and unseen within the visible, and what is said and silenced within the sayable. Two considerations make this weak conception of the political apt. First, for Rancière the *stakes* of politics – *both* the police order with its established practices of domination *and* the disagreement contesting that order – are distributions of the sensible: disagreement is *re*distribution. The sensible is the field over which political agreements and disagreements occur; it is where or that over which power is held and lost. In this respect, speaking of the distribution of the sensible is Rancière's way of focusing on the material conditions of political life in their epistemic and communicative salience. Second, any specific way for intertwining ways of being, ways of doing and ways of speaking is, this side of utopia, a *potential* for redistribution and dissensus, thus for politics in its strong sense. The political in its weak sense is, *sotto voce*, the world calling out for politics in its strong sense as seen from the perspective of the latter. Politics in its strong sense is the activation of the repressed claims of politics in its weak sense. That dissensus *reveals* a repressed sensible/material meaning is what makes politics creative rather than mechanical; forging the terms of material meaning through which that meaning becomes available as what has been impossibly denied.

The juncture of the political in its weak and strong senses entails that there is, necessarily, an aesthetics of politics, and it is this fact that makes the inverse thesis – that there is a necessary politics of aesthetics – so easily available for Rancière's theory.[14] Again, Rancière's metaphysics of the everyday takes all social appearing to involve a range of exclusions, a set of those items that are not simply unsaid, unseen or unheard as such, but are so withdrawn from appearing because implicitly – without argument or contestation – deemed as unworthy or undeserving or not entitled to appear. This entails that every act of bringing to appearance is *ipso facto* a claim to normative authority of some sort, regardless of the specific content in question. The political in the weak sense of the term thus specifies that all appearings are normatively saturated, and that each regime of normatively saturated appearing is actively constituted as such.[15] It is thus unsurprising that Rancière should relocate debates about art in the aesthetic domain. But the gesture back to Kant and Schiller is more precise in its motivation; the constitutive orientation of the arts in modernity involves *a continual movement of dissensus*: a redistribution of the given sensible order, and a becoming sensible of ideas and meanings. Even without Kant's conception of aesthetic ideas or 'The oldest program for a system of German idealism', the thought that incarnation is intrinsic to art practices is patent; that incarnation in modern art is a component of the secularizing processes of modernity is the emphasis that thought is given by Hölderlin, Schelling and Hegel.

Dissensus is built into the series of negatives Kant marshals in his construction of aesthetic judgments of taste. The object of a judgment of taste is approached *without a concept* – that is, without consideration of the kind of object it is or the proper ends to which it can and should be put; equally, therefore, it is to be approached *without interest, disinterestedly*, its further existence playing no part in the estimation of its beauty; if it is truly a judgment of taste, then it concerns not how the object causally affects our sensory apparatus (the way tastes and smells ordinarily do), but its mode of appearing to our senses, hence its *mere form*, its internal purposiveness without consideration of what that purposiveness is for – *purposiveness without purpose*. Now treat aesthetic judgments of taste as if its grammatical elements were elements of an affirmative practice, hence a practice of tearing objects out of their ordinary circumstances, their usual uses and ends, the standard ways they are categorized and conceptualized, their moral significance or insignificance, and considering them in their mere appearing, as things in themselves, all but worldless apart from their imposing claim on the judging subject. This activation of the grammar of taste into a grammar of artistic practice is, broadly, how Rancière configures the aesthetic regime of art.

In his construction of the aesthetic regime of art, Rancière, following Schiller's and Adorno's lead, is re-transcribing Kant's aesthetic reflective judgment of taste into a conception of the work of art, but a conception understood from the perspective of the artwork's relation to the judging subject. I have placed in square brackets the Kantian source of Rancière's core concepts.

> In the aesthetic regime, artistic phenomena are identified by their adherence to a specific regime of the sensible [aesthetics, not the philosophy of art is our topic], which is extricated from its ordinary connections and is inhabited by a heterogeneous power, the power of a form of thought that has become foreign to itself: a product identical with something not produced [purposive but without purpose], knowledge transformed into non-knowledge [without concept; a reflective and not determinate judging], *logos* identical with pathos [a unity of understanding and imagination whose only yield is pleasure], the intention of the unintentional [the artwork must appear as nature], etc.[16]

In order for the sensible to be extricated from its usual circuits of meaning and significance, thought must become foreign to itself by suppressing its typical operations: identifying, classifying, moralizing, appropriating, enjoying, using. Thought becomes foreign to itself because it no longer *serves* the subject; through the artwork thought becomes disinterested in its own governing interests. Works of art are thus material mechanisms through which the mind can/must suspend its own constitutive functions, thereby allowing the sensible object to be emancipated from the implicit police order of the modern age, to potentially allow each and every object to become a full and equal citizen in the republic of appearances.

That aesthetic practice could be a form of radicalism in itself becomes plausible if one assumes, and it is what Schiller argues without end, that the cost of modernity has been a suppression of the sense drive by the form drive; that is, modernity in the form of Newtonian physics, machine technology, the division of labour, the domination of use value by exchange value, universalist morality, and the rights-based, bureaucratically governed liberal state is the triumph of formal reason (what Hegel labelled 'the understanding' in opposition to 'reason', and what the tradition of Critical Theory theorized under the labels of instrumental reason and identity thinking) whose fundamental characteristic is the extirpation of humankind's sensuous-material nature as a *normatively* independent stratum of human living. In this telling, the space of reason (rationality, meaning) and the space of freedom are joined without remainder. This triumph is equally, for Schiller, the cause of the terror of the French Revolution, and the perspicuous malformations of modern life: poverty, repressive morality, the fragmentation of the living subject and so on. Although Rancière does make emphatic reference to Schiller's notion of the play drive – the drive that suspends the form and sense drives, and is thus his version of Kantian disinterest – leading not only to the notion of activity without a goal, but 'an activity that is equal to inactivity', and further contrasts play's freedom with 'the servitude of work', all as ways of considering what is at stake in thought becoming foreign to itself, he nonetheless typically locates the emancipatory movement of the aesthetic regime not directly in opposition to the mechanisms carrying out the form's drive's extinguishing of sensible life, but rather in relation to the regime of art preceding it: the representative regime.[17] In broad terms, the representative regime of art operated through a mimesis of action governed by genre hierarchies in which, for example, high subject matter related to those of noble standing, low subject matter to those belonging to lower classes and hence where there were strong appropriateness conditions connecting action to a character's station. In the representative regime artworks as sensible representations were, primarily, expressions of non-sensible ideals, norms and forms in which a presupposed and abiding conception of human nature sutured doing to affection, story to appearance.

Rancière is not wrong to draw the contrast between the representative regime of art and the aesthetic regime: the modern novel, well before Flaubert and Hugo, blurred the distinction 'between those things that belong to art and those that belong to reality'[18] in a double movement that allowed the bourgeois everyday to become a fit subject matter for art through the normative transformations in accordance with which art became democratized. One can see this same double gesture occurring even earlier in Dutch genre painting where, by repudiating the classical solution of high Renaissance painting, it had effectively detranscendentalized painting;[19] or, now connecting the beginnings of modern painting with the beginnings of modernist painting, Yves-Alain Bois tells us, in his encyclopedia of the *informe*, that Manet's *Olympia* 'refused the various ideological and formal codes regulating the depiction of the nude, whether erotic, mythological, or even realistic (Courbet didn't like it)'.[20] Decoding, demythologizing, denarrativizing: in this, at least, the uprising of modern art against the decorum of those arts still imbued with (Catholic, aristocratic, feudal) hierarchical presumptions and modernism's leveling of even aesthetic form to its material conditions of possibility are joined: the latter's anti-aesthetic just a further twist, a further elaboration of the aesthetic revolution itself.

On its own, however, this is insufficient. While the great decoding efforts of modern literature, painting, music and theatre surely were originally posed primarily against the representative regime as a necessary condition for their vindication/celebration/interrogation of bourgeois life in its secular espousal of the ordinary, after 1848, after the patent failures of the bourgeois revolution – but only just catching up with what early critics of capitalism and industrial society, like Rousseau, Schiller and Adam Ferguson had already clearly diagnosed – the decoding could no longer be opposed solely to past representative orders, but rather had to set itself against the principles of sensible order governing bourgeois life itself. Emancipation could no longer be considered as if from a previous artistic regime (itself representing a past police order), but would henceforth have to somehow engage the social forms governing *our* everyday. Because they construed the aesthetic as a suspension of all (social) cognition, all practical reasoning, and all (social) morality , that is, as being outside the cognitive regimes constitutive of everyday empirical life, Kant and Schiller anticipated the critical dynamic that art inherits in its modernist disposition through which a regime of the sensible and a regime of thought become foreign to themselves, issuing in works whose most constant pulsion is to lodge a dissent against the current distributions of the sensible; at its best, artistic modernism is the ongoing propounding of a dissensus. If Rancière's aesthetic scheme seems to wobble between the original decoding efforts of early modern art targeted against the previous representative order and the radical repudiation of the cognitive regimes of the present by artistic modernism (for as long as it lasted), his allegiance to the protocols of aesthetic theory in its negativistic constitution is what finally holds his account together.

The shift from the representative to the aesthetic regime amounts to a change of orientation from 'ways of doing' (the mimesis of action) to 'ways of sensible being', which is why painting becomes increasingly important to modern culture and the novel, as a narrative form must nonetheless routinely cede equal time to description.[21] Rancière insists that within the aesthetic regime the image always has a double aspect, referring to 'a way in which things themselves speak and are silent', how the function of images rotates 'between the unfolding of inscription carried by bodies and the interruptive function of their naked, non-signifying presence'.[22] *Pace* Wollen/Godard, Rancière contends that within the aesthetic regime the image function can only satisfy its semantic burden – its possession of transitive sense – through an acknowledgement of a moment of intransitivity, a moment of meaningless presence, a moment of recalcitrant givenness. It is as if embedded in the great decodings of Dutch realism, for example, there was already sequestered the meaningless materiality of the *informe*. But isn't this essentially what Proust was already insisting upon in his obsessive engagement with Vermeer's *View of Delft*? Recall the account in *The Captive* where the novelist Bergotte suffers a terminal jouissance in front of the canvas: 'In a celestial pair of scales there appeared to him, weighing down one of the pans, his own life, while the other contained the little patch of wall so beautifully painted in yellow. He felt that he had rashly sacrificed the former for the latter.'[23] Analogously, in *The Future of the Image*, Rancière records the exquisite description by the Goncourt brothers of a Chardin still life where there is an almost indiscernible transition between transitive and intransitive passages of painting: 'In one corner there is apparently nothing more than a mud-coloured texture, the marks of a dry brush, then, suddenly a walnut appears curling up in its shell, showing its sinews, revealing itself with all the details of its form and colour.'[24] It is the 'suddenly' that makes the mud-coloured texture (a standard Chardin background) and the walnut continuous, as if the texture might at any moment burst into meaning or the walnut collapse back into sheer materiality, a wrinkled brown patch of paint. In the full passage, the Goncourts enact this double take for each feature of the painting: emphatic material presence of colour, line, texture as just the reverso of its signifying image: strawberries, orange skin, apples, bread. This gesture, this modern production of 'the splendour of the insignificant' is familiar enough – the democratic thrust of 'the insignificant' held in place precisely through the reversals that allow material form to become meaning, and meaning to dissolve back into its material conditions of possibility.[25] The question that presents itself is: why must transitive and intransitive moments be systematically connected in this way?

Consider the protocols of the aesthetic regime as a response to two different ordinances from which it means to depart: on the one hand, in repudiating the hierarchical arrangements of the representative regime, a floodgate is opened, since if metaphysical order (e.g. some version of the great chain of being) does not give on to aesthetic order, then there are no given criteria in accordance with which ranges of objects and subject matter might be excluded from aesthetic consideration; in principle, everything is 'in'. On the other hand, ontological egalitarianism, the levelling down or levelling up of subject matters is, or can be, at the same time a flattening or emptying of the world, its disenchantment. While Newtonian physics is egalitarian in its reach, it is also dismissive: nothing counts except as an example of universal law. This same thought, as part of the metaphysics of the ordinary, demands that for each object we take to be saturated with history, place, use, as a silent witness to the world of which it is a part, there corresponds a material reserve, a withdrawal, a reticence, a way in which those meanings are not intrinsic to that object but impositions and projections, accretions, requiring the acknowledgement of there being a way in which the object turns away from us. An object cannot be taken as a sign of history, imaged in this way, without the possibility of its being the sign of nothing but itself. So images bearing objects to us must possess the same fracture – being for another and being for itself, expressive and mute, speaking and silent, theatrical and absorptive, full and empty, transitive and intransitive – as the objects themselves. The dual character of the image in the aesthetic regime is thus, I am urging, the merest inflection or translation of the metaphysics of the ordinary, in which contingency is found sufficient for emphatic meaningfulness, into artistic practice.

3 A Question About Narrative

From the perspective of the logic of the image, it is obvious why the transition from the representative to the aesthetic regime might be marked as a movement from 'ways of doing' to 'ways of sensible being', from the primacy of narrative to the primacy of the perceptually given. There is, within a modern frame of reference – as but one more expression of the authority of mathematical physics – a grinding insistence on the primacy of the *thing*, the bare object, the material world stripped bare of every cultural accretion.

Or at least Rancière often writes as if this were the case. It matters here that despite references to Dutch realism or Chardin, Rancière is taking his cue from the history of the novel, locating the emergence of the aesthetic regime in the nineteenth-century novel, in Hugo and Flaubert, in the moment when the pressure and actuality of things could weigh against narrative development, when writing began to read as if the thoughtless clamour of things, their relentless pressure, might impose itself on thought, transforming description from representation to a form of acknowledgement and surrender, a response to a pressing perceptual necessity.

In identifying the aesthetic regime in this way I mean to underline how alike it is, at one level, to the moment of Godard's counter-cinema, to the moment that would conceive reality as a force for interrupting the fictions of narrative. Hence, the notion of the aesthetic regime really is best considered as an alternative to modernism as a framework for the understanding of modern/modernist art, but one which – and I am in full agreement with Rancière about this – locates its defining gestures as intimately continuous with a certain realism, a secularizing of writing and painting, of considering how word and image relate. 'Novelistic realism,' Rancière writes, 'is first of all the reversal of hierarchies of representation (the primacy of narrative over the descriptive or the hierarchy of subject matter) and the adoption of a *fragmented* or proximate mode of focalization, which imposes *raw presence* to the detriment of the rational sequences of the story.'[26] What nonetheless makes this claim historically lopsided is that it presumes that narrative is always mythological, so to speak, always the narrative of the representative regime, as if, implausibly, narrative itself did not undergo a secularizing movement. Rancière implicitly ignores not only the immense gap between, say, Greek tragedy and Shakespearean tragedy; how, for example, Hegel writes about Shakespeare in ways continuous with how he writes about Dutch painting; he emphatically ignores the history of the novel, from *Robinson Crusoe* through the politically significant epistolary novel of the eighteenth century, which, according to Lynn Hunt, by making available for the first time the inner lives of social 'others' – above all, women – contributed significantly to the development of the new universalism with its conception of natural right.[27]

Although he knows differently, because he tends to figure the meaning of the aesthetic regime in relation to its departures from the representative regime, Rancière tends to construe the question of the authority of narrative as if all narrative had the same type of hierarchical commitments as the 'ways of doing' of the representative regime. While the structural view that reads narrative as simply the movement from one equilibrium to another provides a modest justification for this conceit, it patently fails to interrogate how narratives that mean to embrace the secular might manage to do so. All this matters to Rancière's conception of movies because, in his theory, they concern the competing authority of narrative and image – which is to say, the structural meaning of cinematic narrative cannot be solely or only that which is, again and again, undone by the image function; something in the necessity of narrative will require acknowledgement.

4 Film and the Aesthetic Regime of Art

Rancière opens *Film Fables* with a passage from Jean Epstein's 1921 *Bonjour Cinéma* in which he argues that *all* the true drama of film congeals on the mere things presented: 'The cigar burns on the lip of the ashtray like a threat. The dust of betrayal.'[28] It is as if the slow cigar burn – as emphatic as the ticking of a clock – was truer to the suspense of waiting and anticipation than any portrayal of human movement; and hence that although human speech can deceive and the structures of plotting can give meaning where none truly belongs, things do not lie: they are there. The truth of mere things and the truthfulness of the camera are epistemically wed; all that film does is present again the thing in its bare presence. Or rather, that is what attaches us to film; it is the source of our caring and conviction in Epstein's view: 'Is whether they married in the end really all you want to know? Look, really, THERE IS NO film that ends badly, and the audience enters into happiness at the hour appointed on the program. // Cinema is true. A story is a lie.' Therefore the authority of film lies in its recording function, where the image axis accedes to its authority through its excess beyond the claims and needs of the narrative function. Cinema is the great vindication of empiricism; in Epstein's view: 'the art of moving images provides access to the inner truth of the sensible that settles the quarrels for priority among the arts and among the senses because it settles, first and foremost, the great quarrel between thought and sensibility.'[29]

Epstein is propounding at least a core element of the Bazin–Kracauer theory of the film. Consider two of Bazin's core theses: first, 'All the arts are based on the presence of man, only photography derives an advantage from his absence.'[30] In making this claim, Bazin is not denying the obvious – namely, that all the elements that go into shot selection reflect the subjectivity of the photographer. The point is rather that in the case of much photography we understand the photographer less as maker and more as facilitator; as one who finds something worth photographing, and provides the conditions under which the camera can best record the image. Part of the authority, and hence part of the aesthetic claim of the photographic image, depends on the camera's passivity, its being a mere causal mechanism, its interest in its object utterly disinterested. The photographic image is radically *dependent* on the object photographed, and it is our knowledge of this causal dependence that contours our responses to the image perceived. *Pace* Bazin, who thinks the authority of the photographic image is ontological, there is nothing necessary about this shaping of the meaning and authority of the photographic image; it is logically possible that we should have normally perceived only photographic images that had been doctored beyond recognition, and that it was this transfiguration that we loved and admired in our photographic culture. Nor is it necessary that photography should have developed emphatic reporting, documentary and evidential functions; nor, that cameras were pointed at the entire expanse of things in nature and culture, treating high and low equally, making all subject matters legitimate objects of interest and attention; we might have focused all our energies on photographing the human face or babies and the recently deceased or only abandoned objects or just great paintings or only paperclips that were bent out of any useful shape. Acknowledging all those unrealized counterfactuals is what makes the authority of the photographic image cultural and aesthetic rather than ontological; an exploitation of the photographic material means, not its inevitable truth, an exploitation of its mechanical capacities precisely tailored to our democratically inclined positivism. There is an elective affinity between the photograph in its capacity for mechanically recording the world and the infinite effort to authorize intransigently secular things.

Once the photographic image and its cinematic extension are understood as ideas, as particular realizations of the aesthetic regime, then Bazin's second thesis, the one that allows cinema to fulfil Schelling's 'definition of art as the identity between a conscious process and an unconscious process',[31] comes into play: 'Only the impassive lens, stripping its object of all those ways of seeing it, those piled-up preconceptions, that spiritual dust and crime with which my eyes have covered it, is able to present it in all its virginal purity to my attention and consequently to my love.'[32] The camera sees more than can be seen, and thereby, through its passivity, undoes – as the modern arts are meant to do – the reified structures of everyday perception, letting perceptual image dominate conceptual grasp, and sensate satisfaction provide an escape from the vicissitudes of moralized need and desire.

But, of course, cinema never was like this dream of it; even Epstein's cigar-burning image was drawn from a schlock melodrama of the time whose narrative gives to the image its temporal meaning. While Rancière recognizes that Epstein's dream of cinema, the glory of writing with light, belongs to 1920s' 'para-scientific' utopian ideologies, he nonetheless sees the return/embrace/domination of narrative as capitulation: film puts its technical capacities 'at the service of restoring the entire representative order that literature, painting, and the theatre had so deeply damaged. It reinstated plots and typical characters, expressive codes and the old motivations of pathos, and even the strict division of genres.'[33] Talkies and Hollywood are the villains here; once talkies place voice and image together, leading to the inevitable use of shot and countershot, then human action and reaction in objective space raise a claim whose satisfaction is to be found in the stories of those persons' lives. Although ultimately implausible, the claim that true cinema is silent cinema is not without warrant.

Rancière argues, however, that this reversion to narrative cannot be construed in wholly sceptical terms, with cinema arriving 'as if expressly designed to thwart a simple artistic teleology of artistic modernity, to counter art's aesthetic autonomy with its old submission to the representative regime'.[34] The emphasis here is on 'simple artistic teleology'; it is this that Rancière considers historically naïve, and why, for example, in his various accounts of the aesthetic regime, he more than once critiques Clement Greenberg's presumption that there is an (timeless) essence of painting. As we have already seen, the aesthetic regime is idea not essence. Rancière understands film's inheritance of the aesthetic regime as complexly dialectical: '[In virtue of its basic technical equipment] cinema literalizes a secular idea of art in the same stroke that it actualizes [in Hollywood narrative] the refutation of that idea.'[35] However, if we do not regard idea as essence, a simple artistic teleology, then we cannot regard film's refutation of that idea as the culture industry vanquishing true art. Here is Rancière twisting free of that reductionist argument, and with it from Godard's counter-cinema argument:

> The art of cinema has been constrained, empirically, to affirm its art against the tasks assigned to it by the industry. But the visible process by which it thwarts these tasks only hides a more intimate process: to thwart its servitude, cinema must first thwart its mastery. It must use its artistic procedures to construct dramaturgies that thwart its natural powers. There is no straight line running from cinema's technical nature to its artistic vocation. The film fable is a thwarted fable.[36]

I understand Rancière's thought here to be that the achievement of the aesthetic regime's idea of the image function in either its transitive or intransitive form finally *requires the negation of its opposite for its authority* (as the virtuous elements in Godard's theory require the corresponding vices for their authority). Film's natural powers are not natural but a disposition of a material apparatus; that disposition can bear the weight of the idea of the aesthetic regime only through the means through which it declares itself. The image function bursts forth through its defiguration of narration, through its revealing again and again that what seemed natural, fated, was a fable, a myth, a comforting story: the glory of war or the old West shattered as the camera shows the blood spattering, the body writhing, the agony of death. But this means, conversely, that the natural powers of film to lay bare the real must be themselves *first* narratively thwarted. Image can thwart narrative hubris only if narrative first masters film's technical/causal authority.

5 Movies' Democratic Dialectic

Because, in most instances, Rancière uses 'narrative' as equivalent to 'fictional', it typically carries all the connotations of its role in the representative regime. Yet, that is not quite his considered view of the matter; on the contrary, he refuses to contrast fiction as 'pretty story or evil lie' (the Godardian view) with 'reality'. 'Fiction', he states, 'means using the means of art to construct a "system" of represented actions, assembled forms, and internally coherent signs.'[37] Elsewhere, pressing the same idea, he states:

> The real must be fictionalized in order to be thought ... Writing history and writing stories come under the same regime of truth. This has nothing whatsoever to do with a thesis on the reality or unreality of things. On the contrary, it is clear that a model for the fabrication of stories is linked to a certain idea of history as common destiny, with an idea of those who 'make history' ... *[T]he 'logic of stories' and the ability to act as historical agents go together*. Politics and art, like forms of knowledge, construct 'fictions', that is to say *material* rearrangements of signs and images, relationships between what is seen and what is said, between what is done and what can be done.[38]

In the representative regime, what holds doing and sensible appearance together is a posited metaphysical picture of human nature. The untruth of the representative regime is its conception of social hierarchy; from the perspective of modernity, there is a real, an egalitarian empirical order that such representations of the world betray. Now we are told that modern narratives are fictions in a different sense – namely, they are non-detachable products of the freedom to act in a manner of making actual what has not existed before; narratives are the linguistic expression of the human capacity for making history, making the real accord with some idea of how it should be. Art and politics belong together in their shared interest in reshaping a sensible-material medium to accord with a desired end.

Only on this action-based interpretation of narrative does it make sense to say that film is the highest or most complete form of the aesthetic regime combining a maximum of narrative construction with a maximum of responsiveness to the demands of sensate reality. When 'anyone and everyone is considered to be participating in the task of "making" history', then narrative can no longer be regarded as the imposition or projection of an alien interpretive framework onto otherwise indifferent or recalcitrant material. To borrow Paul Ricoeur's phrasing, narrative stands to the temporality of human action as a language game stands to a form of life. If human action, beyond habit, routine and social norms, involves making – breakfast, a house, a town, a constitution, a war, a life together – then the structural account of narrative that moves from equilibrium to new equilibrium (or the former equilibrium returned) after working through the disturbance that brought down the original state of affairs is, precisely, merely *formal*, obscuring that the new states of affairs are items *made* (or suffered in the failure to make the wanted future present). Hence, Rancière contends that the real difference between documentary and fiction film 'isn't that documentary sides with the real against the inventions of fiction, it's just that the documentary instead of treating the real as an effect to be produced, treats it as a fact to be understood'.[39] Although the difference between retrospective fact and prospective effect is indeed fundamental, this contrast is nonetheless slightly off kilter along two dimensions: the facts to be understood in documentaries can be things produced, and hence the explanation is going to be the discovery of the narrative that led from action to end; and often the facts are actions themselves, doings, and what we want to understand is how some individual or group came to commit just those actions. Documentaries can be formally like fiction films, narratives; however, in them the facts are taken as preceding the narrative, and it is the intelligibility of those acknowledged worldly facts and states of affairs that are the stakes of the film.

The convention of film fiction is that there is no worldly set of facts whose explanation or revelation consititute the purpose of the film, although biopics offer a salutary blurring of that convention, a blurring intrinsic to the aesthetic regime. But this is equally to say that film fictions cannot quite be captured by the thought of 'treating the real as an effect to be produced', unless by 'real' here Rancière means the film itself. However, that sense of the real will not hold for his conception of thwarting, and it is the doubled dialectic of thwarting – the thwarting of narrative by image, and the mastery of image by narrative – that is the accomplishment of Rancière's theory. The reasons for this should now be evident: because of its mechanical means, the image function of film accomplishes what is only promised by the image function of aesthetic literature (novel, poem, theatre) and aesthetic art; however, *moving* images, as they bear on human life, must concern human action, and human actions are, in the first instance, made intelligible through narrative structures, where narrative structures are simply the *patterning* of human actions over time. Every non-habitual human action (and most habitual ones) is a narrative in miniature: an antecedent equilibrium is disturbed by the uprising of some desire, need, or want that can only be satisfied (or suffered in the misery of dissatisfaction) through a doing. Because, in films, we directly perceive the actions of agents, then film narrative *must* address itself to the immanent patterning of action, to actions' perceptible consequences and outcomes – both in the narrative present and over time. In movies, as opposed to novels, because actions are perceived in the same way as things, as immediate images – albeit moving images – it is the immanent patterning of action that must be narratively accomplished; while for the novel the accomplishment of the narration is sufficient. The primacy of narrative materials over the act of narration is the consequential upshot of the camera's original passivity. In the novel, biographical form precipitates autobiographical form (narrative the shadow cast by narration); it is just the necessity of this precipitation that the camera's relation to action obviates. Film thus works from the opposing direction of the novel: narration must either acknowledge the demands of narrative material or repudiate the medium's material conditions of possibility.

While image and narrative are not the only matrices necessary for understanding the social world, they are among the social forms of intelligibility central to the micrological level of understanding the everyday. If the authority of the image function of film is that the representing image is an imprint of the world – call it the veil of Veronica thesis – and the authority of the narrative axis is that 'this' patterning of action is in fact intrinsic to the world imaged, then the double dialectic of thwarting is nothing other than the necessary micrological interrogation of ordinary modern life as perceived rather than experienced. It is an interrogation because the two axes, however cooperative, make competing demands: the truthfulness of the image and the intelligibility of the narrative. Narrative intelligibility is only acceptable if it is truthful, and an image truthful only if, finally, intelligible; or rather, over time we will find a narrative acceptable only if in reflecting a recognizable patterning of our life it heeds the demands of worldliness in recognizable ways; and we will find an imaging of the world intelligible if in adequately acknowledging the force of actuality, the force of worldly circumstance, it provides for an intelligible patterning of human action, a world in which agents can make sense of their lives as agents or where we can now understand why such sense making has become impossible. Film simultaneously collapses the two axes into each other at every instant while acknowledging their autonomy from each other as style, emphasis and form of analysis. Their analytic separateness from each other is what permits them, synthetically, to fall apart, how they can come to test each other, thwart each other, correct each other. Rancière's thesis is that the two axes can sustain their authority – which is to say, movies can sustain their *authority* – and it is only their standing as forms of authority that is at stake in the debate about movies, their condemnation or praise – only through processes of reciprocal thwarting, reciprocal criticism. Rancière reads this process as internal to the logic of each significant film, which must be in part true; however, I am suggesting that the dialectic more centrally belongs to the life of movies as an ongoing artistic practice.

6 The Democratic Hypothesis

A movie matters only because movies matter; film fictions are, or have been, the ongoing interrogation of the metaphysical-moral fit between self as agent and a social configuration of the sensible, plural world as an arena for human action;[40] but that interrogation of a given world (as image) as providing or denying the possibilities for living a certain kind of life with others (narratively organized) is not a laboratory experiment but simply the democratic conversation about who we are. Michael Wood is even more modest: 'Movies are a form of talk, contributions to conversations that continue when the movies are over, and while talk can have profound and echoing repercussions, it rarely has loud and immediate ones.'[41] The bar, the coffee shop, the water cooler, the school cafeteria are the proper extensions of the movie theatre since it is in those locales that we engage with one another over our collective life, its possibilities and dangers, its fears and hopes, its temptations and disappointments: is *this* what love, marriage, family, war, work, honesty, vice, civil order, being a woman, being a man *are*? For significant stretches of the past century, major portions of the democratic public sphere occurred in the space stretching from the movie theatre to wherever one's liquid of choice (coffee, soda, beer, whiskey) was consumed.[42]

That movies have been constant companions – instigators, critics, kibitzers, provocateurs – in our conversations does not, I hope, need arguing. What, however makes this conversation emphatically democratic rather than ideological and – in being democratic – a new formation of the very idea of art? The first plank of the democratic hypothesis turns on accepting Rancière's contention that movies belong to the aesthetic regime of art, and that this regime in both its primary versions is essentially democratic and egalitarian in its constitutive orientations: modern art as the materialist, secularizing undoing of the hierarchical protocols of the representative regime of art, and modernism as the self-conscious continuation of that undoing but now ranged against the rationalized abstractions of modern life itself. In making this claim, Rancière tacitly privileges image against narrative (as all but marking the shift from the representative to the aesthetic regime), making the reciprocity between meaning-image and material-image the source of art's power to generate, each time, a dissensus where a police consensus had been, thus letting some new fragment of the world appear, be seen, heard or spoken. In this respect, rather than contesting Godard's schema, Rancière's theory can be thought of as offering a metaphysical mechanism that provides critical autonomy to the right-hand side (difference, writing in images) of Godard's schema, turning scepticism into critique.

The second plank of the democratic hypothesis involves the claim that movies are a fuller realization of the ambition of the aesthetic regime than any other art form. This thesis comes in two parts. On the one hand, there is the Epstein-inspired celebration of the movies as elaborating the full scope of their photographic basis: the passivity of the camera, stretching out towards each object whose presence it records, spontaneously, as it were, imbricating the relation between image-meaning and material-meaning, between the world as seen and the sensible unseen of each seen thing: photographic images reveal objects beyond human powers of revelation. On the other hand, as soon as movies allow speaking individuals in, their scope expands from world as 'thingly' presence to world as arena for action, requiring that the image function in its temporal unfolding be organized through some narrative operation. It was this joining of some thin version of photographic transparency – as promising the real, and keeping that promise through the referential excess in each received image – as harnessed to the portrayal of narrative lives that, simultaneously, made some version of realism, however atrophied in practice, the primary destination of each ordinary film while pressing movies into the mold of a popular art form. The critical interaction in each movie, and over time in the succession of movies – in their conversation with one another – between the image function as representing the claim of a given world and the narrative function as representing the possibilities of action in that world, came to designate the specificity of film. Of course, in almost any modern art form, one might point to the struggle between intelligible form and material content. What distinguishes movies is that the material content to be formed is the disposition of a particular historical world, with form installing the potentialities for successful action in that world, form thus becoming another kind of material content. Hence, movies measure the world as a place for action, and measure the ideals of action against the actuality of the world. Because every movie will contain a photographically elaborated, narratively unsaturated material excess that marks the gap between action and world, between the hopes of narrative form and the demand that such form be 'true to' the world it informs, then every movie opens the space that allows, and even demands, its critical interrogation.[43] The photographic/image excess of each movie marks the limit of narrative reason, the claim of world beyond our powers to make it conform to desire or hope. More simply, because each movie is a formal reconstruction of a photographically depicted world that is spatially and temporally continuous with the world inhabited by the spectator, each movie formally arrives as a fiction of the spectator's own world; but a fiction now in precisely Rancière's sense: the claim of each narrative film is that it provides the conditions for the intelligibility of action in the world it depicts. In this respect, every remotely serious narrative movie of necessity raises the question of its accuracy, truth, authenticity (with only pure entertainments escaping that demand).

If one concedes that the image function of movies is (or has been) secularizing and equalizing, then it follows that in movies the dialectic between image and narrative entails the incremental secularizing of the narrative function itself; that is, the propounding of narrative forms adequate to the demands of a wholly secular social world. This entails the third plank of the democratic hypothesis. I have urged that narrative form is not only intrinsic to the intelligibility of action, but, furthermore, following Rancière, that its fictional character, its excess beyond the doings it informs, is the point of convergence between action as art-making and action as history-making. I now want to urge that narrative cinema, as it emerged from Hollywood, is profoundly about and located in, precisely that point of convergence, and furthermore, that it is no accident that this convergence should come from Hollywood. What is it that Hollywood narrative cinema knew that European cinema has never quite known? How might we explain the role of Hollywood in the construction of the democratic conversation? Hollywood knew (and continues to know when it is true to its American inspiration) what every American knows in his or her bones – namely, that America itself is a massive *historical experiment* in whether there can be a society that is self-made, whose fundamental contours are those it gives itself. There is no question of modernity in America because, in accordance with its collective self-understanding, nothing preceded America in this place.[44] For Americans, the European idea of modernity – say, the project of the Enlightenment, or of the liberal nation state, or of a society built on private property and commodity production – always boils down to the idea of America itself: is this form of life possible? Are 'we' possible? Can there be a form of life that is not composed of some homogeneous group with its shared language, ethnicity, religion and history, but rather a nation of immigrants from different lands that is founded on freedom and some notion of equality, where the right of the individual trumps the demands of the collective, where each is entitled to a life that is self-fashioned, where no caste or class barriers can permanently bar one's acceding to a place in society, where the only laws are those it gives itself, and where the possibility of a life one can call one's own should continue to be available until the moment one draws one's last breath? Providing a surprising parsing of Deleuze's philosophy of cinema, Paola Marrati states the thought this way: 'The American nation-civilization distinguishes itself from the old nations; it wants to be the country of immigrants, the *new world*, but the new world is precisely the one that finally accomplishes the broken promises of the old world.'[45] American life is, or was, always the interrogation of the possibility of America as a form of life; and movies, I am urging, have been the locale in which we have, for the past 80-odd years, constructed our idea of this place – the wilderness, the West, the farm, the city, the suburb – in relation to ways of our inhabiting it.

What this third plank thus entails is that narrative form – for 'we' Americans – is always understood to be a historical a priori; a narrative construction of an identity tailored to or denied by the portion of the American life-form represented. It is just this fact that makes the narrative forms of Hollywood cinema secular rather than mythological, contingent constructions rather ideological rationalizations. Movies propound America, interrogate it and celebrate it; movies have been the mode of our collective self-consciousness, our collective means for projecting who we are or wish to be or fear becoming. This is not to deny that we can deceive ourselves about who we are and what is possible here; but those deceptions appear as deceptions through the effort of other movies, other conversations: the end of the myth of the West in *McCabe and Mrs. Miller* or the end of the myth of marriage in *Marnie* or the end of the myth of family and community in the *Godfather* trilogy. Movies are democratic because in America democracy does not refer simply to a set of political ideals and institutions; democracy in America is the idea of America as a historical project that exists through the troubled conversation about what and how America means, a conversation that has been carried out culturally in the movies as in no other place. It is because the conversation has been emphatic, continuous and intimate that the question as to whether the movies were proper art forms or mere entertainments always seems somehow beside the point, missing how movies matter. In the democratic conversation of the movies, art-making and history-making converge: we cannot desist from telling stories about ourselves because the stories the movies tell are just the ways we have here and now come to understand who we are and what the very idea of America now means.

To understand movies as popular and democratic, transforms the relation of movies to traditional ideas of art. Movies are modern in the way that no other art form is, because, in virtue of the manner in which the image function is tethered to its object world, they are more fully anchored in their time than other modern art forms; the sort of movies we have come to make and care about are such that they finally cannot create their own world – the way a great work of art makes a self-sufficient world – without betraying this one. That is a pressure that no previous art has had to bear; but it is movies' implicit acknowledgement of this pressure, their fatal momentariness and transience, that is, conversely, the source of cinematic authority. The argument is not that movies lack the formal complexities of great art; it is rather that movies place this complexity into the service of an art object that seeks its historical moment rather than seeking to escape it by becoming somehow timeless or classical (letting the preponderance of form generate a closed world of meaning in which each moment is semantically saturated by the schema of the whole). Movies want to be conversation partners, not enduring objects of contemplation. They must want this for themselves because it is demanded by their image function being photographic in character, and because in them, art-making and history-making converge.

Movies date with unspeakable rapidity; their welcome visual contact with their time, and the fact that their presentation aims to be living and realistic entails that the merest shift in fashion (in dress or haircut), linguistic habit, or the material conditions of everyday living can mark a movie as hopelessly 'past'. But these are solely external markers; it is when the practical presuppositions about how social life works – the social necessities that connect individuals one with another, and practices to their conditions of possibility – visibly change that reveal the world presented as not ours, as no longer a blurred hybrid between photographic realism and narrative fiction, but as just a fiction, a fantasy. As elements of our democratic conversation, movies are transient; they are an art form for whom transience is automatic, unlike painting and sculpture, for example, where the exposure of the artwork to transience requires a radical anti-art or anti-aesthetic gesture. The transient character of movies is, more or less, an acknowledged fact; but the usual explanation for this has been that they are mere entertainments, their enticement exhausted by their novel appearance. Once the artistic complexity of classical cinema is granted, then the source of cinematic transience must be relocated so that it becomes a part of the kind of achievement movies want for themselves. That we – critics, theorists, audiences and movie makers – routinely want to place the claim of movies in line with those of traditional artworks amounts to nothing more than our reflective incapacity to recognize their democratic character, to recognize what an emphatically democratic art practice would be.

Throughout most of the twentieth century, 'America' was an idea of the possibility of modernity, its promise, as much as 'socialism'. Hollywood, I am claiming, exploited and bent itself to that idea ruthlessly. It is then no accident that Godard's most vengeful turn against movies should occur at the precise moment that the idea of America shifts from experiment and promise to imperium. I understand the analogous interrogation of Hollywood in the 1950s as one of Europe asserting its own voice as a mode of resistance to the threat of a cultural swamping, hence of marking the difference between Europe's rootedness in the past and its war as opposed to the evergreen America without past and, for all intents and purposes, untouched by the ravages of war. In putting the matter this way, I am suggesting that the emergence of great European cinema of the post-war years can be construed not as modernism replacing Hollywood narrative – there is no such thing as modernism in the movies – but as new forms of narrative cinema that were designed to resist what had come to be seen as the ideological myth-making of Hollywood cinema, which is just the ideological myth-making of America itself. I understand the revival of movie culture in the 1970s – the heyday of Scorsese, Altman, Stone, Penn, et al. – to be a demonstration to the effect that the shift marking the end of the idea of America, an end that seems emphatic with the war in Vietnam, did not necessarily bring with it the end of movies as a democratic art form; a demonstration that movies could remain democratic as long as the idea of America as experiment could remain open, as long as history could remain open. The movies of the 1970s knew this claim, however melancholic in elaboration, as movies' own thought.

The idea of movies as a democratic art form converges perfectly with Rancière's claim at the end of 'Deleuze and the ages of cinema' that the near-total indiscernibility between the logics of movement-image and time-image – that is, between 'the montage that orients spaces according to the "sensory-motor" schema and that which disorients it so as to render the products of conscious thought equal in power to the free deployment of the potentialities of world-images' – entails that the attempt 'to fix a border separating a classical from a modern cinema' is bound to fail.[46] This not to deny that the constellation of film forms, the preponderance of film types, the habits of movie-going by audiences, the practices of criticism and the role of cultural products in society generally could not entail a withering of movies as a democratic art. That this happened is what I meant to flag in my opening sentences. But what has withered is not classical cinema or Hollywood cinema or the movement-image or cinephilia, but, as Susan Sontag mourned, 'an art unlike any other: quintessentially modern; distinctively accessible; poetic and mysterious and erotic and moral – all at the same time … It was both the book of art and the book life.'[47] Because this withering, this death of art, is unlike the exhaustion of artistic modernism, this was arguably no historical fatality but something we collectively did, something that in a fit of distraction or ignorance or weakness or spite we let happen.

Chapter 3

Godard and Rancière: Automatism, Montage, Thinking[1]

Lisa Trahair

A saturation of magnificent signs bathing in the light of their absence of explanation.

(*Jean-Luc Godard, Histoire(s) du cinéma*)

In the fifth episode of his video essay *Histoire(s) du cinéma*,[2] entitled 'La monnaie de l'absolu', a voiceover – Godard's – conjectures that it is often forgotten that the cinematograph (the first cinematographic machine), like modern painting, is a form that thinks, a form made for thinking that 'makes its way toward speech'. Godard says little about what he means by this idea that cinema is capable of thought, yet he implies that it is different from the thought expressed by words. In the third episode, 'Fatale beauté', while remarking on the dissemination among filmmakers of Jean-Paul Sartre's notion of the *camera stylo*, Godard suggests that equating filmmaking with writing precipitated cinema's fall 'under the guillotine of meaning'. He also comments that cinema exists 'for words stuck in the throat and for the truth to be unearthed'.

Godard's resurrection of the cinematograph in this instance results in a certain anthropomorphisation. This machine, unlike its cinematographic successors, but comparable to video, is used for recording and projecting. It is as if thinking were bound up with the operations of the mechanical apparatus itself rather than an ability which is exclusive to living beings with an intellect trained on using their mental capacities and memories to make deductions about external reality. Perhaps Godard conceives meaning to be an effect of thinking and not to be confused with it. Would the extrinsic speech (or discourse) that cinematic thinking approaches be the meaning that comes into effect as a result of thinking? And if this machine's thinking is preverbal, is this because it shows rather than speaks? How then are we to understand the power of words when they play a part in film? Clearly, the words of Godard cited here are not sufficient means for understanding cinematic thinking.

In his writing on *Histoire(s)*, Jacques Rancière develops a theory of Godardian montage that provides some scope for understanding cinematic thinking and its irreducibility to either speech or writing. In this essay, I trace the development of Rancière's interpretation of *Histoire(s)* from his first encounter with it in 'A fable without a moral: Godard, cinema, (hi)stories' in his book *Film Fables*, to his second in *The Future of the Image*.[3] In the *Film Fables* essay, Rancière engages the possibility of cinematic thinking by addressing the tension between form and fable, specifically between cinematic automatism and the narrative conventions established in literature and theatre. In his second encounter with *Histoire(s)*, he rearticulates what is arguably the same tension, proposing that the video essay's aesthetic strategies span two poles of 'the sentence-image'. These poles are dialectical montage and symbolic montage. In following the course of Rancière's engagement with Godard's project, my focus is on how the relationship between automatism and montage assists our understanding of the way cinema is party to thinking. In Rancière's early writing, automatism is conceived as putting thinking on the side of reality, while montage puts thinking on the side of art and indeed the artist's intentions. It is my argument that Rancière starts to complicate this alignment by admitting (without in fact saying it) that montage is not just a technique (for directing perception, as in continuity editing, or equivalent to metaphor in creating symbolic meaning) but a technology that deploys mechanical principles to allow reality to reveal itself. In this sense, montage is not opposed to automatism. My question therefore is: what happens to thinking in this development and how are we to think of it?

1 The Video Essay

Histoire(s) du cinéma is considered by many to be Godard's *magnum opus*. Jonathan Rosenbaum has compared it with James Joyce's *Finnegan's Wake*, emphasizing the way it positions itself after some endpoint in the development of film language in order to cast a backward glance at the history of cinema and the role it has played in twentieth-century culture and thought.[4] Rancière himself places it alongside Gilles Deleuze's cinema books in the paradigm of the encyclopaedia.[5] While the video essay aspires to be both a history of cinema and, to some extent, a history of the twentieth century, it is also a reflection on the developing self-consciousness of cinema as a form of art and as medium imbued with the human spirit.

It hardly needs to be said then that *Histoire(s)* is an almost infinitely rich work. The video essay operates as an archive of the twentieth century, containing a diversity of historical documents: in addition to the books, films (of diverse forms and genres), paintings and photography, it includes newsreel footage and sound recordings both from radio and of popular music. The essay reproduces shots from over 200 films, quotes from more than 50 authors (political, academic and literary), includes the photographic work of more than a dozen professional photographers, images of prints of hundreds of artworks, and citations of musical chords from numerous composers. It runs for 266 minutes in total, but comprises four chapters, each of which is divided into an A and B section.[6] Godard has remarked on the multiple entry points and limitless pathways available to the viewer attempting to make sense of the essay, and compared the work with Walter Benjamin's *Arcades Project*,[7] proposing that it can be viewed as one, four or eight films: 'eight films combined in one … eight chapters of a film that could have had hundreds of others, and even more appendices'.[8] He also underlines his utilization of some of the central motifs of modernity, not only the arcades, but also the flâneur and montage.[9] Indeed, viewing the essay is much like embarking on a situationist *dérive*, involving in this particular instance a *cine-historical* adventure through the cultural residue of the twentieth century.[10]

The essay, for all that, is not a comprehensive archive. It includes no contribution from experimental filmmakers, for example, nor images of abstract art, and undertakes no consideration of the situationist practices that seem to have assisted in the formulation of its aesthetic rationale; rather, the image-track restricts itself to the citation of pictorial and figurative representations. Rancière himself has suggested that the video essay is chauvinistically European in its orientation: *Histoire(s)* limits its palette almost exclusively to images that originate in Europe and the United States because its underlying interest is in the 'destiny of European culture'.[11]

2 The Proposition

Before discussing how Rancière's distinction between form and fable provides scope for unpacking what is at stake in Godard's comments about cinematic thinking, mention should be made of the fact that Rancière acknowledges that the video project is an essay and as such puts forward a proposition, thereby implying that the work is a mode of thought. While acknowledging that the proposition itself and the 'arguments' that support it are not discursive, Rancière nevertheless supposes that they are determinable by the analysis of images, by attention to their sequencing and to the different kinds of operations performed on them.

Rancière suggests that the project propounds a single thesis that cinema missed its date with history by failing to bear witness to the atrocities perpetrated during the Holocaust. In his critical reformulation of Godard's 'narrative', Rancière emphasizes how Godard attributes this to the domination of cinema by the Hollywood juggernaut's production and distribution of a multitude of ideological fabrications; namely, the fabrications articulated by means of the storytelling conventions of classical narrative cinema. Godard admonishes cinema for neglecting the duties that attach to its ontology because it failed to appropriately avail itself of the nature of its ancestry. Of the two aesthetic traditions that spawned the new art form – one pictorial, the other literary – cinema, mainstream narrative cinema in particular, opted for the latter; and in thus aligning itself with literature, cinema was unable to realize the potentialities that derived from its pictorial specificity and the tradition of the visual arts.[12]

As Rancière describes it, the terms of Godard's argument are the same as his own – a conflict between film form and narrative fabulation has operated throughout the history of cinema. The difference between Godard's meditation on this 'awkwardness' and Rancière's is this: Godard, for Rancière at least, wants to redress this subordination of pictorial form to narrative content and redeem cinema of its fall into sinful ways, whereas Rancière wants to critique the thinking that lies behind Godard's stance. In particular, Rancière wants to show the ineffectuality of the methods Godard uses in order to bolster his own argument that the conflict between form and fable in cinema is symptomatic of a much more profound set of aesthetic conditions that operate across the entirety of the contemporary cultural sphere.

3 The Distribution of the Sensible and the Regimes of Identification

For Rancière, neither technological capacity nor medium specificity determine the real particularities of a work of art. Art, including cinema, is rather forged by a contest between different regimes of identification that vie with one another to preside over sensibility in general. The material world is experienced through the senses because of a consensus located in the system of a priori forms (spaces, times, the visible, the invisible, speech and noise).[13] Culture participates in the 'distribution of the sensible' that brings the heterogeneous flux of the world into focus in such a way as to suggest that it is organized.[14]

Rancière identifies three regimes, which individually circumscribe and specify the horizons and modalities of sensory experience (what is seen, heard, perceived) and the capacity to respond to it (whether by doing, making or thinking) – the ethical, the representative and the aesthetic. Each regime has its own distinctive, identifiable and consistent logic, even if its hold over sensibility in general is tenuous. Importantly, the tension that Rancière identifies between form and fable is in fact a tension between two regimes.

In distinguishing between these regimes and specifying how they carve up the material world, Rancière discusses their more or less systematic philosophical elaborations, focusing on the position of the image in the first regime, and the role of art in the second and third regimes. The ethical regime of the image coincides with the philosophy of Plato, and in the first instance occurs at a time when art is not distinguished from other kinds of doing and making. The image is evaluated on the basis of its claim to truth – which is determined in turn by the law of resemblance – and the nature of its impact on individuals and communities.[15]

The representative/poetic regime finds its justification in the writing of Aristotle. In this regime (which Rancière sometimes calls classical) art is distinguished from other kinds of doing and making by virtue of its distinctive substance. In Aristotle's *Poetics*, substance is understood as the poetic arrangement of actions in order to comprise the plot.[16] While mimesis is not absent here – actions, after all, 'represent the activities of men' – the emphasis on poetic fabrication is 'to the detriment of the *essence* of the image, a copy examined with regard to its model'.[17] The conjoining of the concepts of mimesis and poesis here is telling; for there is a sense in which the former looks back to Plato and the latter looks forward to the aesthetic regime of images. While imitative arts are distinguished from craft on the basis of resemblance, resemblance does not operate here as a *law* (which either permits or forbids representation) but as a concept involving the careful articulation of a set of *principles* (such as verisimilitude, appropriateness and correspondence). Most significantly, arts are distinguished from other practices of doing and making because they are poetic. In aspiring towards the ideals of formal beauty, order, harmony and balance, and in specifying the criteria of what, for example, would come to be called the well-made play, it is clear that in this regime, form is permitted to speak to itself, but only insofar as it can produce powerful exemplars (or ideals) for non-artistic endeavour. The poetic thus gives definition to general ways of doing and making. It becomes a means of assessing actions. Analogy is thereby a primary means of bridging the partitioning of the sensible. Representation is not geared to representing reality truthfully but analogically. What is also distinctive about this regime is its development of criteria for distinguishing and comparing arts and for classifying them into genres on the basis of form and content. This system of classification goes hand in hand with a fully hierarchical organization of society.[18]

The aesthetic regime of art coincides with what conventionally goes by the name of modernity. Rancière uses the term 'aesthetic regime of the art' in preference to modernity, however, in order to avoid, in his words, 'the teleologies inherent in temporal markers'.[19] Rancière links the aesthetic regime to the post-Kantian philosophy of Romanticism, predominantly that of the Schlegel brothers and Schelling. As in the ethical regime, in the aesthetic regime art cannot be distinguished on the basis of its substance; that is, because of a division within ways of doing and making. Nor is art responsive to a set of criteria pertaining to the sensibility, taste or pleasure of its audience. Art is whatever is called art. This art in name only strives for complete autonomy from the social and political realms.[20] Its 'speech' is neither imitative nor representational but immanent. It wants to speak only to itself and about itself, and because it is absorbed in its own autopoiesis it reproduces the autopoiesis of the natural world. Art's autonomy thereby makes it equivalent to 'the forms that life uses to shape itself'.[21] Because it achieves an absolute identity with the materiality of non-art it is able to speak truthfully (without in fact saying anything) about the processes of the material world. This new regime emerges in the wake of the Enlightenment, the French Revolution, the spread of democracy and eventually the explosion of the mass media. The same effort to eradicate hierarchies is undertaken in the aesthetic realm as in the social and political realms.[22] The restructuring might appear to be transversal from the outside but it is by way of internal procedures specific to the realms themselves. Within the aesthetic realm, Rancière identifies the dismantling of the hierarchies of the representative regime, such as the hierarchy of genres based on subject matter, of the word over the image, action over character, narration over description and content over style.[23]

The regimes pertain to historical epochs only to a limited extent. As becomes clear in the way Rancière goes on to discuss cinema, it is not the case that one regime is superseded by another, or that the impact of the structural order of one regime disappears under the dominance of another.

In his analysis of the contemporary politico-cultural sphere, for example, Rancière perceives a generative tension between the representative regime and the aesthetic regime. It is as if the logic of one regime goes hand in hand with particular economic, political and technological conditions, but doesn't establish a decisive hegemony over them because of the persistence of previous logics. So it is not the case that the representative proclivity is absent from the age in which the aesthetic dominates. Rather, the core of modernist theorization of the arts, under the sway of the aesthetic regime, promotes the view that art has broken completely with representation, has abandoned analogy by asserting both the separation of the arts into their distinct media and the autonomy of art from the social and political realms.[24]

The struggle of regimes over distributions of the sensible impacts on the tension between form and fable in cinema, and, in turn, on the question of cinematic thinking. We will see that the driving force behind cinematic fabulation is the representative regime's contribution to the medium. Celebrations of the primacy of cinematic form derive from the imperatives of the aesthetic regime. On the question of cinematic thinking, we might suppose, in advance of anything specific that Rancière has to say on the topic, that the ethical regime and the representative regime both limit the capacity of the cinematic image to be involved in thought. The ethical regime does so because it confines the operation of the image within the question of belief– of belief in its truth. The representative regime provides scope for the image 'to speak', but constrains the nature of its operations by containing it within hierarchies that subordinate its operation to the rules of language and to the constative power of the word. Is cinematic thinking possible in the aesthetic regime? Wouldn't such thinking be located precisely at the point that art becomes indistinguishable from what is not art, at the point that it appears to have liberated itself from all external motivations, including that of the artist's intellect? Such thinking, on Rancière's account, is co-extensive with the autopoiesis of nature. And yet the thrust of Rancière's argument suggests that he wants to take issue with this idea that cinematic thinking is co-extensive with the autopoiesis of nature. His articulation of a dialectic between form and fable, for example, provides another means of thinking about what cinematic thinking entails.

4 The Dialectic of Form and Fable in Cinema

According to Rancière, the supposed autonomy of art in the aesthetic regime leads to a privileging of the purity of form over and above everything

else. The purity of cinematic form is expressed in the concept of automatism: specifically, the mechanical nature of the production of the image and
its capacity to operate independently of the intentions of the filmmaker.
Rancière's first mention of automatism in the 'Prologue' to *Film Fables* is
made in the context of his reflection on Jean Epstein's celebration of cinema's ability to record objective reality independently of the eye and the
gaze and constative discourse, to 'see' things 'as they come into being, in a
state of waves and vibrations, before they can be qualified as intelligible
objects, people, or events due to their descriptive and narrative properties'.[25] For Rancière, Epstein's theory of *photogénie* is among the first evidence of a cinematic equivalent to a broader aspiration found at the heart
of the aesthetic regime of art. Cinema is only the technological perfection
of more general strivings towards a purity of style that would allow the natural world to shine through in its singular glory by eradicating all evidence of
both the artist and the medium as mediating filters. The invention of
cinema:

> finally gives life access to an art capable of doing it justice, an art in which
> the intelligence that creates the reversals of fortune and dramatic con-
> flicts is subject to another *intelligence*, the *intelligence* of the machine that
> wants nothing, that does not construct any stories, but simply records the
> infinity of movements that gives rise to a drama a hundred times more
> intense than all dramatic reversals of fortune.[26]

For Rancière, the emphasis on automatism goes hand in hand with an over-
emphasis on aesthetic purity, on the independence of cinematic form from
other media. The 'cinema purists' are those who celebrate what they deem
to be the inimitable function of the mechanical eye of the cinematic camera for recording the irreducible flux of nature over and above any of the
storytelling methods that cinema appropriates from theatre and literature.
Epstein, Bazin, Godard and Deleuze, Rancière suggests, are 'cinema purists' because they champion the idea of cinematic automatism at the expense
of the representative dimension of cinematic art.

This narrowly modernist renunciation of the representative dimension of
art has, in Rancière's view, resulted in a number of lopsided interpretations
of film (and is evidenced in his view in the work of André Bazin, Godard
and Deleuze). When modernist accounts of cinema forget about the story,
the Aristotelian legacy is thrown out the window. The arrangement of the
plot, the structure of events, the protagonist's reversal of fortune, the
alteration of his/her state of knowledge by the concatenation of events are

all forgotten in favour of an interest in cinema's specific ability to passively record the brute materiality of the sensible world.

Despite the essentializing tenacity of theorists and filmmakers who insist that the best cinema issues forth from recognition of the specificity of its technology, one only has to look at the cinematic works in circulation to see that cinema, by and large, does not seek to align itself exclusively with this 'truth', nor repudiate the legacy of Aristotle's *Poetics* in its storytelling capacity and its orientation towards fiction.

On re-examining exactly how it is that Epstein casts his argument, Rancière redefines the reach of cinematic automatism in order to argue for the operation of 'an active dialectic in which one tragedy takes form at the expense of another … Epstein's text, in other words, undertakes a work of de-figuration. He composes one film with the elements of another'.[27] He extracts from conventional melodrama and experimental film, a work of 'pure' cinema, a 'theoretical and poetical fable that describes the original power of the cinema from the body of another fable, from which he erased the traditional narrative aspect in order to create another dramaturgy, another system of expectations, actions, and states of being'.[28]

Moreover, for Rancière, making one fable with another is 'a constitutive fact of the cinema as experience, art and the idea of art'.[29] Godard and Deleuze, as much as Epstein, are involved in the business of extracting 'the original essence of the cinematographic art from the plots the art of cinema shares with the old art of telling stories'.[30] This kind of act is performed as much by audiences and directors as it is by critics and cinephiles. (It is also the case that Rancière himself proceeds in this manner.)

In casting the tension between regimes and the imbrication of the techniques 'proper' to different arts within a given work as dialectical, Rancière approaches the view that thinking derives from the recognition of two encounters: first, between the two regimes within a given work; and second, of cinema and other arts because cinema is an art 'whose meaning cuts across the borders between the arts'.[31] In the first instance, the full scope of cinematic invention is apparent only when it is understood as an encounter between the two different and, in many respects, antithetical regimes of the image – between an aesthetic regime that celebrates aesthetic presence to the exclusion of everything else and the representative regime that subordinates the volubility of pure sensible presence by arranging aesthetic elements in the form of a good story. In the second instance, *Film Fables* recounts the dialectical encounter between 'pure cinema' and other art forms: 'Cinema can only make the games it plays with its own means intelligible to itself through the games of exchange and inversion it plays with the literary fable, the plastic form, and the theatrical voice'.[32] In Rancière's writing, the relation between these two encounters remains obscure. While Rancière appears to maintain with some rigour the idea that the emphasis on film form and cinematic purity belong to the aesthetic regime, it is hardly logical that the other media with which cinema engages necessarily fall on the side of the fable and the representative regime. Despite this obscurity, Rancière is in a prime position to suggest that the productive outcome of such dialectics is a specifically cinematic thinking, that film engages thinking because the cinematographic image in all its excess confronts the movement of the story, and resists subordination to its meaning. Yet his stance is ambiguous in this regard also. At the end of the 'Prologue' he maintains the dialectic between the two regimes, each continually thwarting the other, but implies that 'thought' is on the side of the representative regime: 'the art and thought of images have always been nourished by all that thwarts them'.[33] If the aesthetic retains power, it is on account of its beauty. Writing about Bresson's films, for example, he observes that aesthetic beauty calls narrative meaning into question but he doesn't go far enough in assessing this capacity to question meaning or what the outcome of such questioning is vis-à-vis thinking.

5 Fable and Form in 'Histoire(s) du cinéma'

Rancière's *Film Fables* essay demonstrates how the video project plays out in exemplary fashion the logics of the representative and aesthetic regimes facing off with each other at different moments and taking turns in being subordinated to each other. In the first instance, in Rancière's interpretation, the video project deems the fable to be consistent with the way the story is formulated in accordance with the logic of the representative regime. This is not the story told by the project – the proposition about which the video thinks – but the story as it is articulated in mainstream cinema, where narration is controlled by what is conventionally called 'continuity editing'. Godard's thesis about the role that cinema played in the course of the history of the twentieth century and the obligations that attach to its ontology is a second instance of fabulation. In other words, there is the kind of story that Godard criticizes as any good modernist would and the story that he tells and that will, so Rancière says, see him fall prey to his own criticism.

For Rancière, Godard's idea of cinematic ontology and his means of redeeming cinema by attending to its pictorial legacy, however ineffectual it might ultimately be, relate to automatism.[34] Rancière, however, redefines to some extent what is meant by automatism. Cinematic automatism is conventionally conceived as the passivity of the camera before the drama of real life and the indexical function of the cinematographic image (a function that is understood to involve presence and absence). Yet Rancière claims that Godard's version of it relates to the cinematographic camera's duty to be *present.* He argues that, for Godard, cinema's 'vocation is to the present and to presence', and that *Histoire(s)* pursues the poetics of pure presence that cinema has otherwise betrayed.[35] By being sidetracked by Hollywood into producing a world that conforms to our desire, Godard's *Histoire(s)* contends that cinema failed to be present to the present. For Rancière, this is the 'thought' of *Histoire(s).*

Rancière argues that the video essay is not just critical but attempts to redeem cinema by heeding the duties that attach to its ontology and restoring cinematic purity. Thus, one of the predominant aesthetic strategies in *Histoire(s)* is the deployment of anti-montage to restore the primacy of images over the plot and demonstrate their indifference to the stories into which they were once arranged. By appropriating numerous single shots and sequences from some of the most renowned films of the twentieth century – and some less well-known ones as well – Godard divorces cinematic images from their original stories. Rancière claims that the effect is to turn images into 'icons of the originary presence of things' so that 'the face of things impresses itself like the face of the Savior on Veronica's veil'.[36] According to Rancière, this reinstates an originary sensorium of images, a virtual world that lies beyond the diegetic worlds in which the images were 'originally' inserted.

Godard's quest in this respect is consistent with the more general aspirations of the aesthetic regime of the image. He reverses the logic of the representative regime as it is manifest in the impact of continuity editing on classical narrative cinema. Such editing subordinates the image to the narrative, film form to the arrangement of the plot, events to logical causality.[37] Rancière finds the same idea that Flaubert had of writing in the cinema purists' idea of cinema. Where Flaubert used style as an absolute way of seeing things to attend to the 'ordinary prose' of an otherwise indifferent world, Epstein deemed cinema to be the first art capable of doing justice to the real drama of life by simply 'record[ing] the infinity of micro-movements'.[38] Godard's anti-montage similarly emblematizes the idea that cinema's uniqueness comes from its capacity to record the movement of life itself; that is, from its silent testimony to the noumenon or the in-itself of things.

The restoration of this iconic function of images appears to produce pure images. Rancière calls them 'event-worlds that co-exist with the infinity of other event-worlds'.[39] They belong not only to the once enslaved but now free 'pure' history of cinema, but also supposedly to 'all other forms of illustration of the century'.[40] To be sure, the corpus that Godard hails in *Histoire(s)* is a body of presentations unwilling to gloss over its less attractive features, whether it is the images of Holocaust victims, or the sequence from Pasolini's *120 Days of Sodom* of the libertine, prostrate, arms-out-stretched-in-orans position ecstatically embracing the 'holy' water of the innocent who urinates on his face, or the shots of early twentieth-century pornography, so much more appalling than any contemporary equivalent because of their portrayal of women as children, or, more unsettling yet, the indifferent footage of Hitler seated, gazing out the window of a train.[41] Rancière proposes that the combination of these 'random' images form a new sphere of co-belonging that bears witness to a virtual sensorium of inter-expressivity bound up with cinema's 'historical' power, which is the power 'to put every image into associative and inter-expressive relationships with all other images'.[42] For one brief moment Rancière calls this anti-montage 'fusional montage'.

Rancière contrasts this 'historical power' with a 'dialogical power of association and metaphor'.[43] In a manner that is consistent with the dialectic between form and fable (and between the aesthetic and representative regimes) that he elaborates in the 'Prologue', the relocation of images in Godard's project means that their sovereignty is short-lived. The apparently infinite potentialities of fusional montage settle into a more easily legible symbolic montage (although it will take Rancière until his next engagement with *Histoire(s)* to use this term) and help to sediment Godard's thought.[44]

Rancière's description of one such use of montage perfectly illustrates at a micro level the entire movement from fable to form to refabulation that he argues takes place in Godard's cinema. Rancière interprets a sequence close to the end of the first episode as a triumph of the restitution of symbolic meaning. Instead of recapitulating how Edmund's suicide at the end of *Germany Year Zero* stands as a materialization of the impossibility of innocence in occupied post-war Germany, Rancière sees Godard simultaneously employing a range of video-editing techniques to show how Italian neorealism embraced cinema's power to convey, in Flaubertian spirit, 'the passivity of things with neither will nor meaning',[45] and symbolic montage to redefine the meaning of the same images. Rancière locates the symbol in a superimposition of Edmund rubbing his eyes moments before jumping to his death onto the innocent gaze of Gelsomina from *La Strada*. Between the gazes of the two 'children' Rancière finds an annunciation of the Resurrection, and a rebirth of cinema 'to its powers and duties to see'.[46] By harnessing the power he had restored to the image when he prised it away from its subordination to narrative and resorting to symbolic montage, Godard makes use of the tools of the very order he had sought to subvert. For Rancière, the alleged moral premise of the entire project is sacrificed in this move.

Rancière has thus framed Godard's proposition as his own question and derives his answer from a reading of Godard's work against itself. Viewed from the vantage of articulating the process of cinematic thinking, Rancière's first interpretation of the video essay, seems to locate thinking only in the triumph of the representative regime, of representation sublating the aesthetic. At the same time, however, Rancière proves his point that the film thwarts the moral fable it had sought to demonstrate by arguing that the effect of Godard's redemption of cinema by the methods I have just described doesn't successfully atone for cinema's historical infidelities but trivializes them: it demonstrates both 'the infinite possibility and radical harmlessness of the great manipulation of images'.[47] For Rancière, the final thwarting (or the last turn of the screw) reveals not the purity of the cinematic image, but its innocence. Innocence both alludes to the crime of which cinema was accused and refers to an ontological predisposition which will never allow it to resist being led astray.

But how do we know that such a view was not the one that Godard was at pains to present all along? We are left with the question: whose thought is it anyway?

6 Godard on Montage

Inasmuch as Rancière's first essay on *Histoire(s) du cinéma* exemplifies the broader argument of the book *Film Fables* that cinema brings to the fore a dialectic between fable and form, its thrust places montage in the video essay largely on the side of the representative regime. In the first instance, this is the conventional montage associated with continuity editing, in the second it is the symbolic montage that permits Rancière to read the story that Godard has constructed on the back of another. Automatism, on the other hand, is figured here in terms of a kind of anti-montage and with Godard's fleeting success in restoring the iconic function of images.

In casting montage and anti-montage as opposed aesthetic strategies, Rancière fails to adequately heed both the distinctiveness of Godard's own views on montage and their pertinence to extending the sweep of cinematic automatism. Throughout *Histoire(s)* Godard repeatedly makes reference to an essay he wrote for *Cahiers du cinéma* in 1956 entitled 'Montage, mon beau souci'.[48] This essay provides a means of nuancing the circuit that Rancière describes from the conventional montage of mainstream narrative to the restoration of pure images by anti-montage to the restoration of meaning by symbolic montage, and to consider the problem of the immanence of cinematic thinking.

The concept of automatism has been important to a number of other theorists of photography and film. For Walter Benjamin, the photographic image makes us aware of an optical unconscious because what the camera sees is 'affected unconsciously' and in a way that has not been 'worked through by a human consciousness'.[49] The separation of the artist and his or her vision brings the 'unintended' into play. Automatism, for André Bazin, means forming an image of the world automatically, providing access to 'the natural image of the world that we neither know nor can see',[50] and 'without the creative intervention of man'.[51] Similarly for Stanley Cavell, cinematic automatism involves the removal of the subject from aesthetic form, 'the human agent from the task of reproduction'.[52] I would argue that Godard's conception and use of montage is so thoroughly imbued with automatism that it introduces the operation of the unconscious into the arrangement of images in order to demand thinking.

In 'Montage, mon beau souci', Godard engages in the debate about the pre-eminence of *mise en scène* or montage as the constitutive essence of cinematic ontology to present a very original argument that montage is integral to *mise en scène*.[53] Montage here is shown to be both passive and creative, something that the director can deploy intentionally – whether to orchestrate diegetic reality or to show thought – and something that 'thinks' independently; indeed, something capable of exceeding conscious manipulation. The significance of this essay has previously been recognized for Godard's attempt to reconcile his distinctive interest in montage with the way Bazin formulates cinematic ontology with reference to automatism.[54] The standard, if somewhat inaccurate, reading of Bazin's conception of cinematic ontology sees him giving priority to *mise en scène* over montage on the grounds that montage does not let reality reveal itself through the *mise en scène*, but instead determines and restricts what is visible in the image. Understood in this way, montage is an effective means of limiting the chaos of profilmic reality and of creating a narrative by minimizing the capacity of images to 'speak' to one another.

Godard makes the point that montage is integral to *mise en scène*, or better, the two are integral to each other, by drawing out three significant characteristics of montage. The first concerns its temporal specificity, the second its relational capacity, the third its revelatory nature. Godard observes first that montage does in time what direction does in space: it performs a kind of opening up of the present towards the future.[55] Second, whether it is the décor, the lighting, the arrangement of objects within the shot, the depth of field or the scale of the image – in other words, whether it happens at the level of plastic form or profilmic content – the mere fact of something distinguishing itself from the quotidian appearance of things can be understood as a montage effect. Like Eisenstein before him, Godard thinks of montage not simply as something that happens between shots, but within them as well. Godard says montage is responsible for the emergence or development of an idea when elements *within* the shot cease to function in a purely denotative way *and* between shots when something related to the protagonist's character – his or her motivation or thinking or impulse – dictates the cutting between shots to deliver up the movement of the story.[56] With his second point, Godard both demonstrates the co-implication of montage with *mise en scène* and suggests something about its complexity as well; namely, that montage is cinema's means of creating relation. Montage is what happens between things when what is seen and heard separates itself from an undifferentiated whole to pose itself either in relation to the whole or in relation to another part of it. Godard's third point, which is vital to understanding the presence of automatism in montage, is that montage effects can surpass those of *mise en scène*, and when they do so 'the beauty of the latter is doubled, the unforeseen unveiling secrets by its charm in an operation analogous to using unknown quantities in mathematics'.[57]

To understand how montage both submits to *mise en scène* and acquires the capacity to surpass it in practical terms, let us turn to Godard's formulation and deployment of the cinematic device of 'cutting on the look'. While film studies understands this shot in its capacities of establishing point-of-view and suturing the spectator into the fabric of the narrative by switching their primary identification with the look of the camera into a secondary identification with the look of a character, Godard understands it somewhat differently, suggesting, perhaps a little abstrusely at first, that its effect is 'to bring out the soul under the spirit, the passion behind the intrigue'[58] and then, more tellingly, as almost the 'definition of montage' and evidence of 'its submission to *mise en scène*'.[59]

Cutting on the look is one of the devices used throughout *Histoire(s) du cinéma to* link images together that might otherwise be deemed to be discontinuous, or to put it in Rancière's terms, to resubmit those shots that have been snatched from their original films and recombined in their newly adoptive sequences in the quest of symbolic montage. Remember it was the gaze of Gelsomina in *La Strada* that connected with Edmund on the verge of suicide in *Germany Year Zero*, and that this connection saw cinema reawakened to its obligation to be present to the presence of history. In the second episode, 'Une histoire seule', cutting on the look is employed reflexively to punctuate various sequences of images in the repeated citation of a medium close-up of a man and woman positioned on either side of a movie projector. In all instances of the use of this shot the couple exhibit the same attentive gaze, the same wide-eyed intense expression. The projector between them insists that it is a screen at which they look, even though their gaze, taken together with the composition of the shot, is reminiscent of parents observing their new-born child.

Their gaze, like a shoot, sprouts from their eyes, roots itself in the image that follows, and creates an eyeline match. This means that the matching image is mediated for us by the protagonists; it is a seen image. It shows not the thing-in-itself, but the image seen by another; not just what happens in the objective unfolding of the moments of the diegesis (the orchestration of the plot), but how the turn of events is invested or charged with feeling by the world's inhabitants. In every instance, the coupling of the shot with the images that follow compels the audience to pay as careful attention as the protagonists and to remember that such images are projected images, not 'pure' images that have never been seen.

But what happens when the look no longer submits to *mise en scène?* What would the parameters of its freedom be? And how would such freedom in turn impact on *mise en scène?* What kind of look is it that comes into play when montage doubles the *mise en scène* to reveal the secrets buried in it? To be sure, it is not the eye that looks but the image. This is the special look of the ocellus as it is understood to function in Lacan's discussion 'Of the gaze as objet petit a'. Ocelli are images of eyes that in themselves have no capacity for vision. Lacan recalls Roger Callois' uncertainty over the cause of their power: 'it is a question of understanding whether they impress … by their resemblance to eyes, or whether, on the contrary, the eyes are fascinating only by virtue of their relation to the form of the ocelli.'[60] This conundrum leads Lacan to insist that we distinguish between the function of the eye and the function of the gaze, where the function of the eye is to see, and that of the gaze is to ensure that the object feels the impact of being seen, exists in a world in which it is given to be seen.

I want to suggest that cutting on the look as it is understood by Godard discloses the function of the eye in cinema, but that his conception of montage puts into operation (at least one of) the function(s) of the gaze – a gaze that operates in the first instance without the involvement of a functioning eye. Just as the automatism celebrated by one film theorist after another comes into play precisely because of an absence of sensory vision – because the camera does not see what it gives to be seen – montage as it is conceived by Godard produces 'vision' (the concept and not the sense) in the gap between images.[61] Indeed, it provides us with another way of thinking about his statement that 'cutting on the look' is the ambition of montage. Images are like conceptual seers, in fact seeing nothing of the images that appear to pass before them. Their look, which is the look (or gaze) of montage, embraces exactly the same kind of passivity that Bazin saw in cinema's propensity towards automatism.

This notion of the unforeseen releasing hidden secrets is precisely the kind of montage effect that Godard seeks from the way he sequences images and that makes his editing distinctive. As much as the camera turns profilmic reality into reality that will be seen, Godard's 'plot structures' are generated out of a deployment of montage that tirelessly works at making the invisible visible. Montage does so without pause or complaint because it operates blindly and in the first instance without thinking. But in the second instance, it demands thinking; and between the absence of thinking and the demand for thinking, the question of Godard's thinking comes to the fore – although the very nature of the relation between images and the operation of the gaze means that one cannot distinguish between intentional consciousness and the unconscious.[62] This is how montage surpasses *mise en scène*; and this is not simply the true drama of reality as Rancière suggests Epstein understands *photogénie*, but a more extraordinary drama subsisting independently of both subjectivity and the natural profilmic world as it unfolds for us in real time. It also requires the identification of some kind of consciousness to bring it into existence.

Consider how the shot of the couple on either side of the projector sees other images in the video essay. The shot is in fact from Ingmar Bergman's film *Prison*, and when the text '*le montreur d'ombres*' (the shadow puppeteer) is imposed on their image, one can't but help think of the prisoners who are duped by deceitful appearances in Plato's allegory of the cave. The suggestion of prisoners cooped up in caves works to combine Mum and Dad besotted with the infant cinema with the shot of Jimmy Stewart in *Rear Window*, cocooned in plaster, holding his camera to his face that Godard has used to open the first episode of *Histoire(s)*. These images together also remind us that we are reflecting on cinema as a specific kind of technology that historically has been put to a variety of uses. The second episode begins with an intertitle 'Cogito ergo video', thereby establishing that the episode will have something to do with Godard's interest in using the infinitely more versatile technology of video to reflect on the peculiarities of celluloid. In Hitchcock's film, Jeffries (Jimmy Stewart) has been photographing a crime, and in their episode the couple gazing intently at the projected image bear witness to uses of cinema for ethnographic filmmaking and to celebrations of imperialism in Hollywood films. Dispersed like a refrain throughout the episode is the proclamation that the Lumière brothers' invention of the cinematograph will yield 'neither an art nor a technique', and among the many images with which it combines is a sequence comprising shots from various cinematic adaptations of *Madame Bovary*, and Godard's reminder that, in addition to many technological marvels, the nineteenth century invented stupidity – though it is open to interpretation whether he is referring to Emma's behaviour, the particularity of comicality in Flaubert's writing, a lack of faith in the Lumière brothers' invention, or indeed suggesting that one needs to take care when ascribing something like intelligence to a machine.

7 Fusional Montage

Rancière implicitly acknowledges the importance of this capacity of Godard's montage to double *mise en scène* and release secrets buried in it when he describes how *Histoire(s)* exemplifies 'the most stunning manifestation of the Romantic poetics [of the age of history] of *everything speaks*'.[63] He observes that between the images that have been freed from the shackles of narrative and returned to an originary sensorium and the symbolic montage intended to redeem cinema of its sin of failing to be present to the presence of history, a new fraternity of images, a world of 'generalized interexpressivity' is implied.[64] These images 'become susceptible to striking an infinite number of relationships amongst themselves as well as with all the events of the century'.[65] Rancière, however, calls this a regime of meaning, whose rule is that everything speaks twice, first as pure presence, and second by virtue of the infinity of virtual connections between things.[66]

Rancière, like Godard, acknowledges the complexity of such 'speech' – for him, things speak 'the language of their mutism'.[67] It is arguable that fusional montage is not after all synonymous with anti-montage, but lies in the gap between the image that has had its iconic function of originary presence restored to it and symbolic montage, a place where the image hasn't yet acquired the signifying capacity of a textual symbol. The meaning of the image here is held in abeyance, but I would not go so far as to say that it rests in a state of potentially infinite expressivity, as Rancière critically contends. The video essay, Rancière has observed, is not comprehensive in the reach it extends to film history. I would argue that what is expressible is always constrained by the real conditions in which a work exists, even if those conditions are themselves not readily available to consciousness. In other words, the undetermined is not the same as the infinite. It is also arguable that even while observing fusional montage and heeding the emergence of its aesthetic parameters in the work of the Romantics in the first instance,[68] Rancière fails to acknowledge that this is in fact the condition under which all images (sounds included) subsist in *Histoire(s)*. The symbolic montage that he elucidates by contemplating the sequences where Godard weds shots from *La Strada* with those from *Germany Year Zero*, and comments on George Stevens' documentation of the camps with a collage of a shot of Elizabeth Taylor in *A Place in the Sun* and Giotto's *Noli me tangere*, is largely an effect of his own interpretative reading. This point is brought home when in his second engagement with *Histoire(s)*, Rancière is more circumspect about symbolic montage, taking care to distinguish it from dialectical montage and acknowledging that his interpretations of Godard's sequencing of images are allegorical.

8 Two Kinds of Thinking: Dialectical Montage and Symbolic Montage

Writing about *Histoire(s)* again two years later in *The Future of the Image*, Rancière ascribes significantly more importance to montage and extends its dominion beyond 'narrow cinematic meaning'.[69] Montage now has the general power of 'paratactic syntax' that operates in the sentence-image. The basis for this new formulation of montage is his endeavour to understand the relationship between shots that appear to be 'without common measure' in Episode 4(b) *Les signes parmi nous*.[70] In this context, he argues that the words superimposed on images and used in voice-over to which we are hyperattentive do not hold the pre-eminent position that they had in the representative regime of art – the regime that had foundered precisely because of the image's power to exceed the word was suddenly recognized and 'the textual function of intelligibility' was no longer able to sequester the image to its service.[71] Words no longer assert authority over images and their sequencing but raise further questions about 'common measurement'.[72]

For Rancière, the great parataxis is a mode of articulation that negotiates two different distributions of the sensible, one of which comprises a schizophrenic explosion or breakdown of meaning into bodily rhythms and cacophonous noise, and the other the community dominated by the cliché and consensus, where the commodity and its sign are indistinguishable and bodies choose between anaesthetization or conformity to the rhythms of capitalism. The sentence-image is the technical means of negotiating these two territories.

The sentence-image is not a combination of word and image; it is the combination of two powers – first, the phrasal power of linking that is associated with written syntax; and second, the disruptive power that inheres in the image's excessive polysemy. It could thus be argued that the sentence no longer restrains the function of the word and the word itself starts to function as an image. We have already seen this in the montage sequences of *Histoire(s)*. The word is simply one image among others that look at one another.

Rancière also insists that this idea of montage as phrasing or linking is not to be thought as a subcategory of metaphor, although we will see that his formulation of symbolic montage is somewhat more accommodating than this insistence suggests. Phrasing is not the power of connecting the Holocaust to a horror film because of a certain homogeneity between two things; it is the power of clashing heterogeneous elements.[73]

Symbolic montage and dialectical montage are the major ways through which linking the heterogeneous occurs. Dialectical montage creates clashes between heterogeneous elements either by combining incompatible things or by fragmenting a continuum by inserting great distances between terms that appear to call for one another. While Rancière doesn't say as much, the nature of his examples suggests that whether dialectical montage proceeds by the first or the second method depends on whether the great parataxis confronts the schizophrenic scream or the continuum of consensus and the tyranny of the cliché. Combining heterogeneous elements is a way of managing the schizophrenic scream, and distancing terms that seem to call for one another is a response to the banality of the cliché. In both cases dialectical montage discloses another reality behind the apparent one and draws a contrast between worlds. This other reality might be 'the absolute reality of desires and dreams'[74] that the symbolist poet Lautréamont evoked when he envisaged 'the chance juxtaposition of an umbrella and a sewing machine on a dissecting table' (which the surrealists brought into even sharper relief when they made it the catch cry to sum up the method of all their madness). Or it might disclose the political reality of economic domination, as seen in John Heartfield's photomontages and Martha Ròssler's juxtaposition of American self-representations of domestic bliss and plenitude with photographs of the war in Vietnam. For Rancière, these clashes are used in art to reveal 'a different order of measurement' which is the secret reality of the world.[75]

Symbolic montage does the opposite of dialectical montage: it creates likenesses by drawing together unrelated elements. Rancière says symbolic montage is oriented towards familiarity and occasional analogy (and this is the evidence of his faltering stance against metaphor), thereby once again 'attesting to a more fundamental relationship of co-belonging, a shared world where heterogeneous elements are caught up in the same essential fabric and are therefore always open to being assembled in accordance with the fraternity of a new metaphor'.[76] While dialectical montage actively discloses a secret world, symbolic montage makes use of the shrouds of 'mystery' taken in the sense that Mallarmé meant it when he insisted that the best poetry proceeds by allusion, and recommended that images be used to 'evoke an object little by little, so as to bring to light a state of the soul' and objects in turn manifest 'a state of the soul through a series of unravelings'.[77]

Rancière's second encounter with *Histoire(s) du cinéma* extends the automatism he finds at the heart of the aesthetic regime of art into montage as well. In both dialectical and symbolic montage he writes of the operation of little machineries: '[t]he dialectical way invests chaotic power in the creation of little machineries of the heterogeneous'[78] and '[t]he symbolist way also relates heterogeneous elements and constructs little machines through a montage of unrelated elements'.[79] While Rancière doesn't elaborate further on how such machines are put into operation, or to what extent they are pre-programmed to perform the duties of constructing and dismantling meaning, it is easy enough to imagine the great parataxis negotiating the schizophrenic scream on the one side and 'the anodyne and glorious appearance of the world' on the other by putting these transformers to work.

Rancière starts to build a powerful image here even if he is reluctant to join the dots. It seems that the articulation of the dialectic at its broadest level – as a generative tension between the representative and the aesthetic regimes – has been readjusted to provide a different emphasis. Whereas in *Film Fables*, Rancière proclaimed a dialectic of servitude and mastery, of passivity and activity, and of the melancholic beauty of one being thwarted by the other, in *The Future of the Image*, the great parataxis, sandwiched between the schizophrenic scream on one side and consensual stupor on the other, utilizes two different machinic functions to engage with the two great distributions of the sensible that lie on either side of it. Montage takes either the material of the schizophrenic scream and provides it with the substance of sense or draws apart the clichés of received ideas and subjects them to a process of fragmentation. The dismantled consensus thus becomes indistinguishable from 'the flesh' of the scream that will need to be linked up all over again. While an admirable ethical stance would seem to underpin each pole of montage – insofar as each is intent on dealing with equally intolerable realities by reforming organizations of matter and redistributing the sensible, as it were – the operation of these machines together describe the circular arrangement akin to baling water from a ship that would otherwise sink. Operating in tandem with one another, they disclose a homeostatic reality.

With the development of the broadly applicable concept of the sentence-image, Rancière has rejected the automatism specific to the cinema only to install a much more generalist machinery in its place. While Rancière rails against the pure formalism associated with modernism and rejects in particular the cinema purist's emphasis on cinematic technology, this is clearly not because he disregards the role of technology *per se*. Whether or not this is the image that Rancière means to produce, it is what results when one's investment in the aesthetic regime focuses too much on form and not enough on content, and forgets that acknowledging the productive encounter between the two is where the possibility of thinking lies.

Is there scope for assessing the problem of cinematic thinking in this, it has to be said, ultimately formalist (though not purist) means of reading Godard's project? While it could be argued that dialectical montage can be seen in the 'secret' history that Godard endeavours to indicate behind the fabulations of images that Hollywood cinema took such delight in, Rancière argues that in the years since Heartfield, Rossler and *Pierrot le fou* the general sphere of the production of images and the widespread appropriation of the technique of what would once have been called 'dialectical montage' means that it has lost its functional efficacy: '[T]he procedures for linking heterogeneous elements that ensured dialectical conflict now produce the exact opposite: the homogeneous great layer of mystery, where all of yesterday's conflicts become expressions of intense co-presence'.[80] Rancière concludes his analysis of *Histoire(s)* by proposing that the project embodies the 'neo-symbolist and neo-humanist tendency of contemporary art'.[81]

In *Film Fables*, Rancière endeavours to reconcile two very different traditions of cinema – avant-garde/modernist cinema and classical narrative cinema – by showing that it is possible to ask questions of one tradition which are usually reserved for the other. Rancière thus adopts a posture of taking up the Godard who made *Histoire(s)* as a storyteller determined to show what he most loved and most despised about the medium, the institution and the century over which it held sway, rather than as an essayist and a radical experimenter with film form. Rancière makes Godard a storyteller rather than a thinker because he finds his thesis wanting and his critical method no longer effective. Here I have taken Godard's (admittedly obscure) comments concerning film as a medium for thinking to show that there is scope in both the work and in Rancière's engagement with it for beginning to consider what cinematic thinking might entail. Rancière hits the nail on the head when he conceives Godard's work in terms of a tension between automatism and montage; for these are the means by which his films think. However, by understanding such operations as deriving respectively from the aesthetic and representative regimes he locks himself into a perspective that puts thinking on the side of the representative regime and sees automatism purely in terms of the power to restore the original sensorium of images. Even though Rancière's identification of a dialectic between the two regimes has scope for understanding thinking as something generated by that tension – as does his recognition of the inter-expressivity of images – he arrives at the view that Godard's thinking is expressed in symbolic montage and that such montage has meaning because it works within the terms of reference of the representative regime. Such thinking, for him, is not cinematic but literary. Yet what makes cinematic thinking specific, in Godard's hands, is the degree of automatism with which he is prepared to work and which makes images 'speak' to one another. Godard's essay of 1956 has a much broader conception of montage than Rancière acknowledges – one that is conceived on the basis of looking and heeds the importance of the unconscious in the play of thought. In his later development of the concept of the sentence-image, Rancière conceptualizes montage in terms much closer to Godard's – the polysemy of the image plays a crucial role and the unconscious necessarily resides in the clash of heterogeneous elements – but he continues to maintain that it is symbolic montage rather than dialectical montage that characterizes the sentence-image of *Histoire(s) du cinéma*. It is curious that Rancière argues that dialectical montage has no operational capacity in *Histoire(s)* when his own interpretation stages a series of dialectical turns in the work and in the process not only heeds the form of its images, but provides evidence of the way Godard's images look at one another.

Chapter 4

The Names in History: Rancière's New Historical Poetics

Dmitri Nikulin

In *The Names of History* Jacques Rancière undertakes a bold attempt to establish a new way of writing the history of those who have been so far excluded from and missed in it.[1] The task of the philosophy of history is to provide an outline of a new 'poetics' of historical narrative that would allow the previously silent and silenced to acquire a distinct voice, and thus to obtain the ability to be heard and to become the subjects of history rather than to remain impersonal objects of official historical records. To that end, Rancière provides a careful reconstruction of the modern history writing that, for him, is established on an improbable yet actual 'triple contract' of the scientific, narrative and political. In such a 'contract', the scientific is meant to necessitate 'the discovery of the latent order beneath the manifest order'; the narrative should supply 'the readable forms of a story with a beginning and an end, with characters and events'; and the political should be suitable for the age of democracy.[2] Rancière's claim, then, is that only through a critical reflection on this triple order might we be able to reclaim history and politics to those who did not and still do not have a voice in history.

1 The Scientific: Contra the Annales

In providing the outlines of this new history, Rancière begins by criticizing the Annales school, starting with Febvre. Yet the Annales school becomes both the point of departure and the point of return, insofar as Rancière borrows a good deal of his examples and some central ideas from Braudel (when speaking about the role of a single person who has the pre-emptive right for keeping a name for history), as well as from Le Roy Ladurie (who argues for new history as a democratic 'heresy'). According to Rancière, the Annales school reacted against the previous tradition of 'chronicling', in which every event or person was considered, nominalistically, as being strung onto a thread of linear temporal progression, reduced to just a record in a document. As an alternative, the Annales school strove to provide a 'scientifically' rigorous history based on measurement – on geography, statistics and demography.[3] Instead of providing a haphazard chronicle, one should work out a historiography working with big periods and whole 'mentalities', which are sometimes read into or out of concrete examples of a 'microhistory' (as in Le Roy Ladurie's history of the village of Montaillou in Ariège),[4] and inscribed into a closely inspected place that engenders history by transmitting to it the character of its 'terroir'. (Later, this approach was transformed and reinterpreted in Nora's extensive project of the 'places of memory'.)[5] The Annales revolution in history thus presupposes the science of registration and measurement, of numerical evaluation and statistical analysis of 'objective' data.

Against this kind of historiography, one could argue that in order to know something about past events one should look at them from a particular perspective that is already implicitly loaded with theoretical presuppositions and interpretations, which, however, remain outside of the historical analysis. In other words, the Annales school's approach might in fact shape and construct, rather than discover and interpret, historical material. For Rancière, however, the main problem with the Annales school is that it leads to a complete dissociation of the scientific and the narrative component of history. By promoting a strictly scientific approach, such a history first ignores good storytelling, which results in history being dissociated from the story; and second, favouring 'the great spaces of life formed over long periods',[6] the Annales school's kind of history suppresses and abolishes the uniqueness of events and of proper names, which results in their anonymity and obliteration. From now on, personal names are irretrievably lost for history qua personal and become only raw material for scientific interpretation. Thus, for Rancière, in coupling science *and* history, the Annalistes establish an insurmountable separation between science and narrative (*récit*).[7] However, when history becomes scientifically constructed historiography, it degenerates into a sociology that abolishes history altogether.[8]

2 Michelet, the Ambivalent Figure of the Father

Jules Michelet, often considered the founder of modern French historiography, is also one of the main figures in Rancière's discussion of history.[9]

Since, in the words of Lucien Febvre, Michelet is 'the founding father' of the Annales school, Rancière cannot avoid both an appropriation and a rejection of Michelet's way of studying history.[10] While being critical of Michelet's political views (although progressive for his age), Rancière is fascinated with Michelet's *style* of writing history. Michelet's poetic history, and especially its remarkable appropriation and presentation in Roland Barthes' book on Michelet, becomes the non-foundational stylistic foundation for Rancière's new 'poetics' of history.[11]

In Rancière's account, Michelet overcomes the previous 'royal-empiricist' analysis that concentrates on grandiose king-like figures by inventing a 'republican-romantic' historiography, which attempts to spell out and to account for 'the appearance of a new political entity that is at the same time the new object of love, the native land'.[12] Michelet, then, substitutes the figure of a king as the embodiment of a people with the abstraction of people and country as a nation that is now the historical subject rubbing shoulders and engaging in struggles with other subjects who are also nations. This collectivity of the people for Michelet is embodied in one event that will always have but one inexplicable, true and eternal name: the Revolution.[13] Since, however, this event cannot ever be fully explained, the event of the Revolution becomes a non-event. This can be considered a properly Romantic component in Michelet's writing about history, similar to Schlegel's insistence on recognizing something in a person that can never be fully thematized or spelled out.[14] Hence, Michelet invents a new narrative that, in the words of Rancière, 'is not one and that thereby suits the event that doesn't have the character of an event'.[15]

For this reason, Michelet's narrative is inevitably anti-mimetic,[16] because the subject of history can never be imitated or fully reproduced. A historical event, therefore, can only be hinted at, and the historian can give us a glimpse into it not by an exhausting, rigorous and scientific analysis of all the appropriate circumstances, but only through a poetic description of the event's seemingly accidental appearance.

The following are two examples of Michelet's 'historical poetics' – one in the original, the other in translation. A history of the sea: 'L'eau de mer, même la plus pure, prise au large, loin de tout mélange, est légèrement blanchâtre et un peu visqueuse. Retenue entre les doigts, elle file et passe lentement.'[17] And a history of the revolution: 'What is the old regime, the king and the priest in the old monarchy? Tyranny, in the name of grace. What is the revolution? The re-action of equity, the tardy advent of eternal justice.'[18]

The science of history has thus become altogether abandoned and dissociated from the poetic narrative in Michelet, so that we are presented with a choice: either an accurate dry scientific historical analysis; or an oracular engaging storytelling. Michelet clearly opts for the latter, whereas Rancière hopes to turn the disjunction into a conjunction, while still adhering to Michelet's poetics in Barthes' version.[19]

For Michelet, then, the truth of an event is better 'read in cries than in spoken words, better in the disposition of things than in the ordering of discourse. It is better read where no one is trying to speak, where no one is trying to deceive.'[20] And such is the gasp of a 'silent witness' whom the historian 'brings into a significance without lies.'[21] This means that the historian should become, in Barthes' formulation, a civil servant who is in charge of the good of the dead by explaining the meaning of their actions and lives to both us and the dead who never understand why they lived.[22]

The central idea in Michelet that is scrutinized by Rancière is that the historian is obliged *to lend his voice* to others who have so far remained voiceless and, thus, outside history. But at this point, Rancière becomes critical of Michelet, because for Michelet the meaning of history is *immanent* to history and to the narrative through which it is told, so that the historian as the hierophant of history generously returns this meaning to us in and through narration.[23] Moreover, Michelet *tells* us this meaning, whereas Rancière attempts to rescue history from a precise, finalized and unambiguous speech that signifies history's becoming a stiff scientific enterprise, a division of political science, which only means the abolition of history.[24] Rancière, on the contrary, intends to reclaim the literary 'excess' of what history can possibly say ,and in this way, to allow for a new narrative capable of giving a voice to the voiceless.

3 Metaphors of the Political: The King, the Sea, Death

The 'royal-empiricist' history offers highlights of the biographies of 'great people', represented archetypically by the figure of the king. A 'romantic' way to overcome and suspend this approach is to turn the king into a metaphor. Once the king becomes a metaphor, his life story cannot be fully told and deployed, precisely because it is now only a metaphor. But the metaphor can be elicited and explored in its multiple meanings, which can be further clarified and complicated by other metaphors, such as death and the sea.

The significant insignificance of the figure of the king as a metaphor in which all individual and concrete historical features begin to fade and get obliterated is put forward by Braudel. Yet in his great voluminous book about Philip II of Spain, Braudel mentions the king's death only in passing.[25] The death that took place in September 1598 was not the end that completed the whole period in history called 'the age of Philip II' or simply 'Philip II'. In this sense, the end 'never took place'.[26] If there was no end, then there was no death, at least, no death worth paying attention to. But without the end, a historical event can never get and preserve its meaning. The event is thus displaced, is out of place. Hence, we have to find other ways to speak about it and to communicate it.

Rather than obtaining its meaning at the end – the meaning that can be expressed in words, or speech (of history), passed on and communicated to posterity – the death of the king for Rancière is simply 'becoming silent' (*devenir-muet*).[27] It is not meaningless; it is simply mute and thus cannot be told. Why? Because it is a double event, both a political and a 'paper death' (perhaps, in this way corresponding to the 'two bodies' of the king, the body natural and the body politic).[28] Philip was a bureaucrat king who ruled out of Escorial, the centre of the web of known and hidden connections which he established in order to manage his empire. Almost never leaving his seat, every day he had to go through a pile of paperwork, make decisions on cases, write resolutions, reward the loyal, and punish the apostates. As the head of a bureaucratic system that he single-handedly creates and maintains, the king becomes the epitome of a ruler-bureaucrat who accumulates power in, and emits it from, a single centre that is both real and symbolic. The king, then, becomes ubiquitous and omnipresent through the bureaucratic network, yet is entirely withdrawn from the world, which makes history impossible, other than the history of the organization and distribution of such a power under the generalized and impersonal name of the king.

For this reason, the dead king is nothing more than the silent king who leaves behind him a 'mass of paper'.[29] The king is buried alive under this mound of paperwork and, as a 'paper' king, is already dead long before he dies. The mass of paper becomes his tomb, in which he is buried long before he is dead. Everyone else either is reduced to a record somewhere in the geological layers of paper, or speaks directly, yet in striking opposition to the immense paperwork. This inevitably puts such a speaker outside of truth, the access to which can only be granted through the access to the documents read and approved by the king. The living and the dead cannot speak for themselves and thus are outside of, and remain inaccessible in, history.

Still, there is something so vast that it cannot be missed, even by an inattentive and heedless eye, yet is still overlooked by the meticulous letter-king. It is the sea. In its startling sublimity, with its Micheletist 'whitish' (*blanchâtre*) water, the sea attracts, dazes, and makes stumble everyone who looks at it. But not the king, who is far from the sea, living in his paper tomb. The king does not know what the sea is, what it signifies, even if his empire is the empire of the sea. Michelet's 'Copernican revolution in history', then, is 'a displacement from the history of kings to that of the sea',[30] when the sea can – and does – become a subject of history.

Rancière's own attempt to appropriate the metaphor of the sea, however, appears doubtful: for him, the sea is split into the easily readable yet rather simplistic opposition of the sea of the Mediterranean to the sea of the Atlantic. As a historical subject, the sea, then, should be understood from, and in relation to, epic – *its* epic. For the Mediterranean, it is the *Odyssey*; for the Atlantic, *Moby Dick*, a 'counter-epic'.[31] The apparent difference between the two, for Rancière, is that the former unites – by the ancient but still very much alive communication of trade and culture exchange; the latter divides – by its vastness and especially by its being 'a space without historiality'.[32] The simplistic opposition between the Old World and the New World is unluckily reminiscent of the alleged superiority of the supposed refinement of the metropolis over the vulgarity of the colony. Besides, many other historical 'seas' – the Sea of Japan, the Black Sea, the Pacific, the Caribbean, the Tasman Sea – each comes with its own 'epic' and therefore the implied history.

4 The Excess of Words and the Mass of Paperwork

The sea, for Rancière, is a metaphor that is more than a metaphor, because it is the very basis for a new history that should be turned into a story, which can only be told as metaphorical. Yet the metaphor of the sea still does not allow for the appearance in history of those who are displaced from it by great-man-oriented history-telling. Hence, it is the very *form* of telling history that defines what history is, how history is reconstructed from the past and how history becomes normative for the future.

Therefore, the 'words', or speech, of history (which is the original title of the book in French) do matter. History is not innocent for Rancière but implies a particular kind of politics; and if the current politics of the time does not correspond to the normative evaluation of what the time should be, it is history that needs to be changed, the very form of telling history that might give politics the language and tongue to account for the (democratic) age. It is thus the 'words' or 'names' that need to be liberated in their excessive meanings in order to fit the historical, political and social reality. Unwittingly, the originally Confucian (*Lun Yu* 13:3) notion of 正名, *zheng ming*, the 'rectification of names', thus becomes a metaphor for the revolution in history.[33]

The 'poor use' of words,[34] however, is itself established by the way a particular kind of history is told – by the 'royal-empiricist' accounts of paper deeds of the 'paper kings' that intend to regulate the historical speech as forever finalized and unambiguous. The 'mass of paper' that buries the king also buries everyone else, because people are reduced to impersonal records and faceless inscriptions, incapable of speaking for themselves or of being spoken of in history.

Therefore, the more people use the current 'words' of history, the more they are themselves obliterated from it. This situation is described by Rancière as the 'excess of words' (*l'excès de parole*).[35] Referring to Durkheim's claim, which Rancière regards as 'one of the founding axioms of modern social science' (which, in a sense, goes back to Hippocrates' natural philosophy), that 'the excess of life makes life sick and provokes death', Rancière diagnoses modern society with the inability to release an 'excess of speech' in a non-choking and non finalizing way. Rather, one should pay attention to the literariness of historical speech that is always 'excessive' in that it allows for its reinterpretation and reappropriation by the previously historically mute. Michelet, for him, is the inventor of the 'art of treating the excess of words, "the death by paperwork" of the king', which means the rejection of the 'royal-empiricist' model of history in favour of the new 'republican-romantic' one.[36] However, Michelet's way of telling and accounting for history is dated and is thus unsatisfactory for modernity, because, metaphorically speaking, after the death of the king (i.e. after the revolution) those who were previously deprived of the right and chance to produce their own 'paperwork' begin frantically doing so, which is still meaningless and thus leads to the total loss of any meaning in history.

Schematically put, history for Rancière is the history of the understanding and living up to the expectations of the Event, which for him is the French Revolution that kills the king (already buried under the mass of paperwork), liberates the bourgeoisie and eventually allows the dispossessed to come to the fore of history, leaving behind the previous masters of history. The three stages of modern history are thus the royal, the bourgeois (of which Michelet becomes *the* historian), and the democratic. Democratic history, however, is not yet properly told and thus needs a new language and new poetics, which Rancière hopes to lay out in his book. This new history 'must regulate this excessive life of speakers that has killed royal legitimacy and threatens that of knowledge'.[37]

Thus, the problem with history for the democratic age is that it is indispensable but does not (yet) exist, because 'the excess of speech' that creates modern history[38] currently cannot be regulated. History's very beginning is troubled, because modern history abolishes royal legitimacy but still uses its narrative and the suffocating massive paperwork: 'The history of the masses that belongs to the age of the masses finds its seat only in speaking of the times of kings.'[39] Inherited from the *ancien régime*, the bourgeois abundance of words makes speech frozen and incapable of either grasping or rectifying the exclusion of people from history. This, for Rancière, is the main 'defect' (*défaut*)[40] of modern history.

5 Giving Voice to the Poor

For Braudel, when paperwork becomes available to everyone in the sixteenth century, the 'Renaissance of the poor' occurs, as opposed to the 'true Renaissance'.[41] The former, 'faux' Renaissance is propelled by people's hope to talk about themselves in writing, in the hopes of leaving a trace in and for history through a written document. But the suffocating 'mass of paperwork' buries not only the king, but also everyone around him under 'the paperwork of the poor' (*la paperasse des pauvres*, the 'scribbles of the poor').[42] Those who are eager to write about themselves – the 'poor' – speak 'poorly' and beside the point, outside the truth about themselves, not only because they are not in command of the proper style, but mostly because the truth of themselves, *already* excluded from the 'paperwork' history, cannot be told by the current means of writing. When the symbolic death of the king under the mass of paper is followed by his equally symbolic death after the Revolution, history still remains unable to tell about those who previously have been transparent for and unnoticed in history. Hence, as Rancière concludes, 'the heritage of the king's "force of history" has to be removed from the people of paper that encumbers his desk'.[43]

Braudel's answer to the exclusion of people from the elitist royal empirical history was to 'reverse the order' of history by bringing people back as the 'masses', to write history on a grand scale, as the 'history of mentalities' inscribed into a 'geology of time' over a 'long duration'.[44] However, such an answer still appears unsatisfactory, because the 'poor' are still effaced both in and by the royal empiricist and the Annales school's ways of telling and doing history: in the former, only a chosen few have access to the constitution of history through writing and documents; in the latter, the masses efface the individuality of those whom they embrace and are supposed to represent.

Rancière opts for a different kind of history, which would steer between the Scylla of abstract individualism and the Charybdis of impersonal dissolution. He hopes that the 'poor', who are the dispossessed of history and forsaken in history, can come back in a new history and become its proper subject. To that end, in a book entirely dedicated to the 'poor', Rancière argues that our 'democratic and social age is . . . neither the age of the masses nor that of the individual'.[45] A problem with the 'poor' is that they should include not only the living but also the dead, those 'poor' of the past who need to be restored back to history yet cannot tell and talk about themselves. However, the absent are not in the past, because each of their stories is '*no longer there* – that is in the past; and that never was – because it never was *such as it was told*'.[46] The only way out, then, is to give or 'deliver' to the 'poor' a *voice*.[47] The paradox of bringing the 'poor' back to history is that Michelet tells us what they would have said, whereas Rancière hopes to allow them to say what they should have said – but in whose voice?

At this point, as in his whole historical project, Rancière appears to be influenced more by Barthes' reading of Michelet than by Michelet himself. For Barthes, historical truth can be recovered only if we take documents as a voice, rather than as witnesses.[48] The historical truth, then, is not (only) a factual correspondence of the told to what happened, but much more the recognition, behind a document, of the voice to those who so far were outside of being told. Rancière replicates this position in considering a historian as a contemporary of a speech,[49] which means that a historian should *lend* his or her voice to those who have been missed in and by history.

As an example of those who speak 'in excess', Rancière mentions[50] Tacitus' description of Percennius, who, after the death of Augustus, demands an improvement of the soldiers' situation. Tacitus then gives a convincing reconstruction of the non-convincing speech of Percennius, who is simply considered to be socially not in a position to advocate any change.[51] For this reason, Percennius' speech is not only subversive – it is self-subversive. As Thucydides lends his voice to Pericles, so Tacitus allows Percennius to speak through him. Yet the very language and 'poetics' of Tacitus' history does not allow Percennius to speak for the 'poor' of a Pannonian legion. Percennius, therefore, 'speaks without speaking'[52] and is thus outside historical truth: he simply has *no right* for reason and language, unlike Blaesus (the commander of the legions), which means that Percennius' reasons in support of the exploited cannot even be considered true or false. The historian, then, should give the 'poor' a *proper* voice. But which voice?

To restore the wretched of the Earth to history is to allow people to reclaim not only their dignity, but also their very lives within the life of memory. No doubt, this is a worthy enterprise. However, the 'poor' are speechless because they *do not know how to speak*, and when either a 'royal' or 'romantic' historian lends them his or her voice, he or she makes them speak in well-established 'literate' ways that substitute for, and thus really miss, the unique voices of the 'poor'.[53] But because the 'poor' are speechless, giving them a voice in fact amounts to *assigning* to them a voice, and this voice is always the historian's voice. To give the 'poor' a voice, then, is not only to reinvent them in Collingwood's sense, where to understand a past event is to restore and re-enact the 'mind' of its actors, to reproduce the whole set of mental states and intentions that constitute a historical action.[54] To give the 'poor' a voice in Rancière's sense is *to invent* them, *to ascribe* to them a voice. Nothing guarantees that the voiceless 'poor' will speak *in their own voice*, because so far they have not had it and have had no way to gain a voice for history. Hence, Rancière has to invent a voice for them that would suit their needs as he understands these needs. Yet the voiceless might have a different voice. Moreover, they might have *many* voices; and even more than that: these voices might *change* with time.

Rancière's historical poetics presupposes that the speech of the 'poor' is always meaningful yet they are not aware of its meaning before it is released in history.[55] Therefore, the historian must give them a voice. However, by lending them a voice the historian does not deliver the voiceless a voice of their own but assigns them the voice of the learned historian-writer with all the prejudices (as 'pre-judgements') and implied meanings that come with this voice, which, however, the historian him- or herself might not really know. In Michelet, the sea becomes the subject of a historical account but speaks for the historian in the historian's own voice; in Virginia Woolf, the mark on the wall becomes the subject of a literary novel yet speaks for her in her voice, which is not fully understood until the end of the story. But then one needs to lend a voice to the historian, and then a voice to this voice and so on. The voiceless are thus deprived of a unique voice and are each made to speak in the historian's own voice. Rather than being a 'medium' for the voiceless, the historian becomes the narrator who at the same time is also the playwright, the director and the protagonist on the newly found historical stage. The new historical narrative, then, gives voice primarily to itself, and not to its 'poor' who become an embodiment of the historian's own aspirations, thus turning 'poor' into an abstract historical construction of a solitary historical subjectivity. Rather, if one wants to help the 'poor' out of what Arendt called the 'futility of oblivion', one should give each a possibility to speak to and with others in a personal voice, rather than lending them one's own voice.

Besides, the 'poor' are initially an economic category meant to refer to the poor and exploited: our age, for Rancière, is the 'democratic and workers' age'.[56] But, if the struggle of the working people is far from being over and, as such, should be supported and recognized, one needs to rethink and extend (but not cancel) the democracy of our age beyond the labour-oriented paradigm. By referring to the oppressed as the 'poor', Rancière forever fixates and preserves them as poor and non-equal to others.

The category of the 'poor', therefore, does not extend to those whose systematic exclusion from history cannot, and should not, be thought in purely economic terms – for example, women. Progressive as it is, 'poor' is still exclusive of others. Rancière speaks about the exclusion of any exclusion (of what is 'exclusive of all exclusion', of the 'denial of exclusion', in reference to the English working class)[57] but in fact, his own approach is selective and exclusive of everyone who does not pass the test of being capable of the aspired new history.

Moreover, democracy should also imply a possibility of equal access to history-telling and a place in the memory of history for *all* living beings, both human and non-human, and even for non-living things. The 'poor' refer to a community bound by an economic or social bond (love, fraternity, work); not a universal community of humankind *and* nature. A 'natural history' should be possible in democracy, but Rancière leaves no place for it (unlike, for example, Hans Jonas in *The Imperative of Responsibility*[58]). If the category of the 'poor' has any place in history, it has to be radically rethought in order to be able to include the 'poor' of *nature*, those exploited and endangered precisely because of our transforming economic activity.

Rancière intends to provide a possibility for a universal history – but only for those who fall under its central category of the 'poor'. Yet, paradoxically, the context of his discussion is almost exclusively Eurocentric, with very sparse references to non-Western historiography and history. The category of the 'poor', then, is exclusive of everyone who does not fit into it and thus has no place in a new history. The equality becomes possible only within a community of those who are nominated equals[59] – for radical democracy would rather require radically non-exclusive ways of telling the history of the living and the dead, as well as of the living and the not living (the 'natural').

History, for Rancière, lives off the written words of the past. As such, history is itself a written enterprise whose task is to capture past events and to restore to dignity those who lived through them. Yet the 'poor' remain a constructed collective entity that speaks for a group constituted according to the recognized and newly invented procedures of telling history. It is then up to a historian to decide who can and should be included in this collective entity – and who can't and shouldn't. Moreover, a unique voice of a person might not be heard and lost in this collective voice, for if the dead are to speak through a historian, one needs to restore and preserve their names. But in most cases, the dead remain *nameless*, precisely because they have been excluded from past history with its preferential treatment of either only a certain kind of people – or of the whole masses of people. For Rancière, history faces 'the personal absence of what the names name' (*à l'absence en personne de ce que nomment les noms*).[60] I would think, however, that the problem is not only the absence of those whom the names name – but of the names themselves, which all too often are irretrievably lost from history. In this way, the narrative that would give the 'poor' a voice remains largely a normative but, in many cases, an impossible task.

6 A New Historical Poetics

In Rancière's project of a new history with its 'triple contract' between literature, science and politics, the scientific aspect means the *precision* of a historical account, rather than a set of quantitative methods that allow for the study and interpretation of empirical data. But to make a story historically precise, one should use radically new ways of telling it. Hence, in order to provide 'a poetic regulation of the excess' in history,[61] one needs a literary revolution. For Rancière, only a change in the very *form* of literary historical narrative will allow the 'poor' and dispossessed to gain their voice and to become fully present in history.

For this reason, one needs a new 'poetics of knowledge',[62] which, as Hayden White aptly defines it, 'is a study of a certain technique of writing by which a discourse originally belonging to "literature" escapes from this "literature" and, *by the use of literary techniques*, constitutes itself as a "science"'.[63] For Rancière, the human being is a literary animal,[64] no less than a historical being. Therefore, the task of a historian is to make the human being known through new forms of narrative, which are the new forms of writing, because history, as has been said, is a written narrative. In this way, the human being is also a *written* animal who writes, or signs, him- of herself back into history through a historian, now as a precise scientific *and* poetic enterprise. Only by becoming literature of a certain kind can history again become history; that is, revert back to its name, which presupposes a mode of an engaged storytelling that allows everyone to have a voice. The previously speechless regain a voice. Moreover, they become *visible*, which means that those who spoke as 'illiterate' become literate as visibly *written*.

In recent publications, Rancière appears still committed to the idea of the revolution in history as taking place first of all in literature.[65] But the revolution in history-telling suggests a new construction of the events, rather than their redescription or recollection anew. A historian, then, *must* produce literature,[66] yet the problem is to understand what kind of literature one should produce.

7 Style

One might say that while Michelet wants to invent a poetics *for* the revolution, Rancière hopes for a revolution in the poetics of history. History as literature, then, should be not a mere fiction, but should tell the truth of history by giving a chance to speak to those who so far have been voiceless and deprived of the possibility of speaking in history by either being muffled or being made to speak in improper ways (through 'excessive' speech that does not really tell anything). However, at this crucial junction, Rancière stops short of giving a developed account of the literary devices suitable for his new history. In fact, the truth of history for him lies largely in the very texture of narrative, in its *stylistic quality*, rather than in formal techniques and rhetorical devices:

> History can become a science *by remaining history* only through the poetic detour that gives speech a regime of truth. The truth it gives itself is that of a pagan incarnation, of a true body of words substituted for erratic speech. It doesn't give it to itself in the form of an explicit philosophical thesis, but in the very texture of narrative (*la texture même du récit*): in the modes of interpretation, but also in the style of the sentences (*la découpe des phrases*), the tense and person of the verb, the plays of the literal and figurative.[67]

The historian thus becomes a writer and playwright who suspends – *prohibits* – the traditional forms of history-writing as inadequate, and turns to the modern novel and to drama in search of new and suitable ways of speaking on behalf of the voiceless and 'poor'. The novels of Virginia Woolf, Flaubert and Joyce should supply the new language and forms of narrative, rather than empirical history or the history of mentalities. In the end, Rancière's project for a new history boils down to accepting Michelet's Romantic poetics of writing minus his liberal bourgeois politics. Or rather, it is Barthes' account of Michelet that establishes the new ways of writing history – in Barthes' case, a history of the historian.

Such a new history becomes a fragmented and systematically unsystematic intertextual pastiche of texts, documents, memoirs, references, reflections, poetic excerpts, aphorisms, incantations and oracles. In a sense, because the truth of history lies in the ways of telling of it, in the *style* of narration, the new historical poetics can and should be primarily *exemplified* and *demonstrated* in its very use, rather than strictly described and defined. Most probably, Rancière intends to exemplify this new historical poetics in his very writing about history, which, however, is not itself a history but a philosophical reflection on history.

8 A Critique

Rather than being defined through a number of methods and tropes, the new historical poetics should use a whole arsenal of literary, especially modernistic, devices. But, pre-eminently, the truth of history about those previously absent from it should be told by metaphor. It is in and behind a metaphor that the 'science' of new history seeks precision. For Rancière, Michelet was the first to realize that the truth of history is better told in 'cries' than in a well-ordered discourse. In the new history, literature should disrupt the statistical analysis: one should not hesitate to insert a 'little narrative' (*le petit récit*) of 'the teacher's notebook' or 'the memory of some childhood' into telling of a history.[68] In this way, it should become possible to overcome the gap between the 'poetic' word of myth and the systematic account of scientific historical discourse. The seemingly insuperable Platonic distinction between *muthos* and *logos* will disappear.[69] History, then, will become a mytho-scientific 'discourse-narrative' (*récit-discours*);[70] the poetry of history will become scientific, and as the science of history, poetic.

However, Rancière's history project appears shaky, because, first, the subject of history is a construction rather than a (re)description. In a sense, the new history is overly reflective in being more preoccupied with itself – its new poetics, forms of narrative and style – than with those about whom it is meant to speak. Second, the ideal of 'science' in history is reduced to the precision of metaphor, yet the precision of metaphor is a matter of interpretation left up to the narrator and the reader, and as such can be arbitrary.

Third, Rancière's narrative for a new history tries to avoid any structural classifications of literary and narrative genres. Still, it appears to be morphologically very close to the genre of 'tale' (fairy tale), which, as Scholles puts it, 'takes place in a world which is deliberately set against our own world as other, different, better. The tale is a progress toward justice through potentially tragic obstacles'.[71] But the tale, although being in an *oral* narrative form, has a highly structured plot,[72] which Rancière neither mentions nor employs, thus reducing tale-telling to the use of metaphor.

Fourth, the normative task, giving the dispossessed a voice and a place in history, is entrusted to a poetics that organizes its narrative around a metaphor. Yet in fact most of Rancière's metaphors – 'the sea', 'the excess of words' and others – have a *metonymic* function; that is, they suggest a connection by contiguity rather than by similarity. However, if Jakobson is right,[73] this turns the new history into a novelistic fictional literature.

9 Epic and Parataxis

Therefore, in order to be able to write a new history, the historian should make a literary revolution by inventing a *new poetics* that employs novel forms of narrative. Rancière grants Michelet the discovery of the immanence of meaning to forms of literary narrative,[74] which means that the ways we tell history are not 'innocent', for each one is a *form* of literary speech and thus entails a meaning that goes beyond both a straightforward imitation and a scientific interpretation of the past. But then, again, a particular narrative form provides a *construction* rather than a description of a meaning in history. We only need to choose the right genre of telling history. Yet in this way the dispossessed of history are assigned the voice of the benevolent narrator rather than gaining their own unique voices. The story of their history is then told *for* them, not *by* them.

But because the new history now has to speak through a historian who lends his voice to the new subject of history, history-telling becomes oracular rather than 'scientific'. Yet, the oracle is long dead in and for history, and should remain such if history is to be a reasoned enterprise of understanding the voices of people and things of the past for the sake of the understanding of the present.

Rancière makes an interesting observation which, however, he does not elaborate on but rather mentions in passing: the 'literary revolution' in history should overcome the traditional structure of the novel and turn to epic in order to allow the 'parataxis of democratic coordinations [to] succeed the syntax of monarchical subordinations'.[75] It is not by chance, then, that the metaphor of the sea as representing the new historical poetics is tied to an epic. The new history for Rancière should follow the narrative that makes it possible to break the existing hypotactic – and thus hierarchical – order of speech, where some people are considered to have a privileged access to being told about. Within the epic parataxis, the king is just one of the characters, but he is already dead, a stock character buried alive under the mass of speechless paperwork which constitutes his tomb.

It is well known that the modern novel (in Bely, Joyce, Proust) is very interested in epic, and intentionally uses and reproduces paratactic narrative structure. An important feature of epic, which distinguishes it from other literary genres – particularly from tragedy – is that epic introduces and holds together many narrative parts at once. Epic is therefore paratactic; that is, it allows for the simultaneous co-existence, or co-presence, of a number of different parts of equal value within its plot, which employs a series of mutually independent narratives. The paratactic whole does not take precedence over its parts, so that while each constituent is meaningful within the context of the unified whole, each part is nevertheless autonomous, remains equally meaningful and important, and is not subordinate to or hypotactically subsumed under the whole.

Because epic consists of many loosely related stories about independent characters, its narrative is therefore voluminous and lengthy and can begin and end with any event, which demonstrates epic's intrinsic unity.[76] But such is also the story of real events that often do not seem to have a meaning outside of the way they are told about. However, epic, originally paratactic, is later 'completed' by 'prequels' and 'sequels', which turns it into an enterprise of strict historical and temporal subordination.[77] This is the work of a traditional historiographer, who arranges the described events into a sequence that makes sense within the traditional novelistic or dramatic narrative structure of their entanglement, development and resolution.

Moreover, epic time is gathered into the atemporal 'absolute' past, that of memory and remembrance, removed from the linear and sequential historical time. The temporal setting of epic is the past *par excellence*, the non-existing tense of the absolute 'past present', always already complete but redefined through a renewed interpretation. For this reason, if the modern epic of the dispossessed can be told at all, it would place them in the historical presence of the goal the narrator establishes and attempts to articulate, such as atemporal justice.

Rancière presupposes the possibility of a modern historical epos that would acquit and justify those whom previous historical narratives have been systematically missing. Yet history is epic-oriented from its very inception as written history. Hecataeus of Miletus, who became the model for later historians – Hellanicus, 'the father of history' Herodotus, Eratosthenes, Strabo and Diodorus – already composed in the 'epic' mode.[78] In its very structure, Hecataeus' *Periēgēsis* is very similar to Homer's catalogue of ships in Book II of the *Iliad*. Hecataeus' history provides detailed lists and accounts of names – of people, peoples, countries, cities, mountains, rivers, islands – that became known in history as inscribed into a concrete place through the accompanying narrative of travel, founding and naming of a city, war, genealogy and so on. Such a history is structurally similar to epic in that it too consists of a great number of episodes that involve many people, and is thus very detailed, but its basic plot is rather simple and can be expressed in just a few words – although this plot is always capable of being further refined and finely tuned. One might say that this epic structure in fact is the historical invariant in any history. Epic has thus been the pattern for writing history from history's very inception and can also be taken as the model for new history.

10 Names of History and Names in History

Rancière criticizes Michelet for establishing the difference between word (*mot*) and name (*nom*) as a 'generalized synonymy'; that is, taking the name of a historical character to stand for a whole range of related phenomena and events, to 'all the places and all the generations that find voice in his speech'.[79] He too wants to get rid of such synonymy, as well as of proper names of chronicles and of common names of science in favour of the names that stand for concrete people.[80] However, as I have argued, this cannot be achieved, because the voices assigned to these names are reduced to the same unique authorial and authoritative, even if often implicit, voice of the narrator. The others' voices are then dissolved into various tonalities and registers of literary devices and writing techniques within the searched historical poetics. In this way, personal names get substituted for literary words.

Although this new historical poetics should be epic-oriented, Rancière mentions rather disparagingly 'the mnemonic fancy of the Homeric catalogue';[81] and yet, proper and personal names – unique but not mutually isolated – are handled in and by epic with great care. In an epic 'catalogue of names', each name is both independent of any other but at the same time appears in – but is not subdued to – a story that can be thought of as a historical narrative. Within the same history and the same set of names one can tell different and independent stories, which means that history is not teleological and dominated by one master narrative but allows for many histories. Each history that uses epic narrative is constituted by a detailed and elaborate account of names – the 'who' of history, as well as a relatively simple narrative account of the story – the 'what' of history, which can always be 'zoomed in' on with more details. These names are personal unique names that can be the names of people, events, things – including living things – which allow for a new 'natural history' of the world that is absent in most modern accounts of history, including Rancière's.

Such a history – which has the structure of the 'catalogue of names' that are further specified by a narrative – is, again, very similar to epic, which also uses a narrative plot (even if often skillfully hidden in some modernistic novels) and an ordered set of characters.[82] Yet Rancière's poetic narrative, however progressive it is intended in its design to be, is still selective and thus privileges one 'borrowed' voice – eventually, the voice of the narrator – at the expense of others who are therefore excluded from this constructed history. This makes this new history uniform, even if it might use fragmented narrative techniques. But if we want to conceive of everyone as a subject of history – of *a* history – we need to limit the exclusive power of narrative by limiting the very narrative itself, by reducing it to a 'minimal' narrative that is closer to the spoken word of mouth. The properly 'historical' thus resides in the detailed account of the names of those who should become the subjects of history.[83] Therefore, one should preserve and account for proper names as kept *in* history, rather than for the names *of* history.

If history is not monolithically universal and does not evolve towards a telos or an extra-historical purpose (which in Rancière is established by the voice of the narrator-historian), it must admit of a co-existing *plurality* of histories. This means that everyone always participates and lives in several histories at the same time. As I have argued, Rancière's new historical poetics supplies a new narrative that should justify those previously excluded from history by giving the dispossessed their place in history or, rather, making history the place for them. However, in such a history justice comes from and with a narrative that gets primacy over the names, because narrative constructs and constitutes the names of history by the 'words' of history.

I would think, however, that each history depends on, and is constituted by, its names, which are then its *proper* names. These names should have priority over the narrative, if they are to be the names in history; that is, not produced but shown and told by a history. Moreover, the names in history can be those of *any* people, things and events. The names in history, then, constitute the properly historical and should be carefully preserved, organized (of which epic poetic catalogue or genealogy are the examples), supplied and clarified by a narrative. Yet, contrary to Rancière, this narrative can in principle use *any* narrative techniques, and not just one poetic narrative that is thought of as both epically paratactic and modernistically aphoristic. History should care for those about whom it speaks and tells, and thus become properly democratic, not exclusive of anyone or anything. Every history, then, has the structure of the historical that provides the form for a history supported by the interpretative narrative that gives a history its content.

Chapter 5

Equality in the Romantic Art Form: The Hegelian Background to Jacques Rancière's 'Aesthetic Revolution'

Alison Ross

In his book *La Parole muette*, Jacques Rancière seems to agree with the key theses of Hegel's account of the Romantic art form. For Hegel, Romanticism institutes a new category of aesthetic value that admits the entry of the everyday and the ordinary into the field of art. According to Hegel's powerful account, Romantic art removes the classical restrictions from *what* art can represent, and *how* it should be represented. Similarly, Rancière treats the art of what he calls the 'aesthetic regime of the arts', which includes what is typically classified as Romanticism, in terms of its peculiar knotting together of the prosaic and the poetic. He revises the Hegelian formulation where art practice was cut loose from the classical hierarchies that had determined appropriate topics and techniques in terms of the political vocabulary of 'equality'. It is significant that for each, the entry of prosaic material into the field of the arts complicates the meaning of the category of the 'arts'. Like Hegel, Rancière singles out the literary arts of the 'word' as *the* historically significant form of Romantic art; for Rancière it is in literature that the 'disorder' affecting the modern category of the 'arts' first becomes visible. In this regard, he points specifically to the Romantic presumption of a plenitude of meaning in the world that literature would 'speak' as a case study of 'equality'.[1] Rancière's analysis is, however, again like Hegel's, no celebration of Romanticism, no simple recounting of its revolutionary impact. For each thinker, the intrusion of 'equality' that marks the field of Romantic art as a disturbance of the traditional hierarchies which had governed classical topic and technique does not just imply the eventual dissolution of the Romantic art form – and along with it, perhaps, the semantic integrity of the very category of 'art' – but also draws attention to the need for a critical, systematic articulation of the contradictory features of Romanticism.[2]

Nonetheless, the criticisms each makes of the Romantic art form service the claims of radically incompatible frameworks: Rancière is frustrated at the uneven recognition of equality in Romanticism and thus coordinates his discussion of the 'aesthetic regime of the arts', to which Romanticism belongs, with a political conception of equality able to locate and describe particular cases of deficient treatments of this theme in the Romantic paradigm. Hegel, in contrast, identifies in the prosaic material of Romantic art the justification for his historical thesis that art, as a mode of access to the absolute, is at an end. In other words, what Rancière identifies as the nascent signs of equality whose promise is deliberately curtailed, Hegel uses as evidence for the new hierarchical claims of the reflective dominance of philosophy.

Rancière's analysis of Romanticism aims to locate and defend the evidence of the efficacy of what he terms 'the aesthetic revolution'; briefly, the ways in which aesthetic practices are conceptualized as (and capable of being) engaged in the redesign of life. However, it also puts forward an explanatory schema that would make the different narratives of art – from Schiller and Benjamin to Adorno and Lyotard – intelligible as positions that endorse aspects of this aesthetic revolution. The critical motivation of this schema can be seen in the way that Rancière highlights the paradoxical commitments regarding the modes and effects of the communication of new perceptual modes of experience in each of these thinkers. Considered in relation to the stakes and implications of this critical reflection on the legacy of Romanticism, Hegel occupies an unusual position. In fact, Rancière equivocates on Hegel's significance for his analysis of the aesthetic revolution. In some writings he insists that the positions associated with Hegel are not exclusively tied to the proper name of Hegel but articulate a general narrative structure regarding the place of the arts in modernity that underpins the cogency of diverse positions.[3] In other places, he defends the specific pertinence of Hegel's formulations regarding the arts against the meaning that has been assigned to them.[4] To my mind, this equivocation is indicative of the over-determined position that Hegel occupies in Rancière's reflections on Romanticism.

At first glance, Hegel's writing on aesthetics recommends a comparative treatment with Rancière's work because, like Rancière, his *Aesthetics* defends a thesis regarding the significance of modern literature for conceptualizing the porosity of the modern category of the arts. However, what sharpens the implications of this comparative point is the fact that it is Hegel's conception of modern aesthetics, more than any other, which presents a competing position regarding the significance and implications of the 'aesthetic revolution' to the one that Rancière builds up and defends through an appeal to literary and philosophical examples. In this respect, the figure of Hegel may be used to qualify the seemingly compelling reasons often given for the selection of Kant and Schiller as the historical precursors for Rancière's use of aesthetics.[5] Neither Kant nor Schiller provides a critical and systematic perspective on literary Romanticism, which is the core reference for many of Rancière's recent writings. My intention in this essay is to provide an account of the significance that Rancière's writing arguably gives to Hegel against the background of their respective treatments of literary Romanticism. Rancière's engagement with philosophical aesthetics is a critically motivated one. Careful study of how this engagement positions Hegel can help identify and assess the assumptions that guide Rancière's contention that aesthetic topics and, in particular, the Romantic literary word, has political salience.

1 The Poetic Word in the Romantic Art Form: The Origins of the 'Aesthetic Revolution'

Hegel's treatment of the theme of the modern rise of the prosaic in art functions as an account, but also endorsement, of a particularly marked historical tendency: the diminution of the so-called 'absolute' significance of the arts in modernity. The entry of prosaic material into the field of art is, for Hegel, the precursor to the increasing importance of 'the prose of thought': such prose becomes, in modernity, more adequate than the sensuous mediums of art for expressing the increasing complexity of the Idea of freedom. To some extent, this thesis receives its historical corroboration in the indispensable role of criticism for the reception of the arts in the age of their aesthetic autonomy. According to Hegel's triadic conception of art forms, the earlier symbolic and classical forms of art had provided a depiction and rendering of immediate religious significance and meaning, first in the 'universal' architecture of temples, and then in the sculpture of the statues of the Gods that, in Hegel's idiom, 'particularize' the divine. In contrast, the modern arts of the Romantic art form depict, he says, the 'singular' religious 'community'.[6] The emancipation of Romantic art from the function of the depiction of God in the reflective age of Protestantism leaves art free to explore its own mediums and techniques, but also hollows out the significance of such reflection: art's modern, Romantic fate is ultimately a self-commentary on historical art forms. The final indication of its newfound status, which is also a further corroboration of Hegel's characterization of the modern, reflective age, is that these new art forms are no longer 'luminous' enough to be understood without the elucidations of criticism. They are no longer a direct mode of access to the absolute, but for this very reason no longer 'absolute' in the sense of self-standing forms; art continues, but does so in the mode of deficient, criticism-dependent works.[7]

The point of transition to this situation is marked out by the altered status of the poetic word in Romanticism. This word 'passes from the poetry of imagination into the prose of thought' because unlike the other Romantic arts of music and painting, the word strips back the material mediums of art forms: 'Poetry is the universal art of the mind which has become free in its own nature, and which is not tied to find its realization in external sensuous matter, but expatiates exclusively in the inner space and inner time of the ideas and feelings.'[8] Hegel's treatment of the modern arts depends substantially on the contrasting functions and values of an 'inner' field of ideas and feelings and the 'external' sensuous terrain that is the impoverished stage that 'ties' the alienated, unhappy consciousness to external matter.[9] It is striking that the form of the Hegelian vocabulary, which pits 'matter' this way against 'ideas' and 'feelings', is used in adapted form by Rancière to drive aspects of his own conceptual vocabulary, and especially his treatment of words. In particular, he uses the separation between words and the incarnation of their meaning in bodies as a conceptual schema to characterize literature: 'Literature lives only by the separation of words in relation to anybody that might incarnate their power. It lives only by evading the incarnation that it incessantly puts into play.'[10] This dynamic of failed incarnation of literary meaning, which has its parallel in his account of the failed transition from 'words' to new 'worlds' in philosophy is, for Rancière, the promise of the aesthetic revolution, which Hegel's division of spheres shuts down. Hegel's very description of the different vocations and features of poetry and the prose of thought reveals, in Rancière's telling, an inadequate assimilation of the (Romantic) insight of equality, which Hegel's general position on the arts otherwise seems to absorb.[11]

Rancière's writing stresses the fragility of the distinction between the fields of 'art' and 'non-art' and explains how the Romantic incorporation of the 'ordinary' as subject matter for 'art' evocatively displays this fragility. He captures something significant about the status of modern art when he holds that art is art insofar as it is not entirely distinct from non-art. He credits this insight to Hegel.[12] More specifically, he describes modern art as both a point that courts its self-dissolution into everyday objects and forms, on one side, and a 'life of forms' able to be distinguished from the everyday, on the other.[13] Ultimately, many of his critical points regarding Romantic literature concern the different ways in which Romantic writers suppress their own insight into the porous line between the exceptional, sublime figures of art and their democratic distribution of aesthetic value to the everyday. Rancière analyses the modern 'idea' of art as that which is practised, conceived and played out between these poles of absolute heteronomy (dissolution into the everyday) and qualified autonomy (a life of forms beyond this). At the same time, it is clear that he is much less interested in debates over the constituent features of 'art works' than he is in the defence of a concept of 'aesthetic experience'. He understands this concept in onto-logical terms as the field of the sensory settings of experience. He specifies these settings in the language of equality, being prior to any specific distri-bution of social functions and capacities. In fact, it is this highly specific understanding of 'aesthetic experience' that orientes his treatment of the contradictory conception of 'art' in Romanticism and regulates the signifi-cance he attaches to the 'prosaic'. Among other things, this position on aesthetics has consequences for the partitioning of intellectual fields. Aes-thetics concerns the 'configuration of a common world'. This means not just that the 'aesthetic experience reaches far beyond the sphere of art', but that 'reflection on these "aesthetic" issues requires ... a form of aesthetic discourse which is not a specialization within philosophy, but, on the con-trary, crosses the frontiers of the disciplines and ignores the hierarchy of levels of discourses.'[14]

Rancière's criticisms of Hegel's re-functioning of the prosaic world raise two inter-related issues: 1) the specific question of what is involved in the aesthetic, material dimensions of words when these are treated under the lens of 'equality'; and 2) how to deal with the general implications of the story that Hegel tells regarding the modern restrictions on aesthetic meaning.

These issues are related because the prosaic features of word-use that Hegel identifies in his analysis of Romanticism are presented in such a way that, in Rancière's terms, 'a configuration of modernity as a new partition of the perceptible, with no point of heterogeneity', is formed. 'In this parti-tion, rationalization of the different spheres of activity becomes a response both to the old hierarchical orders and to the "aesthetic revolution."'[15] The 'old hierarchical orders' entailed established ways of organizing perception in advance, whereas the 'aesthetic revolution' disregards these traditional hierarchies and holds out the 'promise' of a perpetual dissolution of such schemas of perception. This promise, however, depends on the 'heterogeneous sensible' that Hegel's partition of spheres dissolves in its re-articulation and re-functioning of the 'sensible' into specific spheres of activity. With the term 'heterogeneous sensible', Rancière intends to signal what is not assimilable into assigned tasks and capacities, but also what in Romantic and Marxist aesthetics attracts 'double' meaning as the 'ordinary' thing that might also be 'extraordinary'. The idea here is that the term 'heterogeneous' signals that something is 'unavailable' for the straightforward allocation of functions and capacities and that this 'unavailability' points specifically to the potential for alterations in the established circuit of the meaning and experience of things. In this respect, the term recalls aspects of Rancière's understanding of the 'distribution of the sensible' [*le partage du sensible*] in which a contingent ordering of shared perceptual meaning is imposed. This point can be expounded in relation to the general significance ascribed to the category of the aesthetic. For instance, unlike the wide scope of sense and meaning that Rancière endorses in the vocabulary of 'aesthetics' as the perception and experience of the social partition of functions, Hegel begins his 'Aesthetics' by complaining about the general reach of this term in its definition as the 'science of sensation' as opposed to the precision of the vocabulary of 'the philosophy of art'.[16]

Rancière asks whether the proposed comprehensive re-functioning of the material sensible is possible and finds that Hegel's narrative of modernity is not, on this point, a compelling one. It is significant that Rancière's treatment of the thesis of the 'partition of the sensible', as proposed by Hegel, and the 'promise' of the 'revolution' that it repudiates, comport the literary features of a story. Hegel's story, he argues, is overtaken on one side by the profusion of other plots in Marxist and Romantic aesthetics that conjugate art and life together in contradictory, but efficacious ways; and on the other, by Hegel's own use of words. Words are ways of evoking the sense and significance of things; but they are also a material medium that is never entirely transparent to the meanings and ideas they articulate. In this way, Rancière defends a version of the Romantic presumption of the plenitude of meaning. In his version, this presumption does not refer to the inscription of the field of 'things' with expressive hieroglyphs of meaning that need decoding; rather, these potentialities of meaning are the province of the 'equality' of words, which bear the capacity to reconfigure hierarchical distributions of sensibility into polemical common worlds.

The significance that Rancière ascribes to words constitutes the core of his alternative to the Hegelian narrative. It is important therefore to clarify what 'equality' could mean when it is transposed like this into the aesthetic field of the operation of 'words', and to also ask in what respects, and with what implications, this manoeuvre weights the field of 'words' with emancipatory expectations and significance.

2 Words

For Rancière, contra Hegel, the word of the 'prose of thought' remains a 'literary' or 'poetic' word. Words entail a structural equality. This means that they are indifferent to the use made of them or meaning assigned to them. Rancière expresses the implications of this idea by describing 'words' as 'silent' or 'mute'; that is to say, they always stand ready for further elaboration or adaptation and they do so on account of the fact that they are 'orphans' and hence without any authorizing figure able to police the way nor by whom,they are used and understood.[17]

The main elements, however, of the conception of literary equality are not structural, but historical. The historical context of modern literature as part of the age of social revolutions brings with it the specific settings of literary equality, which we might phrase in the following terms: insofar as literature uses words to voice the latent meaning of things, and insofar as anything at all in the modern regime of the arts is able to bear expressive meaning, 'equality' is crucial to understanding the significance and effects of the modern poetic revolution. Modern literature disregards the hierarchies of the old representational systems. As such, its 'aesthetic' functions are immediately 'political' because its use of words points in particularly powerful fashion to the *possibility* of setting up new relations to things that promise to reconfigure the sense data of experience. It is for this reason that Rancière is interested in the different ways that the writing of Flaubert and Deleuze, in depicting a world without defined 'purpose' and 'function', may be seen to question how social perception is organized in advance (through specific distributions of functions, values and capacities). Thus, in *Madame Bovary*, he focuses on the way that the dust swirling over flagstones becomes accessible to aesthetic description. This is not because Flaubert gives voice to mundane experiences, but because he displays in poetic form the microphysics of mute, prosaic atmospherics, a scenography of which his characters seem unaware.[18] As Rancière puts it:

When Emma falls for Rodolphe, she perceives little gleams of gold about his pupils, smells a perfume of lemon and vanilla, and looks at the long plume of dust raised by the stagecoach. And when she first falls for Leon, 'weeds streamed out in the limpid water like green wigs tossed away. Now and then some fine-legged insects alighted on the tip of a reed or crawled over a water-lily leaf. The sunshine darted its rays through the little blue bubbles on the wavelets that kept forming and breaking' (Madame Bovary, 107). This is what happens: 'little blue bubbles' on wavelets in the sunshine, or swirls of dust raised by the wind. This is what the characters feel and what makes them happy: a pure flood of sensations.[19]

Rancière also understands Deleuze's ontology as a form of such a micro-physical account of 'reality'. This interest in the new microphysics of percep-tion that Flaubert and Deleuze each propose is, however, no enthusiastic endorsement of either writer, and Rancière uses the idea of literary equality to make specifically critical mention of the ways that each articulate a new perceptual order that confounds the precepts of their 'impressionist poet-ics'. Hence he criticizes Deleuze's mistaken view that the field of forces he describes in words is the way things are primarily, as if 'words' would provide passage to a Deleuzian 'world'. He also points out Deleuze's dependence on literary 'characters' in Melville and 'plot' lines in Kafka to elucidate his pre-personal ontology of a field that is supposedly without structure and direc-tion. Similarly, he complains that Flaubert still wishes to defend the semantic integrity of the concept of art against the democratic intrusions of the merely prosaic. These critical points are best seen as a form of fidelity to 'aesthetic equality'. According to this idea, literary meanings should be considered in the perspective of an ongoing process of productive reception that reshapes the existing basic categories and boundaries of sensory experience as such. Against Deleuze's use of Kafka's *Metamorphosis* to corroborate his ontology of micro-transformations, therefore, Rancière holds that Gregor's transforma-tion is and is not 'literal'.[20] Similarly, the entry of prosaic material into the field of art really does mean (despite Flaubert's condemnation of Emma Bovary) that anything can have aesthetic significance for anyone.

It is worth emphasizing the understanding of the 'aesthetic' that this posi-tion entails: from the modern awareness of the porous line separating the prosaic from the poetic arises the consequence that the 'aesthetic' refers to the democratic field of sensory experience, rather than (as Hegel, for instance, had wished) the restricted field of the philosophy of art.

The implications of this point are especially clear in Rancière's writing on politics. Above all, Rancière understands politics to be the exercise of a kind of speech, and thus defines it as a particular use of words that may occur anywhere. 'Politics occurs wherever a community with the capacity to argue and to make metaphors is likely to crop up.'[21] In his well-known reformulation of Aristotle's description of man as an animal with the additional capacity for politics, Rancière highlights the way that the literary condition of politics is what effects a dis-incorporation of established meanings from bodies: 'Man is a political animal because he is a literary animal who lets himself be diverted from his "natural" purpose by the power of words.'[22]

He disagrees therefore with Hegel's restriction of politics to the operations of a specific sphere. Hegel's philosophical account of the modern, bureaucratic state – in which struggle is a stage that has been surpassed – is at the antipodes of Rancière's 'politics of aesthetics' in which neither history nor institutions can fully remedy the causes nor quash the prospects of continuous 'political' struggle. Thus Rancière describes political philosophy as the antithesis to 'politics' precisely because, in his view, this region of philosophy constitutes the project of reflecting on and refining the institutional mechanisms that represent and advocate the interests of identifiable social actors. 'Politics', in contrast, consists in those speech acts that come from anywhere to contest even the ontological order, what he terms the 'divisions' of the sensible. In this sense, politics is 'aesthetic' for Rancière because it consists in altering and reframing the field of sensory experience; but as it is specifically 'words' that bear the capacity to reorganize the sensory field, the topic of how words exceed the meanings they embody is a recurrent theme in his writing and one that joins together his treatment of literary and political topics. The reasons for the emphasis he places on the contradictory features of literary Romanticism can be understood in terms of his view that 'words' are the mechanism of equality. Literary equality is thereby used as proof of the contingent nature of any re-functionalization of the 'sensible'. This proof, however, needs to be qualified: the literary word only has the *potential* to reframe experience.

3 Word Scenes

It is clear that neither in the literary nor the political domains are 'words' themselves sufficient to alter socially established modes of perception.[23] Accordingly, Rancière stresses that it is the 'account' made of speech (how and when speech is understood to configure a polemical world) rather than the fact of speaking that is important for any consideration of its political force[24]; and he makes a similar point in the context of literary

words, when he claims that it is not 'mere words' alone that are at stake.[25]
In the theoretical field he holds that theoretical discourse is 'always simultaneously an aesthetic form, a sensible reconfiguration of the facts it is
arguing about'.[26] These caveats raise the question of the significance of the
story motif in his critique of Hegel's proposed narrative of the re-functioning of the material sensible; and they emphasize the distinction that needs
to be made between the promise of the 'aesthetic revolution' and whether
and how the presentation of this promise can be understood to be politically effective.[27]

Rancière claims that Hegel's analysis of the Romantic art form is symptomatic of one of the main plot lines of the 'aesthetic regime of the arts'.
These plot lines sustain the promise of extra-aesthetic significance for the
arts. The thesis of the 'end of art' is 'not simply', he argues, 'a personal
theorization by Hegel'.[28] Hegel's position:

> clings to the plot of the life of art as 'the spirit of forms'. That spirit is the
> 'heterogeneous sensible', the identity of art and non-art. The plot has
> it that when art ceases to be non-art, it is no longer art either. Poetry is
> poetry, says Hegel, so long as prose is confused with poetry. When prose
> is only prose, there is no more heterogeneous sensible.[29]

Like most plots, this one needs a temporal scope to unfold. This plot ends
in such a way as to raise the problem of how to 'reassess the heterogenous
sensible' since it invalidates the 'formula of art becoming life … a new life
does not need a new art. On the contrary, the specificity of the new life is
that it does not need art.'[30] The implication is that Hegel formulates the
positive contradiction of post-Romantic art, but he fails to see the productive role of this contradiction and accordingly opts for an ending in which
it is resolved: material forms as eloquent bodies of meaning in the religious past of art on one side, and meaning as it is disclosed and clarified
in the thought of prose on the other. In other words, Hegel 'frames' aesthetic experience; he transfers the properties of the aesthetic experience
to the work of art itself, 'cancelling their projection into a new life and
invalidating the aesthetic revolution'.[31] Hegel's version of the story is thus
contrasted to the various Romantic and Marxist attempts to retain a 'heterogeneous sensible'. These latter attempts operate through a kind of
doubling of materiality: things are not just things but are also the meanings, such as the extra-aesthetic promise, that can be attached to them.
But in Rancière's view, the legacy of such attempts to poeticize the prosaic
also has troubling aspects. This is because these attempts end in the

practice of an endless deciphering of the meaning of the sensible experience.

> This new poetics frames a new hermeneutics, taking upon itself the task of making society conscious of its own secrets, by leaving the noisy stage of political claims and doctrines and sinking to the depths of the social, to disclose the enigmas and fantasies hidden in the intimate realities of everyday life.[32]

Such meta-politics – and among the examples he cites are Benjamin's literary-styled analysis of the commodity form – borrows the plot invented by so-called realist literature. It documents the depth to be found in its poetic presentation of the prosaic: 'Telling the truth on the surface by travelling in the underground, spelling out the unconscious social text lying underneath – that … was a plot invented by literature itself.'[33]

In a sense, Rancière does not quite get away from the narrative. Maybe he sees no need to do so. In contrast to the other plots in which the narrative drama concerns how prosaic things bear significant meaning, and which concerns itself with how to decipher this meaning, Rancière's 'politics of aesthetics' commits him to a version of the story in which it is the 'words' rather than the 'things' that harbour new expressive contents and possible contestable meanings.[34] This is the way that he corrects Marxist meta-politics. The plenitude of meaning attached to words is not exhaustible, and he invests accordingly in the promise that the materiality of the word is a field of new possibilities of meaning. Words are the material forces whose meaning is doubled; they both mean what they say and are silent. This silence is their aesthetic 'promise'. The other side of this 'promise', in which Rancière might be seen to be close to Hegel, is that the political (or for Hegel, the scientific) use of words is guided by the intelligibility of meanings rather than the mysticism of depth hermeneutics.

4 Conclusion

The dynamic of heterogeneous sensibility that Romanticism discloses as the narrative core of art is the historical precursor and the aesthetic form used in Rancière's defence of political equality. The story's promise of aesthetic efficacity is the pivot of his conception of politics, which turns on the possibility not of a mere redistribution of the sensible, but a redistribution that has the political force to alter social perceptions, possibly at fundamental levels. Finally, this requirement of politically significant redistribution couples Rancière's aesthetics to the formative capacity not of mere 'words', but 'stories' – including the terms of the story he tells regarding the contradictory form of prosaic words and literary meanings.

Alain Badiou has claimed that 'Rancière is an heir to Foucault' because his 'approach consists in a rebellious apprehension of discursive positivities'[35]. It seems to me that in its distinctive features, some of which are set out above, Rancière's thought happily inhabits the assumptions of the post-Marxist way of practising politics, which is firmly rooted in literary utopianism. Michel Foucault did not belong to this particular academic community. When he commented on it, however, he was critical of the 'very heavy political blockage' that occurs around the use of literature or literary motifs – and here we can include 'words', 'stories' and 'plots' – as a path for the diagnosis of political circumstances.[36]

Even as it calls into question certain aspects and patterns of formation of this practice, Rancière's thinking belongs within the discursive field that articulates the stakes of political topics in literary terms. Above all, this can be seen in his idiosyncratic understanding of politics being about word-use, and the literary-philosophical examples that his most recent work uses to explore the potential alteration of established modes of perception.[37] The 'discourse' that consists in looking to literature to articulate alternative political meanings, as Rancière does with the category of the 'equality' of words, is, as he well knows, an heir to post-Kantian Romanticism. In this tradition, ideas that would otherwise be experientially poor are given cogent form. It is Rancière's peculiar achievement to have charted the logic of the field of this particular academic community as an efficacious 'plot' (as opposed to a sociologically correctible error) and in so doing, to have found a new way to inhabit and extend it. Looked at this way, it may well be that it is the potential communicative force of the new meanings he ascribes to the word 'politics' that will be the ultimate test of Rancière's 'aesthetic revolution'.

Chapter 6

No Time or Place for Universal Teaching: *The Ignorant Schoolmaster* and Contemporary Work on Pedagogy

Caroline Pelletier

When the editors of this book asked if I could write something on how Rancière had contributed to pedagogy as a discipline and what educationalists might have to say in response to his work, I thought this might make for a short chapter. Rancière has nothing to say on how schools might improve their methods of teaching and learning. His work is not an addition or an alternative to disciplines laying claim to pedagogy as their object, such as the sociology of education and educational psychology. In terms of how his work has been received in education, it has generated less discussion than in philosophy or history, judging by the number of references in these subjects' respective journals. Anecdotal impression suggests that *The Ignorant Schoolmaster*[1] is more widely read among artists than among teachers.

Part of this picture is changing as a result of secondary literature, which has brought Rancière's work to the attention of people working in education. For example, Bingham and Biesta's recent book draws on Rancière's ideas to explore contemporary debates in education, and also to read texts from other disciplines as instances of pedagogy – a move which shows pedagogy to be a problem about how to write, read and speak; what it is to teach and learn in any place or time, rather than a specific concern for educationalists and schools only.[2]

However, the relative patchiness of reference to Rancière's work in education is not solely due, I think, to lack of awareness. There is also something unreadable about his argument, in the sense that it does not appear relevant to the field of education. I say this on the basis of responses I have had to a couple of articles about Rancière's work,[3] from colleagues in my own and other education departments. Although these have generally had a positive response, a recurring comment is that Rancière's ideas are also untimely. This is usually attributed to one or both of two posited phenomena.

First, pedagogic thinking and practice have evolved since the time of Jacotot: teachers are no longer masters, with much greater emphasis in schools now on student projects, collaborative group work and the personalization of the curriculum. The valorization of constructivism is said to have, for better or worse, removed knowledge from its central position in the classroom and allowed the teacher to become a facilitator of students' self-directed efforts to generate their own understandings. Second, Jacotot's 'method' – universal teaching, by which a teacher ignorant of the subject matter demands of the student the manifestation of intelligence – is already widely practised, in the sense that teachers commonly teach subjects they know nothing about, not only particularly in higher education, but also in schools. This follows partly from the curricularization of aspects of life which have previously not been subject to certification, such as childcare, happiness and well-being or social science research methodology. It also follows from the marketization of education, with courses emerging and disappearing in response to identified markets rather than as developments within a discipline.[4]

These responses have perplexed me, in part because the significance of *The Ignorant Schoolmaster* did not appear to me to rely on the validity of Jacotot's method, in the sense of whether it 'works' or not as a way of teaching and learning. The 'untimeliness' of universal teaching as an idea also seems to echo responses to *The Ignorant Schoolmaster* upon its first publication, as described by Ross in her introduction to the English edition. She notes that it was not immediately apparent to readers in 1987, when the book was published, how Jacotot's nineteenth-century adventures could contribute to debates within the then French socialist government about how to reform the school system.[5]

One way of responding to these criticisms would be to point out that universal teaching is not a pedagogic method to be applied in schools or universities to generate emancipation. Unsurprisingly, this is indeed what this chapter will say. But this is what Rancière and Jacotot have said before, without apparently always being heard as saying such – perhaps because *The Ignorant Schoolmaster* raises troubling questions about what one does every day, when one works as a teacher in the state system of education; what one's method is, and how it might be different. So, partly in response to the editors' request to treat pedagogy as some kind of discipline, but also to examine further the perpetual untimeliness of universal teaching, I will read *The Ignorant Schoolmaster* or, more specifically, the idea of universal teaching, in the light of contemporary theories of learning and teaching, in order to examine how Rancière's argument can appear at once very familiar and yet out of place, or out of time. This is what I do in the first part of this chapter. Subsequently, I examine how the problem of inequality appears 'timely' in education. The conclusion returns to the question of how one might find a place for Rancière's work in contemporary educational practices.

1 What is it to Learn and to Teach?

Is it possible to read *The Ignorant Schoolmaster* as a tract advocating a way of teaching and learning? If one were to try and answer this question positively, one could point out that many of the claims made in that text resonate with contemporary learning theory, especially those that have emerged through engagement and argument with the work of Vygotsky, the Marxist psychologist who wrote in the 1920s and 1930s, and whose ideas remain central to many teacher education courses. Whereas Vygotsky's work differentiated between spontaneous concepts (acquired in everyday activity) and scientific concepts (acquired through systematic instruction) and figured the move from the one to the other as a process of 'internalization', more recent social-cultural theory has endeavoured to move away from metaphors of assimilation and transmission and foregrounded instead terms such as 'participation'. This concept of 'participation', for instance in the work of Lave and Wenger,[6] challenges many conventional views of learning. It works to collapse the boundary between interiority and exteriority, or, in other words, mind and activity. Intelligence, as the property of a mind or the potential of a 'habitus', thereby ceases to be a relevant, and sensible, distinction; the object of analysis is activity patterns rather than individual capacities or socially structured dispositions. Learning, or knowing, consequently ceases to be a condition, and is instead identified in terms of evolving and continuously renewed relations among people and artefacts in activity. 'Understanding' becomes a material practice; an act rather than a state, and therefore a negotiated, mediated process of transformation rather than acquisition. By extension, learning is important not so much because it sustains the transfer of knowledge, but because it is concerned with the transformation of individuals.

This conception of learning, widely referenced in contemporary education literature, resonates with the principles of 'universal teaching' as described in *The Ignorant Schoolmaster*. It figures knowledge as a position within an evolving set of relations, a move which focuses analysis on the principles by which knowledge is recognized within a collectivity, rather

than on whether knowledge·is possessed. The emphasis on activity transforms knowledge into a practice: it is something that is done. This collapses
the distinction between doing, meaning-making and knowing: or, in terms
deployed in *The Ignorant Schoolmaster*, between translation and understanding; between manual and intellectual work, in the sense that both are
treated as material activities. By extension, if knowledge is done, it cannot
also be said to be done 'to' anyone: if the unit of analysis is patterns of participation, experts cannot be attributed as causal determinants of anyone
else's knowledge. With learning/knowing defined as the transformation of
persons, the most relevant distinction for differentiating between pedagogic practices pertains to the distribution of positions rather than to the
content area or subject of knowledge. In other words, distinctions cannot
be sustained between egalitarian and illusory knowledge, science and mis-
recognition, or even science and opinion (insofar as both are treated as
material practices characterized by particular ways of legitimizing themselves).

Having described these continuities between universal teaching and contemporary socio-cultural theories of learning, there are several aspects of
universal teaching which, from the perspective of socio-cultural theory,
appear problematic. One of these concerns the constitution of 'will'. Universal teaching proclaims: 'an individual can do anything he wants',[7] since
man is a will served by an intelligence. What differentiates poorer work
from better work, then, is not intelligence but attention; the strength with
which will has been exercised.[8] So, although intelligences are equal, wills
are differentiated in terms of their power. This raises a question about what
might account for these stated differences in will-power, or attention. In *The
Ignorant Schoolmaster*, Jacotot's response to this question is to reiterate that
'all intelligences are equal', while denying that this reduces thought or
intellect to the slogan 'whoever wants is able to'.[9] Therefore, intellect serves
the will, but the question of how will comes to constitute itself, and differ-
entially, is left rather open. Vygotsky's work, and much socio-cultural theory,
emphasizes the mutual determination of will and intellect, a move intended
to avoid the 'spiritualistic principle of absolute free will', as well as the
notion that thought is mechanically determined by external circumstances,
bypassing the necessity for a will altogether.[10] Thus, for instance, whereas in
The Ignorant Schoolmaster, people come to Jacotot because they want to learn
the piano or to paint, with will here apparently preceding the manifestation
of intellect, a Vygotskian argument might say that it is in learning to paint
or play the piano that one also develops the will to do so and the intellect to
know how: intelligence does not so much serve the will, but rather the two

emerge together, or are mediated by each other.[11] Hence, the importance of instruction in Vygotsky is in contrast to the more voluntaristic approach to learning subject matter in universal teaching. Instruction in 'scientific concepts' is emancipatory, in Vygotsky's argument, precisely because this is what enables the will to exercise greater self-determination.[12] *The Ignorant Schoolmaster* shows how this point of self-determination is infinitely deferred by explanation/instruction; but it does not really address the reason for Vygotsky's argument, which was to reconcile a concept of will with that of emancipation, while avoiding equating emancipation with freedom from constraint (i.e. 'whoever wants is able to').

One could, however, argue that the will, in universal teaching, is not so much a free-wheeling spontaneous force, but *is* exercised in relation to material things; the ignorant schoolmaster teaches by establishing an equal distance to the material object of knowledge and demanding that the will be exercised in relation to its interpretation. For example, Jacotot teaches students how to read French by telling them to read a book in French, rather than explaining the French language to them. The material object of knowledge – in that instance, a bilingual edition of a book – is a means of verifying the equality of two minds: in learning to read, the book, as material artefact, works as 'the only bridge of communication between two minds'; it is 'what keeps two minds at an equal distance'.[13] Similarly, in learning to paint, a painting by Poussin can be a starting point for verifying the 'unity of feeling', that is to say, the meaning of the painting that the student can speak about and respond to.[14] Equality is *verified* here in the distance to an object of knowledge, in the capacity of anyone to interpret it.

The problem with this argument is that for such verification to work, and such distance to be maintained, the value or status of the object has to be assumed: it has to be taken as an instance of 'French language' or 'painting'. Therefore learning to paint, in *The Ignorant Schoolmaster*, involves interpreting Poussin's 'masterpieces'. Jacotot's students make the claim 'me too, I'm a painter'[15] only by treating the common object as an instance of (a great) painting; by treating this meaning of the object as given. So, while the ignorant schoolmaster divests himself of knowledge but retains authority, the material object of knowledge conjoins both. As Nina Power argues: 'The danger of shifting the master from person to object doesn't necessarily overturn the hierarchy of student and teacher, just shifts it from the classroom to the library.'[16]

This danger is illustrated in *The Ignorant Schoolmaster* in the separation of learning and 'assessment'. When Jacotot is accused of having developed a method which simply involves the blind leading the blind, and which consequently separates the science of scholars (those who produce 'masterpieces' or write books, presumably) from a science of the people, the response is as follows: 'one must be learned to judge the results of the work, to verify the student's science. The ignorant [schoolmaster] himself will do *less* and *more* at the same time. He will not verify what the student has found: he will verify that the student has searched. He will judge whether or not he has paid attention.'[17] This distinction between what ignorant schoolmasters do and what scholars do implies that what scholars do is somehow different from – 'less and more' – verifying that others have searched with attention. But what is this difference; on what basis can it be maintained? And if one does maintain it, how does this constitute a counter to the accusation that, in universal teaching, there is a science for scholars and a science for people? If learned scholars *must* 'judge' the work of students, how does this avoid re-inscribing the mastery of the explaining teacher/scholar? For instance, when the results of universal teaching are examined in the instance of learning to paint, the stated disappointing results are justified as follows: 'Undoubtedly, there's a great distance from this [what students endeavoured to do] to making masterpieces … But it's not a matter of making great painters; it's a matter of making the emancipated: people capable of saying, "me too, I'm a painter."'[18] But what is the nature of this distance separating masterpieces from students' work? Why is making the emancipated *not* a matter of making great painters (what then is a matter of making great painters)? And if the former is distinguished from the latter in kind (in 'matter'), then on what basis can students claim 'me too, I'm a painter'?

The materialism of post-Vygotskian, socio-cultural theory avoids inscribing the object of knowledge with authority by focusing on the practices within which objects emerge as meaningful rather than on the meaning/status of the objects themselves. Learning to paint, in this sense, is not about an individual's response to a painting but is more concerned with participating in the activity of seeing, discussing, imitating, judging and creating particular kinds of objects. What distinguishes one object from another is not ascribed to inherent virtues (painterliness, literariness) but to the practices for classifying such objects and identifying their unity. Hence the concept 'community of practice',[19] which denotes a unity constituted by particular ways of doing, seeing, judging and so on. 'Unity of feeling' is derived from sharing a practice rather than an object.

Although there are similarities between universal teaching and contemporary learning theory, the differences are also stark. In universal teaching, the determinant of learning is displaced from intelligence to will, a move which splits the two from each other. Learning is the demonstration of strength of will exercised in relation to an authoritative object of knowledge, whose speech or meaning can be heard and responded to by any intelligence. In socio-cultural theory, the determinant of learning is displaced from intelligence to participation in practices, a move which conjoins will and intelligence – in the sense that will is exercised in relation to joining a community, with intellect developing through such participation. Learning is participating in practices of knowing in increasingly authoritative ways, with no distinction made between learning and its legitimization. This implies a vision of community as something with a periphery and a core – learning means moving from the former to the latter.

So, does the emergence and recent development of a materialist argument about what learning is make universal teaching redundant/untimely or insufficiently elaborated to inform contemporary work on pedagogy? One way of answering this would be to say that Rancière's writing provides other definitions of 'will', art and literature from those that appear in *The Ignorant Schoolmaster*. In *The Nights of Labour*, will is not so much an individualistic and indeterminate exercise, but precisely the demand to participate as a member of one collectivity (those who work) in the practices of another (those who have leisure).[20] This does not account for any presumed differences in will-power, but it does imply that will emerges in relation to concrete circumstances. Also, Rancière's book on images, among others, unpicks the category of art, and examines it in terms of modes of perception rather than an object's attributes.[21] Again, this does not resolve the question about how to judge the quality of (artistic) work, but it does imply that such qualities are not authoritatively imposed by the work itself. *The Ignorant Schoolmaster*, therefore, is not Rancière's book on education: one could read all of his books – and the differences between them – through the lens of this idea, since they all address the issue of how subjects (learn to) think and feel the world in particular ways.

However, identifying differences between contemporary theories of learning and universal teaching does not really address how the latter can appear 'untimely' in education. To return to this concern, I will develop a little further the comparison between universal teaching and contemporary work on learning and teaching in education.

2 Pedagogy and Community

Lave and Wenger's concept of communities of practice avoids equating learning/pedagogy with schooling. The argument that learning takes place through participation contrasts with the historical emphasis, in education, on instruction and methods of teaching. Their representation of community as something with a core and a periphery, and their focus on trajectories that move from 'legitimate peripheral participation' to 'full participation', is a reminder of their background in anthropology: they are concerned primarily with the maintenance and generational redevelopment of cultural orders – in contrast to Jacotot's/Rancière's emphasis on the suspension or redistribution of social order. However, recent developments of their work have developed the idea of 'non-legitimate' forms of participation and emphasized the multiplicitous and overlapping nature of communities. They have also clarified that their theory makes no presumptions about newcomers' status as novices (in the sense of ignorant/lacking capability), nor of their inevitable progression towards mastery.[22]

In the area in which I work, around new media and education, the 'communities of practice' concept has been eagerly taken up to study pedagogy in settings which do not feature official instructors – for instance 'online communities'. In particular, there has been much interest in education in the practices of media fans – the individuals that celebrate and document their relationships to diverse forms of entertainment (including videogames, television, film, music and media celebrities) – which are seen to demonstrate pedagogic processes, with fans learning from one another through processes of affiliation to a common object of interest.[23] This interest in sites of activity lacking institutionalized intellectual hierarchies contrasts with the arguments Rancière analyses in *Hatred of Democracy*,[24] which betray a fear that education has become *too* democratic, with students thinking themselves equal to their betters, and lacking respect for the authority of the teacher and his/her knowledge. In research on the pedagogy of new media, there has been a different movement, with enthusiasm expressed for the pedagogic productivity of students' 'popular culture'.

In some respects, these accounts of communities of practice echo arguments from *The Ignorant Schoolmaster*. I will briefly give one example, taken from the work of Gee, who has done extensive work on how players learn to play videogames – including through participation in fan communities. His interest in these activities stems from the opposition he perceives between pedagogy in 'popular culture' and in schools, as denoted in the title of his book *Situated Language and Learning: A Critique of Traditional Schooling*.[25] Contemporary sites of game play – especially online – are seen to offer a model of enculturation into skilled practices, which stands in contrast to the apparent failure of schools to achieve a similar level of productive participation. Gee recruits Lave and Wenger's work to offer two contrasting narratives: in the first, videogame players and fans learn how to play, act, interact, value and feel through increasing participation in the gaming community, progressively learning the meaning of words and symbols in context; in the second narrative, set against a background of 'traditional schooling', students are stupefied by drill and testing, simply memorize facts and learn abstract systems of thought detached from experience. Consequently, schools should learn from communities where there are no 'teachers', just 'leaders' who 'don't and can't order people around or create rigid, unchanging, and impregnable hierarchies'.[26]

In gaming communities, then, there is, according to Gee, no instruction, because there is no unjustified authority, indeed there is only 'porous leadership'.[27] Participating in such a community of practice means becoming increasingly expert in a game's design, rules and values – and anyone, with sufficient will-power, can gain this expertise. The game, as the common object of thought, generates 'unity of feeling', in the sense of common ways of being and thinking.

However, it is perhaps already clear that I have selected this example because it also enables differences to be drawn out between the precepts of universal teaching and current work in education on pedagogy. To do this, I would first like to identify the curious transformation of the 'communities of practice' concept as it moves from ethnographic/anthropological research to work on education and schooling.[28] Two things seem to happen in this move.

First, 'community of practice' ceases to be a concept to guide analysis, and becomes the attribute of a setting. In other words, a 'community of practice' is no longer what is constructed through research, but its starting point, the characteristic of a site of research – a move which transforms research narratives into *explanations* of social order. Therefore Gee's account *explains* why players occupy a specific position in the community: they do so because they have reached different points in the development of their knowledge. This implies a predetermined end-point and direction to their learning. The *reason* why the community is ordered as it is, including with its porous leadership, is because of the level of knowledge that players have gained about the object of 'affinity' (e.g. the game *Age of Mythology*). What makes leadership porous then is that 'leaders' are simply those that have the most knowledge: since this knowledge can always be improved, equality and the collapse of unrighteous hierarchy is achieved in the measured progress towards this common goal. Thus, whereas Lave and Wenger's work identified social order in terms of a perpetually moving loci of 'full participation', Gee's work identifies it in terms of levels of knowledge of the common object.

The second transformation in the concept 'community of practice' in work on schooling and institutionalized education is that features such as legitimacy, participation and authenticity become essentially the attributes of communities, rather than of the positions comprising them. Therefore, concern is expressed about how a community of practice can be built, or strengthened, made *more* participative, inclusive or authentic. In Gee's work, this concern is expressed in the principles of learning characterizing fan websites and videogame play which 'traditional schooling' could incorporate in order to make learning more 'active' and 'critical'. This recommendation is based on the idea that learning in schools is 'passive', and that students lack 'criticality' because they simply memorize knowledge for tests – a situation to be remedied through more participative, authentic (as in, grounded in experience) methods of teaching and learning. The principles of learning in gaming communities are therefore viewed as treatment to the passive situation of the school student. The problem with 'traditional schooling', then, is that it fails to fulfil its purpose of making people participate 'actively' in community life, because it makes them into passive consumers of knowledge (unlike good videogames, which sustain 'active', 'critical' communities).

These transformations in the 'communities of practice' concept are consequential, in that they make the basis of community a shared ethos (a common way of being and knowing, a shared love of the common object) rather than shared practices. The transformations also have a temporal dimension: learning involves moving towards an end-point, a future state of full participation/full knowledge of the object. Indeed, in Gee's work, the argument for learning from videogame communities is that they demonstrate the latest learning theory, with schools needing to 'catch-up' with recent research on learning, as well as contemporary popular culture.

It is the positing of a shared ethos as the goal of learning, to be realized at some point in the future, which is refused in *The Ignorant Schoolmaster*. And it is this refusal which, I think, makes it appear perpetually out of date. This 'out of dateness' appears when universal teaching is read as a method which has not yet 'caught up' with a future in which full participation/full knowledge is realized, and manifests itself as shared community ethos. In other words, universal teaching appears out of time when it is framed as a means to an end.

Chapter 5 of *The Ignorant Schoolmaster*, as well as Ross' introduction to the English edition, suggest that universal teaching is repeatedly read as a means, despite Jacotot's and Rancière's statements to the contrary. This reading negates another: that universal teaching is a demolition of the *jus-tifications* for pedagogy as means, justifications which pertain to the relation-ship between schooling and community. In *The Ignorant Schoolmaster*, the justifications are described as follows. First, what holds a community together is shared knowledge: becoming a member of a community involves adopting its ways of knowing, valuing, perceiving and so on. A community, from this perspective, is a common regime of sensibility, into which new members are initiated over time, using pedagogic techniques. This claim can be seen in Gee's argument, when he states that what makes game play-ers a community is a shared, consensual knowledge of games; and that what makes them an exemplary community is their pedagogic effectiveness in initiating new players into the community's rules and values. Second, if knowledge is the basis of community, then those who lead that community, who govern it, are those who know best; who have the most knowledge, and who govern simply to help others catch up. Therefore, in Gee's argument, leadership and authority are simply the dues that are owed to those who know games best, and are only enacted to help less-experienced players achieve 'full participation'. What makes gaming communities appear more active and critical than schools – more successful pedagogically – is that their authority structures are no longer enacted in the imposition of abstract knowledge and meaningless tests, but rather emerge 'naturally' from the varying levels of experience of the community's members. The distribution of social rank, the distinction between leaders and followers, here, is not the result of unreasoned, uncritical authority, but simply the differentiated distribution of expertise gained over time.

The principles of universal teaching emerge from a different, opposing conception of community. The demand, in *The Ignorant Schoolmaster*, that intellect manifest itself in the confrontation between the will of the student and that of the ignorant schoolmaster posits community as a polemical encounter: in other words, what binds the schoolmaster to the student is not a common set of values, interests or sensibilities to be achieved by the student in some future, but confrontation between what is common, and over what is common. If one were to define a gaming community in this light, one might look to interactions in terms of ongoing confrontations over what a game is and is not, what it is to play and not play, what it is to be a fan and who can claim to be one, and so on – not with a view to checking their validity or the display of pre-existing social power, but in terms of con-frontations or disagreements about what constitutes the community. If such confrontations are explained in terms of different levels of experience, what becomes perceptible is not disagreement but inequality: the incapacity of most community members to know as much as its porous leadership, and the good news that they are slowly catching up as a result of appropriate scaffolding. This perspective turns confrontation over what knowledge consists of, and the basis on which one can claim to have it, into temporal trajectories stretching from incapacity to capacity – a move which makes innocent the organization of community into a core and periphery, and which transforms disagreement over the object of knowledge into a call for those with more experience to enlighten those with yet-to-be-developed intellect.

3 Inequality as a Present Concern in Education

When *The Ignorant Schoolmaster* is read as an attack on the presuppositions of pedagogy, it raises questions about the assumptions underpinning endeavours to treat learning as an instrument of more reasonable hierarchy, or 'porous leadership'; greater self-determination (as in, more active, critical community members, an argument which treats self-determination as a matter of degree); and, with these, better community bonds (a common ethos).

Such endeavours are apparent in arguments that make use of concepts of 'participation' and 'communities of practice' to criticize the hierarchies and authority structure of schooling and institutionalized education. They are, of course, apparent more widely than this. To pick one contemporary UK example: in recent debates about higher education funding, a common objection to the rise in tuition fees is that it will deter people from poorer backgrounds from applying to university, and so will impede social mobility. One argument against the rise in fees, put forward by Aaron Porter, the President of the National Union of Students, is that university education should be about 'ability, not ability to pay'[29]. To address these concerns about social mobility, various measures have been floated by the current government, including encouraging universities to admit students on the basis of 'potential' rather than academic attainment exclusively; offering reassurance and clarification to working-class people to remedy their culturally-ingrained fear of debt; and improving state-funded education so that students in the state sector have the same chances as those in private schools. These arguments stem from different perceptions about what inequality is, emphasizing either the inability of the poor to pay for education or their inability to benefit from it (in the sense of having lower educational outcomes). However, both lines of argument treat higher education, and the knowledge it confers, as a way of rectifying the illegitimacy of the community's social order, and of ensuring that individuals are able to find a place suited to their capabilities in the community's division of labour.

Rectifying the community's order through education is also an important ambition of many sociological studies of the curriculum.[30] The role of schools in remaking the inequalities of the social order is a prominent theme in this literature, although there is extensive debate about how/whether the school operates as an independent force, and how sociological analysis might open up prospects for altering existing patterns of authority and control (see, for example, Frandji and Vitale[31] for a recent examination of the debate between Bernstein and Bourdieu on this point). Bernstein's attention to the relationship between disciplinary boundaries and social boundaries/order is an endeavour to identify the autonomy of the school, and thereby to move the sociology of education away from its historical emphasis on reproduction.[32] There is some affinity here with Rancière's argument about the poetics of disciplines and their war on 'allodoxy' (the antonym of orthodoxy).[33] Both writers view disciplines (and, in Bernstein's case, the curriculum) as a principle for policing/maintaining social hierarchies and 'controlling sentiments',[34] or, in Rancière's terminology, sensibilities: 'For the many, socialization into knowledge is socialization into order, the existing order ... discipline then means accepting a given selection, organization, pacing and timing of knowledge realized in the pedagogical frame.'[35] What disciplines/curricula work to achieve is the imposition of coherence and epistemological hierarchy where there is none: 'the ultimate mystery of the subject [in the sense of a discipline taught in school] is not ... order, but disorder, not the known but the unknown', a mystery, Bernstein argues, that is revealed only late in the educational life, and then only to the few who demonstrate successful 'socialization'.[36] It is this conception of discipline which underpins Bernstein's and Rancière's shared scepticism of the claims of 'progressive', anti-authoritarian pedagogies to reduce 'social control' (Bernstein's terminology), since these do nothing to challenge an orthodox (i.e. anti-allodoxy) conception of knowledge – as demonstrated by Gee's analysis of gaming communities. However, whereas universal teaching treats the concordance of social and disciplinary order as an occasion to ignore both, Bernstein emphasizes the importance of developing disciplinary identity. Failure to achieve this results in 'wounded' individuals.[37] This wound is characterized by low educational achievement, understood as the failure to achieve a sense of time, place and purpose[38] – in other words, a failure to find a place in the existing social order. In this version of the sociology of education, then, a balance needs to be found between giving individuals a sense of time and place within the community's social order, while maintaining the openness or malleability of these identifiers. Failure to achieve this – or educational failure – results in suffering, or 'wounded' individuals.

The Ignorant Schoolmaster – and Rancière's work more widely – challenges these two ways of being concerned about community, which I summarize as follows: (1) concern about the illegitimacy of the community's order; and (2) concern on behalf of, or in the name of, those who suffer as a result of the community's order.

With respect to the first of these concerns – A claim central to *The Ignorant Schoolmaster* is that there is no relationship between one's intellect and one's position in the social order. In this respect, universal teaching is no threat to the social order or to the division of labour, since it denies that intellect/ education is, or should be, the basis of social organization. This is because there is no legitimate basis for social order – no rational explanation or legitimate principle for role allocation in the division of labour. Equality means precisely this: that there is no reason or explanation for inequality. The issue then, for Rancière, is not the lack of social mobility, or the way in which people are assigned occupational destinies by their educational attainment. The problem, rather, is that the division of labour is justified in the name of ways of being and feeling; that a relationship is posited between particular aptitudes (and ineptitude) and particular occupations. The verification of equality, in universal teaching, works to deny this, to affirm 'the capacity of anyone to be *where he can't be* and to do *what he can't do*'[39] – an affirmation which frames work/the division of labour as the *condemnation* to be in a particular time and place, and to be nowhere else. Work, then, has nothing to do with aptitude or ability – it is an assignation to a particular time and place in the community's order, which denies the capacity of anyone to contribute to the community in any way. Rather than endeavouring to find better matches between aptitudes and occupations, the emphasis, in universal teaching, is on the capacity of anyone to do anything.

With respect to the second way of framing concern about how community is ordered, there is much work in education research which concerns itself with addressing the marginalization and educational failure of particular social groups; for instance, ethnic minorities, women, working class children, children with 'special educational needs' and so on. This concern can take the form of identifying curricula or pedagogic techniques which promote the academic achievement of, and thus the inclusion of, such identified groups, giving them a legitimate place within the order of the

school. By contrast, Jacotot/Rancière present universal teaching as precisely that: universal, rather than in the interests of, or the name of, particular social groups/identities (on this interpretation of universal teaching,
see Rancière's contribution in this volume). The problem is not, from this
perspective, that some social groups fail and others succeed, and that the
former 'suffer' as a result of their failure; rather, the problem is remedying
the contempt which fuels belief in inequality, including by those who fail. It
is worth emphasizing here that the principles of universal teaching do not
spring from Jacotot's sense of empathy with 'the poor' or their 'suffering'.
He sees claims such as 'I do not understand' and 'I cannot do this' as statements of contempt concealing themselves behind false modesty: one recognizes one's inferiority in one sphere of life in order for one's superiority to
be recognized in another, a sphere one also judges as superior. So it is in
recognizing the teacher's intellectual superiority that the student is able to
claim intellectual superiority over others (e.g. peers or younger children);
ι is in recognizing the intellectual superiority of the university professor
that the school teacher is able to claim intellectual superiority over students. Recognizing one's inferiority, or legitimate peripheral position in
the community, in relation to superiors, or those who are closer to 'full
participation' in the community, is what the education system treats as
learning – the development of disciplinary identity. The challenge, therefore, is not to legitimize this claim, but to suspend the whole system of recognition, and the perverse satisfaction that it affords.

4 Surviving *The Ignorant Schoolmaster*

When one works in the state system of education, how does one survive
reading *The Ignorant Schoolmaster*? Although the book is clearly not an attack
on the work of individual teachers, nor a call to them to stop teaching, its
demolition of the justifications for pedagogy brings into unforgiving light
the paradoxes of working in an institution where one continuously sorts
students (and colleagues[40]) hierarchically according to a notion of ability,
while upholding a commitment to equality and social justice.[41] Universal
teaching does not provide the reassurances offered by the work of Bourdieu or even Foucault, both of which often feature on professional development courses aimed at teachers, and which can be read to demonstrate
either that 'resistance' is futile, or that the possession of 'critical' knowledge is a way of distancing oneself from the malevolent workings of the
education system. In portraying equality as a practice, rather than a state,

universal teaching makes much greater demands on those who work in education.

The book does not tell its readers how to respond to such demands, a move which differentiates it from the literature on 'critical pedagogy', including the work of Paulo Freire. The demand is not for a particular approach to teaching, but for an exploration, or an experimentation, in response to the supposition of equality. Universal teaching was one such experiment, but there is no suggestion in *The Ignorant Schoolmaster* that it can, or should, be repeated: its description serves to locate a moment of transformation in the practice of 'doing' equality, rather than to resurrect the past.

Although universal teaching was an argument against all systems of instruction for the People, it is hard to avoid thinking about learning and education without considering this system, even if only in opposition to it – as the literature on communities of practices makes clear. The way in which this system is considered has changed since *The Ignorant Schoolmaster* was first published: the debates which Kristin Ross describes portray a time when the curriculum was a subject of some public argument.[42] Today, discussions on the curriculum (in the UK at least) – for instance, about how to teach reading and writing – often refer themselves to matters of 'best evidence' and expertise.

Therefore, if universal teaching is not a pedagogic model to be followed through, and if debates about education have evolved since *The Ignorant Schoolmaster* was first published, what is there to make of each today? What I have endeavoured to explore in this chapter is the way in which pedagogy continues to be imagined as a means to a better ordered community: it was this dynamic which universal teaching refused and which *The Ignorant Schoolmaster* set out to undermine. Education institutions, and those who work in them, have something to gain from this representation of community, not least their funding: in the UK in the last fifteen years, there has been a huge increase in expenditure on schools and education research, with the justification that this was a way of tackling social inequality and social injustice; and despite the current economic crisis, funding for schools remains protected according to the same rationale. At the same time, however, the education system is commonly described as 'failing' – failing to ensure social mobility, to raise educational outcomes and especially of the poor, to reduce inequality; in other words, failing to deliver a just communal order, in which everyone is in their proper place. Education research which draws on the 'community of practice' concept to identify the failures of the education system reiterates many of these complaints.

The arguments constituting universal teaching make a case for a different problematics, a different justification for education – one which starts from the 'illusion' of equality and experiments with ways of demonstrating this. This would involve seeing education as an occasion for confrontation, in which what is at stake is the demonstration of equality. The problem of teaching and learning might then be formulated in terms of judging better and worse ways of representing the world, or the community, while presuming the equality of those creating such representations. This is uncertain, experimental work; its easy statement is not intended to deny the sporadic way in which such work is thinkable and doable in education institutions;[43] but it is a more optimistic enterprise than mourning the symbolic violence of the school, retracing the unchanging contours of its discourses, or finding more effective ways of assigning people to their proper place in the social order. It opens up again the possibility of seeing teaching/learning as a hopeful endeavour, concerned not with knowing the world, but with creating it anew.

Chapter 7

Rancière and Anarchism

Todd May

Democracy first of all means this: anarchic 'government,' one based on nothing other than the absence of every title to govern.[1]

Démocratie veut dire d'abord cela: un 'gouvernement' anarchique, fondé sur rien d'autre que l'absence de tout titre à gouverner.[2]

This essay can be read as an attempt to understand the above sentence: its meaning, its motivation, and its significance for the theoretical tradition of anarchism. Among recent French thinkers, only Rancière has been willing to align his thought with the term *anarchism*. (Foucault, for instance – a thinker one might consider anarchist, at least in inspiration – dismisses the movement with this brief gesture equating it with a racist form of bio-power.[3]) Only Rancière has been willing not only to reject the Marxist spectre which hovers over progressive European thought, but also to refer in a positive way to the tradition that, during most of the twentieth century, was thought to have been left to the dustbin of history. With a return to anarchism in political action and, more recently, in political thought, Rancière's gesture of embrace is both timely and deserving of reflective attention. He has much to offer contemporary anarchism, and his thought can itself be better understood in dialogue with that renewed tradition.

Understanding the meaning and significance of the above sentence will require some hermeneutical work. Rancière's pronouncements, while not gnomic, are sometimes a bit programmatic in character. His texts are often short and suggestive. This, one might argue, is in keeping with the requirements of his thought. It seems to imply the equal intelligence of his readers. His writings do not tease us with obscure references or jargon, and neither do they explain themselves exhaustively. This invites the reader to engage with his texts; but this invitation is one not only to read, but also to think and to work. One might consider this essay to be an acceptance of that invitation. Rather than being a violation of Rancière's presupposition of equal intelligence, I hope this essay will be read instead as one person's attempt to see what can be made of the role of anarchism in Rancière's text.

One might begin reflection on the citation by noting the paradoxical character of the phrase 'anarchic "government"'. There is a double difficulty here: first, anarchists are thought to be opposed to government, so it appears that there may be a contradiction operative in the phrase. Second, however, and opposed to this, the term *government* is placed in quotes, thus indicating that something other than a traditional view of government is at stake. Indeed, the term *government* is used in one sense literally and in another ironically. Later in the chapter in *Hatred of Democracy*, in which this sentence appears, Rancière tells us, 'democracy is neither a society to be governed, nor a government of society, it is specifically this ungovernable on which every government must ultimately find out it is based'.[4] Democracy, then, in Rancière's view, seems both to be and not to be a matter of government. In what sense is democracy a matter of government, and in what sense is it not?

The sense in which it is a matter of government has to do with the entitlement to govern. Rancière refers to Plato's discussion of entitlement to govern from the *Laws*, where Plato distinguishes seven forms of entitlement. The first six are unsurprising; they have to do with birth, power and strength. It is the seventh one that catches the reader's attention: 'the title of that authority that has the "favour of heaven and fortune": the choice of the god of chance, the drawing of lots, i.e. the democratic procedure by which a people of equals decides the distribution of places'.[5] But the drawing of lots is not a qualification at all. It is precisely the absence of qualification: it is pure luck, the favour of heaven. As Rancière points out, this implies that one of the entitlements to govern is nothing other than the absence of any specific entitlement. It falls to those who receive it not by virtue of some quality they possess, but simply as the product of a random selection process.

But if one of the seven entitlements to govern is the absence of any entitlement, then what does this imply for the other six? What status can they have as justifiers for the position of governing if they stand alongside the absence of any entitlement? It is as though one said that the entitlement to govern lay in having a particular quality that justified governance, or not having any such quality. The existence of the seventh entitlement undercuts the justification for any of the others. Or, put another way, there is no justification for an entitlement to govern. Anyone at all is entitled to govern.

To say that anyone is entitled to govern, however, is not the same thing as saying that no one is entitled to govern. Instead, it is to say that everyone is *equally* entitled to govern. This begins to get us to the meaning of the citation. If there is to be some kind of government, it must be had on the basis of a recognition that everyone is equally entitled to govern. Or, to put it another way, there is no justifiable distinction between those who occupy the position of governing and those who do not. As Rancière puts the point in *Disagreement*, 'political activity is always a mode of expression that undoes the perceptible divisions of the police order by implementing a basically heterogeneous assumption, that of the part who have no part, an assumption that, at the end of the day, itself demonstrates the contingency of the order, the equality of any speaking being with any other speaking being.'[6]

This, however, does not allow us to understand the significance of the quotation marks around the term *government*. It does not enlighten us as to how democracy both is and is not a matter of government It only tells us that nobody is any more entitled to govern than anyone else. However, if we attend to the citation about the ungovernable on which every government must ultimately be based, we have our clue. Immediately preceding the citation beginning 'democracy is neither…', Rancière writes: 'State government is only legitimate insofar as it is political. It is political only insofar as it reposes merely on an absence of foundation. That is what democracy means when accurately understood as a "law of chance". The customary complaints about democracy's ungovernability in the last instance come down to this: democracy is neither…'[7] The complaints about democracy's ungovernability that had taken up much of the earlier part of *Hatred of Democracy* are complaints about people's unworthiness to govern themselves. Allow people to choose their government and they all become animalistic consumers, dedicating themselves to the first pleasure that comes along.

Rancière turns this idea on its head. The complaints about democracy's ungovernability are, in fact, complaints about democracy itself. They are complaints that democracy 'reposes merely on an absence of foundation'. They are a form of resistance to the idea that everyone is equally entitled to govern, an attempt – through a denigration of the people – to reintroduce the idea that there are some more worthy of governing than others. There are those who are capable of governing, and others who are not; in fact, those others are hardly capable of governing themselves in their private lives, much less governing others in a public arena. These latter are, in the terms of *Disagreement*, those who do not have a part, those who do not count. The fact that democracy is a denial of this distinction between those who do and those who do not have a part to play in governance is precisely what the elites hate about it.

The ungovernabililty characteristic of democracy, then, is the equality upon which every attempt to govern must rest. Even when it denies that equality, it presupposes it. This is an argument Rancière makes at the outset of *Disagreement*:

> There is order in society because some people command and others obey, but in order to obey an order at least two things are required: you must understand the order and you must understand that you must obey it. And to do that, you must already be the equal of the person who is ordering you.[8]

The presupposition of equality is the presupposition of ungovernability – it is not the ungovernability of those who are too unruly to govern themselves, but instead of those who are equal to those who seek to govern them. It is, we might say, a normative rather than descriptive ungovernability, if we keep in mind that the recognition of that normative ungovernability is often an explanatory element in the arising of what Rancière calls *politics*.

If ungovernability is the characteristic feature of democracy, then when Rancière places quotation marks around the term *government* in the citation at the outset, does he mean that we should take the term ironically? We think of democracy as a form of government. By 'anarchic "government"' does he mean, in conformity with the idea often associated with classical anarchism, that democracy is not a matter of government at all, and that therefore there should be no government? I want to claim that matters are a bit trickier than that, and to hold on to the idea that democracy in one sense is not a matter of governance, and in another sense it is. We might approach the idea by saying this: if there is to be anything like democratic governance, it must reflect the ungovernability previously described, the ungovernability that lies in 'the equality of any speaking being with any other speaking being'. Much of what goes under the name of democracy is a betrayal of that ungovernability; and that is perhaps why, when Rancière writes *Hatred of Democracy*, he focuses not upon those who offer their empty encomiums to democracy while betraying it at every turn, but instead upon those who find democracy a threat. These latter, at least, have in their sights the radically unsettling character of democracy, even if, for their own reasons, they fail to see it aright.

As we saw a moment ago, the claim that everyone is equally entitled to govern is not the claim that nobody is entitled to govern. The question before us, then, becomes this: what would be a form of governance that reflected the idea that everyone is equally entitled to govern? What would an anarchic form of governance look like? It might very well, in one sense, be a form of governance. At certain points, some might be entitled to give orders to others, who might be obliged to obey them. On the other hand, it would not be a form of governance that presupposes that those giving the orders would be entitled to those orders in the sense of being justified by any quality they possessed. If they were justified to give any orders at all, that justification would have to rest upon another basis. This, I want to claim, is why the term *government* is placed in quotation marks. It is not because Rancière wants to mark an irony with respect to the term, but instead because the idea of governance based upon democratic ungovernability is not at all the same thing that we have come to associate with any form of government with which we are familiar.

How might such a 'governing' order look? The central feature would be that everyone is considered to be equally capable of governing. This would require that, in some form or another, each person has a say in the ongoing governance of the group. That can happen in many ways. The most forceful expression of this might be said to be a consensus form of governance, where anyone in the group could veto a group decision. However, it is not clear that consensus in fact preserves the equality of everyone. One might ask whether veto power creates an inequality between those who favour a proposal and those who are against it. Often the complaint among groups that work by consensus is that one member can hold up the business of all the others, simply by vetoing whatever proposals are made. Another form of governance might be to appeal consensually to a meta-level: to create consensual agreement on rules of procedure, and then to proceed from there. A group could, for instance, consensually agree on a set of rules that allow for majority or supermajority voting on a variety of issues. This would circumvent the problem of consensus without marginalizing any of the participants. It would be a form of governance akin to the discursive community endorsed by Jürgen Habermas, who promotes a view of norm-setting that requires the actual ratification of those involved in the group.[9]

This meta-level approach is not without its own challenges. First, it is possible, although less likely, to repeat the problem of consensus at the meta-level if someone were to decide to veto all proposals for forms of voting. Second, what happens when a new member joins the group? If he or she does not have a say as to the procedural norms, does that signal that he or she is considered less entitled to govern? There are no easy answers to these questions. However, the fact of their being raised would already indicate a sensitivity to the equal entitlement to govern that lies behind the citation at the outset.

Mark Lance argues that equality cannot be assured simply by finding the right process.[10] He claims that it is not only the process that needs attending to, but also the participants in that process; they must cultivate the particular skills that would lead to cooperative deliberation and a recognition and acceptance of other viewpoints. In line with Aristotelean thought, Lance claims that by developing certain abilities – for instance, to recognize the significance of the viewpoints of others, to have a sense of when to press on and when to let go of one's position – one can become a better participant in processes that seek to ensure the equality of all participants. These virtues, one might maintain, are simply the virtues associated with the ability to recognize the equal entitlement of others; they reflect at the personal level what Rancière envisions at the political level.

Inasmuch as processes like this can be developed, there is no reason to think that there cannot be the giving and receiving of orders involved in a form of governance that would still preserve the equal entitlement to govern. For instance, I might be part of a group seeking more rights for undocumented workers, whether or not I am an undocumented worker myself. The group, with my participation, may have delegated a person as press liaison. At a demonstration, if a member of the press seeks to interview me, it would not violate my equal entitlement to govern for the press liaison to approach the press, turn to me, and say, 'I'll cover this'. There would be the giving and receiving of orders, and yet I would be involved in the process by which those powers were delegated.

One might wish to suggest that certain types of liberal constitutional orders would also meet the criterion of the equality of governance. Take, for instance, John Rawls' famous example of the original position, where everyone is asked to choose principles for social governance from behind a veil of ignorance. This would seem to allow equal participation in the setting of social principles. There are, however, two problems with this proposal, one specific to Rawls and the other characteristic of constitutional orders generally. The problem for Rawls is that the original position is a theoretical model of deliberation, not an actual deliberation. As Rawls notes: 'The original position is also more abstract: the agreement must be regarded as both hypothetical and nonhistorical.'[11]

Second, and this problem applies to any constitutional order, once the governance is set in motion, those who are not governing lose their status as real participants in the system. They vote, or perhaps run for office; but these choices are between being represented and representing, not participating. As we know from historical experience and our current situation, representation is a betrayal rather than an expression of the equality of governance. It places people in a position of passivity relative to their governance, which creates or recreates the distinction between those who have a part and those who do not. This does not mean that representation can never be utilized in an arrangement of equal participation. One could, for instance, delegate a representative from a smaller group to a larger one in order to facilitate specific decisions. However, a constitutional order that has representatives whose position allows them to make decisions on a variety of fronts with the justification of representing others tends towards a division between a governing class and a governed one. (Moreover, as we have all seen to exhaustion, this division is reinforced by and reinforces other divisions – especially, but not solely, economic ones.)

In any case, absent a constitutional order, there are more informal but nevertheless stable ways to ensure an equality of governance. Recently, Rancière has recognized this point by distinguishing between institutions and cooperatives: 'The power of the people', he notes, 'itself is anarchic in principle, for it is the affirmation of the power of anyone, of those who have no title to it. It is thus the affirmation of the ultimate illegitimacy of domination. Such power can never be institutionalized. It can, on the other hand, be practised, enacted by political collectives.'[12] If this is right, there can, then, be forms of governance that sustain the equality of everyone. These forms of governance are nothing like what has traditionally been conceived under the rubric of governance – hence the quotation marks in the opening citation. Nevertheless, they open the possibility of cooperative governance without betraying the one quality that entitles one to govern; that is, the absence of any title to govern.

One might raise the objection at this point that groups with governance like this cannot substitute for a constitutional order. They are bound to be too small and dispersed for the kind of governance required over a territory or diverse social grouping of any size. Rancière is sensitive to this point. In his view, a politics of equality – which is, for him, the only form of politics worthy of the name – is something that should not be confused with the policing of a society. This is why it is 'neither a society to be governed, nor a government of society'. Police orders, constitutional or otherwise, will always be with us. However, because these police orders are necessarily inegalitarian, within those police orders there must always be ground for challenges by and alongside those who are marginalized by a given police order.

In Rancière's terms, police orders always invite dissensus. What we are describing here, then, is not a blueprint for a type of governance that is to substitute for what has gone under the name of government. Instead, we are investigating what type of governance can be associated with those who resist a police order, those who act collectively under the presupposition of the equality of all speaking beings. To put the point another way, we are asking about what governance might look like if it were truly democratic. Rancière insists that 'The test of democracy must ever be in democracy's own image: versatile, sporadic – and founded on trust.'[13] We are asking about the character of a governance based on trust, and we should not be surprised to find that it is necessarily versatile and sporadic.[14]

As the reader will likely have suspected at this point, as the discussion has unfolded it has tracked not only the issue of governance, but, at the same time, that of anarchism. The types of governance suggested a few paragraphs back are in keeping with those discussed by the anarchist tradition. Anarchism has always been focused on the equality of participants and on the processes by which each participant can have his or her voice heard in the context of political decision-making and political movements. When Rancière uses the term *anarchic* to qualify 'governance', his term appeals to a tradition of thought that converges with the interpretation of the passage we have given here. The idea that everyone is equally entitled to govern, that politics is a bottom-up rather than a top-down affair, and that the process of decision-making displays whether or not there is real equality in a particular group: all of these are staples of anarchist thought and practice.

This is not to insist that everything Rancière says, at least under the interpretation offered here, is seamless with everything that has been claimed by the anarchist tradition. The reason for this is that the anarchist tradition is not seamless. In particular, there has been a deep ambivalence in that tradition between an embrace of liberty and one of equality. I have discussed this issue at length elsewhere,[15] and will only reprise the idea here briefly in order to focus instead on how the idea of the equal entitlement to govern displays itself in an important contemporary anarchist text. The leading idea is that while anarchism has historically split into two streams – individualist anarchism, focusing on liberty, which now might be called 'libertarianism'; and collective anarchism, focusing on equality.[16] The latter group, which is the leftist form of anarchism, is itself often ambivalent about the role that liberty plays. Often, maximal liberty is embraced as a value that converges with equality, when in fact there can be tensions between them, as anyone who has seen the recent effects of unbridled economic liberty will recognize.

This confusion can be traced to nineteenth-century anarchist thought, where, as George Crowder has pointed out in *Classical Anarchism*, there is thought to be no tension between liberty and equality. In his view, the classical anarchists of the nineteenth century hold 'the optimistic belief, generated by the rise of scientism, that moral truth, seen as inherent in the laws of nature, will eventually be the object of universal agreement.'[17] If there is a natural convergence on universal moral agreement, then allowing people to act freely will only enhance the emergence of that agreement. While I think that Crowder underestimates the role that equality plays for the classical anarchists, there is no doubt that there is a bond between the embrace of liberty and optimism that such an embrace will ultimately not conflict with the equality of everyone. Rancière's thought, with its privileging of equality rather than liberty, stands as a corrective to the legacy of this confusion.

Many contemporary anarchists are not prey to this confusion. Colin Ward, perhaps the most seminal writer among contemporary British anarchists, describes a form of anarchism that can be seen to reflect the interpretation of the passage I have offered here, even though he does not always spell it out theoretically. In the first instance, Ward is not a utopian anarchist. He does not believe, contra someone like Bakunin, that top-down relationships can be overcome through a revolution that sweeps them away: 'The choice between libertarian [anarchist] and authoritarian solutions is not a once-and-for-all cataclysmic struggle, it is a series of running engagements, most of them never concluded, which occur, and have occurred, throughout history.'[18] In his view, anarchism is not a new idea. The project of bottom-up struggles on the basis of equality has been with us 'throughout history'. Like Rancière, his examples do not come solely from recent history but from earlier periods too; and, also like Rancière, those examples are of particular forms of resistance to hierarchy by those who are its objects.

One example is close to home for Ward. It concerns a squatter campaign that was initiated in 1946 by those left homeless from World War II. The British government was gradually seeking to address the problem, but in Lincolnshire people took matters into their own hands – they decided to occupy army camps that had been emptied after the war. The movement spread: 'By October 1,038 camps had been occupied by 40,000 families in England and Wales, and another 5,000 families in Scotland.'[19] Although the British government initially opposed the movement, claiming that the squatters had leapt their position in the line for housing, it eventually offered the camps official recognition, something that, of course, the squatters were not seeking.

The camps were run on an egalitarian, bottom-up basis. As Ward describes them: 'They organised every kind of communal service in the attempt to make these bleak huts more like home – communal cooking, laundering and nursing facilities, for instance. They also federated into a Squatter's Protection Society. One feature of these squatter communities was that they had very little in common beyond their homelessness – they included tinkers and university dons.'[20] Reading of these camps, one is reminded of some of the spontaneous activity characteristic of the days following Hurricane Katrina. While the media was reporting widespread looting and chaos, most people on the ground (and water) were organizing informally in order to preserve themselves and their neighbours during a period in which the local, state and federal governments were exhibiting a staggering failure to act.[21] The difference between Katrina and the squatter's camps lay in the longevity of the latter – a longevity that gave birth to informal but sustained organizations, or what Rancière calls *cooperatives*. In one case, Ward notes, the squatter's camp lasted for twelve years.

The history of these squatters' camps not only exemplifies anarchist 'government' of the type Rancière depicts, it also displays the difference between those for whom equality is a presupposition of political action and those who rely on the police order. Ward notes that once the British government officially recognized the squatters' camps, it began to move other homeless families into them. However, these latter families did not have the same relation to their surroundings as the original squatters. They had not appropriated them or been involved in their refashioning. In fact, there arose a distinction between what were called 'the goats' and 'the sheep', the former being the original squatters and the latter the official ones relocated by the government. The former had started from scratch, appropriating the camp grounds, turning it into habitable space. The latter, by contrast, did not have a hand in creating their space. The government had not only located them into the camps, it had also provided some basic improvements like partitions and sinks. It became evident that those who had appropriated the space were more active in relation to their surroundings. They, the goats, worked on improving the camps and ensuring their smooth running, while the sheep settled into a more passive and depressed state.[22]

This distinction between the goats and the sheep points towards an element of Rancière's thought that we have not yet touched on: emancipation. The difference between them can be seen as a difference between those who accept and those who do not accept the government's claim that they do not have a part to play in the creation of their lives. (After all, the line jumped by the goats was created by the government, which arrogated to itself the role of dispenser of dwellings.) The former subject themselves to the police order, while the latter do not. Their way of refusing the

government's claim did not consist in challenging the government to provide them with housing. It consisted in seeking housing for themselves –
that is, in presupposing their equality to those in the hierarchy who had a
part to play. In doing so, they cut not only their legal but also their psychological moorings to the hierarchy that governed them. This is in contrast to
the sheep, who continued to rely on the police order. In a word, by acting
on the presupposition of their equality, the goats *emancipated* themselves.
Rancière writes that living from the presupposition of equality 'is the definition of a struggle for equality which can never be merely a demand upon
the other, nor a pressure put upon him, but always simultaneously a proof
given to oneself. This is what "emancipation" means.'[23]

Rancière believes that movements like these, anarchist movements of
equality, do not arise often. He writes that 'politics doesn't always happen
– it actually happens very little or rarely.'[24] I am not sure I agree with this.
Elsewhere, I have documented several recent movements of equality: the
Zapatistas, the Algerian refugee struggle for equality in Montreal, the anarchist publishing company AK Press, and others. And, if we look to Katrina,
or the MST (*Movimento dos Trabalhadores Rurais Sem Terra*) – the movement
of landless workers in Brazil to claim unused land for cultivation – or the
Argentine workers' takeover of factories earlier in this millennium, one will
see evidence of equality at work. Many of these movements do not call
themselves anarchist, and none of them (to my knowledge) call themselves
Rancièrean, but they exhibit the characteristic presupposition of equality
that animate these two forms of political thought. As Rancière reminds us,
equality 'is a mere presupposition that needs to be discerned within the
practices implementing it.'[25] To be sure, politics in this sense may not be as
visible as the police order that surrounds us, but it remains a constant theme
– what Ward calls one of the 'running engagements' – of collective resistance to that police order.

The egalitarian, anarchist impulse seems to run deep, which is likely one
of the reasons that, among elites, there is such a 'hatred of democracy'.
This hatred, as the citation at the outset notes, is a hatred of self-governing,
a hatred of governing by those whose qualifications to govern consist in the
absence of any title to govern. To be self-governing in this sense, however, is
neither to be without governing nor to submit to a representational form of
government; it is, instead, to act alongside others in a common creation of
governing that stems from a common presupposition of equality. Moreover,
it is the emphasis on this form of action emerging from this presupposition
that ties Rancière's thought to that of anarchism, and both of them to the
most significant – and most persistent – people's movements of our time.

Chapter 8

Rancière's Utopian Politics

Paul Patton

Rancière denies that he is a political philosopher in the sense of one who is interested in the foundations or the structure of a stable and well-ordered political community. Rather than these concerns that define much of what currently passes for political philosophy or political theory, he is interested in what he calls the 'edge' or the limits of existing political communities.[1] Rancière is an egalitarian of sorts and this 'edge' is expressed in his idiosyncratic concepts of equality, democracy and politics. In this chapter, I explore the ways in which Rancière's approach to politics repeats certain theoretical gestures common to other French post-structuralist thinkers, while differing in the details of his elaboration and use of these concepts. I focus especially on the limits of this political approach, considered as political philosophy but also considered as a form of philosophical intervention in or commentary upon the present.

1 Politics

Rancière redefines politics so that it encompasses only a very particular activity confined to the margins of what is generally considered to be politics. Politics is commonly thought of in terms of the struggles over power and resources that take place on the stage defined by legal and political institutions, public reason and public opinion. By contrast, for Rancière, politics is a matter of conflict over the very existence of this stage as well as the make-up and status of the performers who are entitled or able to appear. Politics so conceived is not the day-to-day business of argument over public policy, nor is it the perpetual struggle of political parties, interest groups and others seeking to exercise or to influence executive government power. Rather, politics, as Rancière defines it, is manifest in 'whatever shifts a body from the place assigned to it or changes a place's destination. It makes visible what had no business being seen, and makes heard a discourse where once there was only a place for noise.'[2]

Rancière renames what is generally considered politics as *police*, which he defines as 'the set of procedures whereby the aggregation and consent of collectivities is achieved, the organization of powers, the distribution of places and roles, and the systems for legitimizing this distribution.'[3] He uses this term in a sense much broader than law enforcement, with explicit reference to the seventeenth- and eighteenth-century 'science of police' discussed by Foucault in the course of his 1978 governmentality lectures.[4] However, while he notes that 'police', in Foucault's work, refers to a mode of government, his own usage is even broader than this: in addition to the extensive regulation of social and economic order envisaged by the eighteenth-century theorists of government, it includes an order of discourse. Rancière defines police as encompassing 'an order of bodies that defines the allocation of ways of doing, ways of being, and ways of saying, and sees that those bodies are assigned by name to a particular place and task; it is an order of the visible and the sayable that sees that a particular activity is visible and another is not, that this speech is understood as discourse and another as noise.'[5] Rancière's approach effectively limits 'politics' to those relatively rare occasions on which a given order of 'policing' the society in question is subject to challenge by those on the wrong side of a particular hierarchy. Politics involves processing a specific form of 'wrong', where this is expressed between parties that did not exist prior to the appearance of the wrong in question, and where 'processing' implies a reconfiguration of the ways of doing, being or saying that define the organization of a community.[6] Politics thus involves superimposing over the police order that structures a given community 'another community that exists only through and for the conflict, a community based on the conflict over the very existence of something in common between those who have a part and those who have none'.[7]

Rancière's redefinition of politics relies not only on an idiosyncratic concept of police, but also on a concept of equality that departs from the usual understanding of this term. Politics, as he redefines it, is not simply a matter of whatever challenges a given distribution of bodies, statements and roles, but of whatever does so in order to demonstrate the 'sheer contingency' of the order in question and 'the equality of any speaking being with any other speaking being'.[8] Politics in his sense of the term essentially involves a relation to equality: 'Politics is the practice whereby the logic of the characteristic of equality takes the form of the processing of a wrong.'[9] The 'characteristic' of equality here must be understood – first, in the negative sense that equality is the presupposition of any challenge to the existence or legitimacy of a particular form of hierarchy or inequality; and secondly, equality must be understood to involve an activity: in this sense, equality is always expressed in collective action on the part of those excluded or discriminated against. As Todd May points out, politics in Rancière's sense of the term involves an equality that arises only in the context of collective action, or 'only when the mechanisms of what are usually called "politics" are put into question'.[10]

Rancière allows that policing is an inevitable feature of social life and not something that could be avoided.[11] In this sense, his concept of police is 'non-pejorative.' There will be better and worse forms of police, but all of these are opposed to what Rancière calls politics; namely, whatever challenges or disrupts the distribution of social and discursive places and roles. Once the claims advanced by newly emergent political subjects become the bases of reform to existing laws and practices of government, they have already passed from the realm of politics to the realm of police. Chambers suggests that Rancière's framework 'makes possible and gives value to an analysis of the variations and differences between and among police orders'.[12] In fact, he does not devote much attention to the differences between different forms of police, although he does suggest in passing that the better forms of police are those that have been most often jolted out of their natural logic by egalitarian revolts.[13] What are these exactly? Examples include the activity of nineteenth-century factory workers who formed unions in order to challenge the privatized organization of the workplace; the activity of demonstrators who turned public thoroughfares into spaces in which public policies can be resisted, denounced or simply debated; or the activity of civil rights protestors who challenged racially discriminatory laws.

Rancière's conception of politics involves a specific conception of the logic of political situations, which he calls disagreement (*mésentente*). Perhaps not surprisingly, given his reliance on the classical texts of Plato and Aristotle as the primary corpus for developing his concept of politics, this concept and its associated form of disagreement seems especially suited to conflicts that arise wherever there are entrenched caste differences in society – whether these are based on birth, sex, race, religion or socio-economic status. Politics, as a term of art in Rancière's work, finds expression in a variety of more or less fleeting episodes of conflict, contestation and revolt. It refers to 'an evanescent moment when tensions arising from a human-being-in common produce instances of disruption, generating sources of political action'.[14]

Since politics occurs only at the borders of public agreement over particular ways of seeing or saying, disagreement involves a particular kind of speech situation where what is involved is not the possibility of mutual understanding, agreement or consensus, nor even the contents of what is said, but the very standing of the interlocutors:

> The problem is not for people speaking "different languages," literally or figuratively, to understand each other, any more than it is for "linguistic breakdowns" to be overcome by the invention of new languages. The problem is knowing whether the subjects who count in the interlocution "are" or "are not," whether they are speaking or just making a noise.[15]

Disagreement is the characteristic speech situation of newly emerging social movements, such as the successive feminisms that have challenged entrenched views about the natural differences between men and women, or about the consequences of such differences for the economic, social and political organization of basic social institutions – in other words, the 'police' in Rancière's extended sense of the term. Such disagreement is also a common situation in colonial societies, particularly those where the colonized are considered less than fully human, or at the very least uncivilized, and so not peoples with anything recognizable as law, property or rights to participate in the government of the territories in which they live.

This concept of disagreement is explicitly polemical, aimed on the one hand at the Lyotardian schema of the heterogeneity of language games that make up a given community, and on the other hand at the Habermasian schema of communicative action as the basis of political justification. Against Lyotard, Rancière does not deny that such heterogeneity is a constant source of conflict in contemporary societies, but only that the negotiation of such differences is the essence of politics in his sense of the term. It is hard to see how such redefinition amounts to a refutation of Lyotard rather than simply the insistence on a different conception of politics. Against Habermas, he argues

> that no *telos* of agreement is involved in the uttering and understanding of statements, because political dissensus is not the accomplishment of linguistic capacity. It is, first of all, the framing of the stage on which the argument may be heard as an argument, the objects of the argument as visible, common arguments, the speaker himself or herself as a visible speaking being, and so on.[16]

Since it is difficult to see how such framing occurs without recourse to communicative action, this is hardly a compelling argument against Habermas.

Rancière is not the first to object to Habermas by questioning the supposition that communicative action is governed by a telos of mutual understanding or agreement. Moreover, he is right to suggest that, while interlocution always presupposes comprehension of the content of what is said, the issue is what follows from this for our understanding of politics. A more comprehensive discussion of his differences with Habermas would need to take into account his acceptance of the idea that the inequality of social ranks only works because of the equality of speaking beings.[17] The important difference between them then returns us to the question of the nature and function of political philosophy: to outline normative bases for the constitution of democratic political community, or to point to the ways in which existing political communities always fall short of this egalitarian ideal.

2 Post-Structuralist Utopianism

Rancière's stipulative and restrictive definition of politics repeats a stance that we find in the work of a number of other French thinkers deeply affected by the events of May 1968 and the radical movement-based politics that followed. Deleuze and Foucault provided a canonical formulation of this ethos and its implications for their own activity in their 1972 interview 'Intellectuals and power'.[18] They argue that the political role of intellectuals is not to bring knowledge to or from the people, but to work within and against the order of discourse within which particular forms of knowledge appear or fail to appear. More generally, the role of intellectuals consists of struggling against the forms of power of which he or she is both the object and the instrument. Their subsequent work provided different formulations of this fundamentally critical attitude towards what passes for politics in the present, as did the work of others such as Lyotard and Derrida. Rancière's occasional references to one or other of these philosophers, along with his usage of terms such as 'differend', 'police', 'aporia' and 'order of the visible and the sayable', carry the traces of his debts to their work.

These philosophers see their work as political philosophy in a very particular sense. Each in their own way is critical of contemporary liberal and democratic politics in favour of a more profound form of politics at the border of what is possible, even if in their capacity as private citizens they continue to participate in such politics. In contrast to the aims of liberal normative political philosophy, they do not aim to spell out or to justify the principles on which societies made up of diverse kinds of people with their own particular conceptions of the good might function as more or less stable and just systems of cooperation.[19] They do not include among their philosophical goals the orientation of political society that comes with identifying reasonable and rational goals of cooperation and showing how these might be compatible. Nor do they list the goal of reconciliation that is achieved by showing the limits of consensus in democratic societies in which there is an inescapable plurality of comprehensive religious, moral and philosophical views. Nor, finally, do they list the goal of reducing conflict by searching for common ground between protagonists deeply divided on religious, philosophical or moral grounds. However, they are all, in their distinctive conceptual vocabularies, utopian political thinkers – even if their utopianism takes a very particular form. It does not consist in elaborating a conception of what a just and democratic society could be like 'under reasonably favourable but still possible historical conditions', thereby providing a standard against which existing democracies can be measured.[20] This is how Rawls describes his own 'realistically utopian' political philosophy which seeks to probe the limits of the politically practicable. Rawls recognizes that there is a question about how we determine the limits of our social world and what is politically practicable under historical conditions that could in fact obtain. He notes that these limits are not simply given by the actual, since we can and do change existing social and political institutions.[21] This question is precisely the focus of the different forms of post-structuralist utopianism.

Post-structuralist political philosophy presents a variety of more or less unrealistic utopianisms, defined by their respective relations to the outside (Foucault), the impossible (Derrida) or the absolute deterritorialization of actual societies (Deleuze and Guattari). They all share a concern with the limits of existing social and political arrangements, and the different ways in which these limits might be transgressed and the borders of the present reconfigured. Foucault describes his own work in these terms as seeking to identify those points where what was previously considered immutable can now be considered open to change. In this manner, his genealogical enquiries seek to show the singularity, contingency and arbitrariness of those limits to present ways of being and acting that are presented as universal, necessary or obligatory.[22] Derrida described the aim of his analyses of aporia in relation to political concepts such as justice, hospitality, forgiveness and democracy as an attempt to show how, in each case, the possibility of invention, reconfiguration or transformation in existing, historically conditioned and contingent forms of the phenomenon in question is guaranteed by the existence of the pure and unconditioned form of the concept.[23] Deleuze and Guattari describe their philosophy as utopian in the sense that it aims at those encounters in which the absolute deterritorialization effected in thought engages with one or other form of relative deterritorialization underway in the society in question: 'In each case it is with utopia that philosophy becomes political and takes the criticism of its own time to the highest point. Utopia ... stands for absolute deterritorialization but always at the critical point at which it is connected with the present relative milieu, and especially with the forces stifled by this milieu.'[24] Rancière shares this concern with the limits of actual social arrangements. His definition of police as a certain partition of the sensible and distribution of occupations and places within society allows him to assert that the 'essence of politics ... is to disturb this arrangement by supplementing it with a part of the no-part identified with the community as a whole'.[25]

3 Becoming Democratic

Just as he undertakes an extensive redefinition of the concept of politics, so too does he substantially alter what is generally understood by democracy. He renames democracy – in the sense in which it is widely understood, including the constitutional system of elected assemblies, guarantees freedom of speech, expression, universal franchise and so on – as consensus democracy or 'post-democracy'. This is the form of government and legitimation of a given police order from which the *demos* and genuine politics have disappeared. Rancière's own concept of democracy is tied to his narrow definition of politics and his 'activist' concept of equality. 'Democracy', in this sense, is neither the parliamentary system nor the state but rather the mode of subjectification associated with movements that assert the equality of those who are not considered equal: 'Democracy is more precisely the name of a singular disruption of this order of distribution of bodies as a community that we proposed to conceptualize in the broader concept of the police. It is the name of what comes and interrupts the smooth working of this order through a singular mechanism of subjectification.'[26] As such, democracy involves three things: first, the appearance of some new aspect of the people or the appearance of the people in some new light, 'the introduction of a visible into the field of experience'.[27] Second, it involves a 'people' that amounts to the superimposition of a part of those who have no part on the recognized or accepted sum of the parts of the society in question: 'Democracy is the designation of subjects that do not coincide with the parties of the state or of society, floating subjects that deregulate all representation of places and portions.'[28] Third, this appearance of the people under a new aspect or a new people occurs in the context of a disagreement in the sense defined above. Rather than conflicts of interest between constituted parts of the population, these are conflicts over the very count of those parts, interlocutions that undermine the very situation of interlocution: 'Democracy is not a regime or a social way of life. It is the institution of politics itself, the system of forms of subjectification through which any order of distribution of bodies into functions corresponding to their "nature" and places corresponding to their functions is undermined, thrown back on its contingency.'[29] In this narrow sense of democracy , Rancière points out that politics (in the sense in which he defines it) is always democratic to the extent that it amounts to 'forms of expression that confront the logic of equality with the logic of the police order'.[30]

Thus far, Rancière has outlined a stipulative concept of democracy based primarily upon his reading of the classic texts and his own redefinitions of politics, equality and disagreement. This is a concept of democracy that is consistent with the underlying idea of democracy found in political philosophy from liberal egalitarians such as Rawls to communicative rationalists such as Habermas and post-structuralists such as Deleuze and Derrida. Moreover, it underwrites a conception of democratic politics that is consistent with the extravagant utopianism of his post-structuralist contemporaries. All of these political philosophers engage in a process of specifying determinate concepts of equality and democracy on the basis of a common underlying idea. In Deleuzean terminology, different conceptions of democracy may be considered as determinate specifications of the philosophical concept or pure idea of democracy. Rawls formalizes this procedure in terms of a distinction of progressively greater specification in passing from ideas to concepts and conceptions of political values such as fairness, justice or equality. In his later writings, he freely admits that there are a number of versions of liberalism that are compatible with his underlying idea of society as a fair system of cooperation, and that the content of liberal public reason is given by a family of liberal conceptions of justice rather than a single one.[31] In these terms we can allow that the philosophical concept or idea of democracy is compatible with a range of possible determinations of its component concepts. Different historical forms of democratic society can then be considered as the actualization or realization of those more or less specific conceptions.

At this point, there emerges a further 'horizontal' sense in which the institutional and legal forms of democratic government are open-ended. By making the institutions and laws accountable to those governed by them, democratic government leaves open the possibility that these might be revised as the fundamental convictions of the people change over time.

This happens, for example, when basic political rights are extended to those formerly excluded, such as women, slaves or colonized indigenous peoples. It happens when societies accept that individuals may be entitled to assistance to feed, clothe, shelter or educate themselves as a result of circumstances for which they cannot be held responsible. It happens, finally, when changes in comprehensive moral views lead to changes in the law relating to capital punishment, homosexuality or assisted suicide. When such changes are brought about and justified – either at the time or retrospectively – by appeal to one or other element of the complex idea of democracy, they amount to instances of what Deleuze and Guattari call 'becoming democratic'. What they mean by this term, I suggest, are those actual processes of resistance to present institutions and practices in modern societies along with the ideals or opinions that motivate or inform them: the forms of what is said as well as what is done. Inevitably, what is said will draw on elements of existing political normativity to suggest ways in which the inegalitarian, unjust or oppressive character of present institutional forms of social life might be removed. 'Becoming-democratic' is therefore one kind of deterritorialization that is available in contemporary neo-liberal societies. It points to ways of criticizing the workings of actually existing democracies in the name of the egalitarian principles that are supposed to inform their institutions and political practices.[32] Derrida makes similar use of his concept of 'democracy to come' when he suggests that it underwrites the criticism of 'what remains inadequate to the democratic ideal'.[33]

Rancière's concept of democracy lends itself to a parallel conception of becoming-democratic. In *Hatred of Democracy*, he defines democracy as a process rather than a juridico-political form. As soon as there is a form of government, there is a public sphere that he defines as the sphere of encounter and conflict between the opposed logics of police and politics. Government inevitably tries to control this public sphere and to relegate the interventions of non-State actors to the private sphere of non-political life: 'Democracy, then, far from being the form of life of individuals dedicated to their private pleasure, is a process of struggle against this privatization.'[34] In other words, democracy is the process of enlarging this public sphere in which challenges to the established political order can be undertaken. Historically, this has unfolded in the form of struggles to admit to the public sphere those categories of persons excluded because they belonged to their masters, employers or husbands, or because they lacked the requisite property qualification. It also took the form of 'struggles to assert the public character of spaces, relations and institutions regarded as private'.[35] Rancière affirms the open-ended or limitless character of democracy understood in these terms by describing it as a 'movement that ceaselessly displaces the limits of the public and the private, of the political and the social'.[36]

4 Equality

At the heart of the idea of democracy is the equality of persons. However, the concept of equality can be cashed out in a variety of ways. Liberal egalitarians tend to cash it out by means of a universal principle of the equal worth of individuals such that no person's life, beliefs or values are inherently worth more than those of anyone else. Within a democratic society, each person is entitled to live according to his or her own conception of the good, subject to the limits imposed by the principle that their doing so should not adversely affect the freedom of others to do likewise. Each person is also entitled to have his or her own say on matters of public policy. Minimally, such a democratic society is an association of equals in which there is no justification for the exclusion of individuals or groups from the widest possible system of basic civil and political liberties. More robust forms of liberal egalitarianism involve the further claim that there is no justification for the arbitrary exclusion of particular individuals or groups from the benefits of social and political cooperation. Rawls bases his commitment to this kind of equality on what he calls the idea of society as a fair system of cooperation. Deleuze appeals to a related idea of the unfairness or injustice of unequal distribution of the benefits of social cooperation when, in his interview with Negri, he contrasts the universality of the market as a sphere of exchange of commodities and capital with the manner in which it generates poverty as well as enormous wealth and distributes these unequally.[37] The benefits of market economies are not universally shared and inequalities of condition are handed down from generation to generation in direct contravention of the principle that all are born equal.

Rancière offers a different specification of the principle of equality in terms of the equality of all speaking beings or the part of those who have no part. One could be forgiven for thinking that this is a substantive concept of the ways in which people are equal or the ways in which they should be treated as equal. However, he resists any particular determination of the concept. Equality, in his use of the term, is bound up with politics, but not in any particular way: 'All equality does is lend politics reality in the form of specific cases to inscribe, in the form of litigation, confirmation of the equality at the heart of the police order.'[38] Rancière's 'equality' is thus a principle or a presupposition of actions that challenge particular inegalitarian features of a given politics. It has no such determined object or issue of its own, since to do so would render it a matter of policing in Rancière's sense of the term.

Several things follow from this. First, this is a concept of equality that sets Rancière's egalitarianism apart from the commitments to equality of condition, resources, opportunities or capacities that characterize all contemporary liberal political philosophies, even though Rancière does suggest that it is a concept of equality that is incompatible with the division of society into rich and poor. Todd May explains the difference in terms of the difference between an equality that is granted, protected or created by the state and an equality that is acted or enacted by individuals engaged in political action : 'Politics, in short, a truly democratic politics, is collective action emerging from the presupposition of equality.'[39] The civil rights activists who sat at lunch counters in cafés for whites only and asserted their right to be served like any other patrons expressed equality. Once the discriminatory laws are changed and black people enjoy the same rights as whites, it is no longer the same equality that is expressed: 'Equality turns into the opposite the moment it aspires to a place in the social or state organization.'[40] It is important to note that the opposition assumed here between two kinds of equality derives entirely from Rancière's distinction between politics and police. The equality that is expressed in basic rights and protected by law is a matter of policing rather than politics. For Rancière, the equality that is expressed in genuinely political action is at once entirely singular and without content. It is not positive equality in any particular respect but rather a negative equality that is expressed in the refusal of a particular form of discrimination or differentiation. Equality in this sense, May suggests, is 'an empty term. It signifies the rejection of the classifications characteristic of a given police order.'[41] Equality in this sense would be not only constitutively unachievable, but also non-evaluative. This concept of equality would be perpetually open in the same way that Foucault's limits to the present, Deleuze's and Guattari's processes of deterritorialization or Derrida's unconditional concepts of justice, hospitality, forgiveness and 'democracy to come' are open. These are names for a process of challenging a given social or political order but not the name of any particular outcome or end state. Challenges to a particular hierarchy might well be egalitarian in this sense, but this does not settle the issue: we have to take sides.

At this point, however, the lack of content threatens to undermine any normative force associated with this equality. Rancière's conception of politics and its associated concept of equality are open to the criticism that has been leveled at every post-structuralist political theorist at some point;

namely, that they fail to draw normative distinctions that would enable them to discriminate, for example, between certain kinds of criticism of the present, certain forms of deterritorialization or certain kinds of deconstructive openness to the future. He might seek to maintain the distinction between policing and politics, and to maintain a non-evaluative concept of equality and politics, but it is not clear that he can do so. I noted above that he admits that there are better and worse forms of police. This implies that some forms of discrimination or differentiation are worth preserving and should not be removed simply because they disqualify the voices of some: racial or sexual supremacists, religious or other zealots who believe that violence against non-believers is justified and so on. Faced with this dilemma, the temptation is to draw the line at certain forms of expression of equality and further delimit his concept of politics. May starts down this path when he suggests that there is some content to the concept of equality: we are all equal in being 'capable of constructing a meaningful life alongside others'.[42] If 'alongside others' here means in a civil condition that does not permit harm to others, or that enjoins a degree of respect for the different ways of constructing meaningful lives, then we are dealing with a normative concept of equality. Not only does the distinction between police and politics become less clear than it initially appeared, but there is an obligation to elaborate the content of this conception and to draw out its consequences for the concepts of politics and democracy.

5 Actually Existing Democracy

Rancière is less concerned with questions of legitimacy or justification than he is with 'the actual meaning of what is called consensus democracy'.[43] In *Disagreement*, he offers an extended analysis of how this works in contemporary neo-liberal democracies such as France. He identifies several features of this regime of contemporary neo-liberal government, which he calls 'post-democracy', but the overriding feature is the disappearance of politics in the sense that he has defined it: post-democracy denotes 'the paradox that, in the name of democracy, emphasizes the consensual practice of effacing the forms of democratic action'.[44] *Hatred of Democracy* introduces a further dimension to this critical analysis of contemporary neo-liberal post-democratic government – namely, its oligarchic character. By this, Rancière means government by professional politicians who are repeatedly elected to the same or different public positions, who attended the same schools as their opponents from competing parties along with their advisors and public servants, who sometimes rotate between public roles and positions in private companies, but who invariably serve, in legitimate or illegitimate ways, the interests of wealth: 'We do not live in democracies ... We live in States of oligarchic law, in other words, in States where the power of the oligarchy is limited by a dual recognition of popular sovereignty and individual liberties.'[45]

Rancière argues that the primary function of contemporary neo-liberal post-democratic government is economic management in accordance with the requirements of global capitalism. On this point he is in agreement with Deleuze and Guattari's view that national governments have become sites for the management of local nodes in a global network of markets in capital, people, goods and services: 'The absolute identification of politics with the management of capital is no longer the shameful secret hidden behind the "forms" of democracy: it is the openly declared truth by which our governments acquire legitimacy.'[46] *Hatred of Democracy* modifies this claim by suggesting that contemporary oligarchy is actually constrained by two principles of legitimacy: the first is the familiar janus-faced liberal principle of popular sovereignty combined with a commitment to liberal civil and political rights, which compels governments to return to the polls every few years. The second is the principle of economic management in the interests of the local population but not at the expense of the limitless expansion of capital: 'At least in the short space of time that the battle for acquiring and preserving power leaves them, our governments make managing the local effects of necessity on populations their essential task.'[47] The suggestion that good economic management is a source of legitimacy for contemporary governments is, in effect, a generalization of Foucault's hypothesis regarding the form of neo-liberal government that emerged in post-war Germany. This was, he suggests, a radically economic state in the sense that economic development on the basis of a free market produced not only a political consensus among the population, but also sovereignty: 'in contemporary Germany, the economy, economic development and economic growth produces sovereignty ... The economy produces legitimacy for the state that is its guarantor.'[48]

According to Rancière, the elimination of politics in consensus democracy is achieved by 'the conjunction of a determined regime of opinion and a determined regime of right'.[49] The post-democratic regime of opinion is one in which the people are constantly and completely represented to themselves, in their totality, by means of opinion polls. However, at the same time, the people are reduced to the range of opinions represented in the polls and, as such, effectively homogenized. The totality of the people becomes identified with the identified categories or parts, with nothing left over: 'The quality of anyone and everyone becomes identical to the total distribution of the people into its parts and sub-parts.'[50] There is no longer any possibility of an uncounted part, and therefore no possibility of politics. The post-democratic regime of right is one in which the community is defined by its subjection to the rule of law and by the rights assigned to each citizen and protected by the State. Political differences then become reduced to problems to be solved by the passage of laws and the modification of government policy. Since the overriding condition of liberal government remains a rule of law that protects the freedom of each subject to the equal right of all citizens, the State ensures its own legitimacy by the evacuation of politics. The spread of law throughout the social body is accompanied by the proliferation of expertise in social policy and the constant polling of the population to gauge its opinions. The proliferation and constant modification of legal rights aims to bring the rule of law and social relations into perfect harmony so that 'the legal ideal' circulates throughout the social field 'adapting to and anticipating all the movements of society'.[51] In this manner, for example, family law seeks to emulate and even to anticipate new attitudes, moral values, along with the looser family ties that these imply. Property law is ceaselessly modified to keep up with the intangible forms of intellectual property that result from new technologies: 'Committees of savants, gathered together under the name of bioethics, promise to clarify for the legislator the point at which man's humanity begins.'[52] Rights to work and at work become more flexible to adapt to changes in the labour market and in the forms of economic activity. Citizens themselves become a kind of mini-enterprise seeking to maximize the return on their individual and collective capital, including human capital: 'The old "rigidities" of law and the struggle for "rights" are opposed by the flexibility of a right mirroring social flexibility, of a citizenship that makes each individual a microcosm in which is reflected the identity with itself of the community of energies and responsibilities that look like rights.'[53]

Under this post-democratic regime of government or 'police', even the exclusion of marginal social groups is transformed into a problem to be solved by legal and policy expertise, at the expense of genuine political struggle. In the old days, divisions within society were overt and visible, able to erupt into political struggle. By contrast, what is nowadays referred to as 'exclusion' represents 'the very absence of a representable barrier. And so it is strictly identical to the law of consensus'.[54] At this point, Rancière's account of the workings of contemporary neo-liberal democracies begins to sound like nostalgia for older forms of politics where barriers were clearly drawn and where 'The uncounted could make themselves count by showing up the process of division and breaking in on others' equality and appropriating it for themselves.'[55] This nostalgic tone continues in his analysis of the sources of the 'new forms of racism and xenophobia' that emerged in Europe during the 1990s and that accompanied the pre-emptive inclusion of the parts of those who have no part under the name of 'exclusion'. These new forms of racism and xenophobia were, he argues, a consequence of the 'mode of visibility' that accompanied post-democratic consensus government. The reason for this consequence is that the loss of political forms of identity and otherness for immigrant workers left only 'a sociological identity, which then topples over into the anthropological nakedness of a different race and skin … It is the loss of the *one-more* of subjectification that determines the constitution of a *one-too-many* as phobia of the community.'[56]

It is difficult to know what to make of this argument. Why is the reverse hypothesis not equally plausible? Why should we not allow that the reappearance of atavistic antagonisms directed at other races and other religions is entirely political in Rancière's sense of the term? All kinds of sociological explanation may be offered for why these views should have reappeared at this historical juncture, but the fact that they were able to do so is evidence that the attitudes, beliefs and visceral reactions that accompanied earlier forms of political subjectification have not entirely disappeared from our enlightened modern communities. All it took to unleash them in Australia during the same period was a series of campaigns waged by vested interests against court-awarded rights for Indigenous peoples and a conservative politician determined to confront the pieties of late modern political correctness and to stand up for 'traditional' attitudes and beliefs. Are not rebellions such as these also political reactions against the predominant opinions of the educated elite who participate in oligarchic rule? Rancière's analysis of this, as of other contemporary political phenomena, relies on no empirical evidence and no criteria to identify genuinely political challenges to the existing consensus. It resembles the just-so stories of postmodern social reality that Baudrillard candidly described as 'theory-fictions'. Just as Rancière is right to refuse the label of political philosophy for his stipulative redefinitions of politics and democracy, so we should refuse to accept such analyses as political sociology.

Acknowledgement

I am grateful to Alison Ross and Jean-Philippe Deranty for the invitation to present this paper at a workshop at Monash University, and to Alison Ross and Andrew Schaap for their helpful comments on an earlier draft.

Chapter 9

Hannah Arendt and the Philosophical Repression of Politics

Andrew Schaap

Jacques Rancière and Hannah Arendt both disavow political philosophy even as they place the conflict between philosophy and politics at the centre of their philosophical analyses. In response to a roundtable on his 'Ten theses on politics' in 2001, Rancière declared:

> I am not a political philosopher. My interest in political philosophy is not an interest in questions of [the] foundation of politics. Investigating political philosophy for me, was investigating precisely ... what political philosophy looked at and pointed at as the problem or obstacle ... for a political philosophy, because I got the idea that what [it] found in [the] way of foundation might well be politics itself.[1]

These remarks echo a similar declaration made by Hannah Arendt in an interview with Günter Gaus for German television in 1964. Following Gaus's introduction of her as a philosopher, Arendt protested that she does not belong to the circle of philosophers. If she has a profession at all it is political theory:

> The expression 'political philosophy', which I avoid, is extremely burdened by tradition. When I talk about these things ... I always mention that there is a vital tension between philosophy and politics ... There is a kind of enmity against all politics in most philosophers ... I want to look at politics ... with eyes unclouded by philosophy.[2]

Arendt and Rancière followed parallel intellectual trajectories, 'turning away' from philosophy in response to the shock of a historical event and the disillusionment with a former teacher.

Hannah Arendt attended Martin Heidegger's lectures at the University of Marburg in the 1920s, which formed the basis of *Being and Time*. Arendt, a German-Jew who had a brief affair with Heidegger while studying at Marburg, was appalled by his support for the Nazi regime as Rector of Freiburg University in the early 1930s. In 1946, she wrote bitterly that Heidegger's 'enthusiasm for the Third Reich was matched only by his glaring ignorance of what he was talking about'.[3] She recognized in Heidegger's characterization of 'das Man' the philosopher's characteristic disdain for public life and, in his support for the Nazis, the philosopher's tendency to prefer the order of tyranny over the contingency of politics.[4] Subsequently, she was preoccupied by the problem of how 'such profundity in philosophy could co-exist with such stupidity or perversity in politics'.[5] In exile from Germany, Arendt undertook the extensive historical research that resulted in *The Origins of Totalitarianism*.[6] Only once she had settled in America did she turn her attention directly to political philosophy in *The Human Condition*.[7]

Rancière constributed to Louis Althusser's reading group on Marx's *Capital* at the École Normale Supèrieure in Paris in the 1960s. Rancière became disillusioned with Althusser due to his opposition to the student protests of May 1968 and his insistence on the privileged role of the Party intellectual. In 1974, Rancière wrote: 'Althusser needs the opposition between the "simplicity" of nature and the "complexity" of history: if production is the affair of the workers, history is too complex for them and must be left to the specialists: the Party and Theory.'[8] In Rancière's view, Althusser reproduces a symbolic hierarchy that empties the words and actions of political agents (such as the 'working class') of any intrinsic worth due to the division he insists on between manual and intellectual labour.[9] Henceforth, Rancière became preoccupied with the problem of the transmission of emancipatory experience, seeking to avoid philosophy's impulse to either fetishize *concepts* on the one hand, or to fetishize *praxis* on the other.[10] Turning away from philosophy, Rancière engaged in archival research that resulted in the publication of two anthologies and *The Nights of Labour*.[11] Only later in his career did he begin to write about political philosophy, leading to the publication of *Disagreement*.[12]

Rancière and Arendt are both praxis theorists who want to escape political philosophy's reduction of political issues to questions of government. For each of them, Plato seems to stand in for their former teacher, exemplifying the philosopher's antipathy towards politics. Both look beyond the canon of political philosophy to find a more authentic mode of political thought, sometimes highlighting apparently marginal figures as exemplary political actors. For instance, while Arendt valorizes Gotthold Lessing for his passionate openness to the world and love of it, Rancière celebrates Joseph Jacotot as the ignorant schoolmaster who presupposes an equality of intelligence between teacher and student. Arendt and Rancière both understand politics as aesthetic in nature, concerning the sensible world of appearances. They are both preoccupied with 'events' or exceptional moments of political action through which social worlds are disclosed to the senses. Given these affinities, sympathetic readers of Arendt might be surprised by Rancière's claim that Arendt's political thought, in fact, *represses* politics in a way paradigmatic of the tradition she sought to escape from. On the contrary, it might appear that rather than offering a rival view of politics, Rancière actually amends and extends an Arendtian conception of politics.[13]

I want to caution against such an interpretation. It is true that Arendt is an important influence on Rancière, despite his polemic against her. Yet, as Rancière observes in a different context, 'the power of a mode of thinking has to do above all with its capacity to be displaced'.[14] Arendt's understanding of praxis seems to resonate within Rancière's work. However, those apparently Arendtian notions that Rancière makes use of are fundamentally transformed when transposed within his broader thematization of dissensus. To develop this argument, I first examine Arendt's own account of the tension between philosophy and politics in order to understand the phenomenological basis of the political theory that she sought to develop. I then consider how persuasive Rancière's characterization of Arendt as an 'archipolitical' thinker is. In the final section, I discuss some key passages in *Disagreement* in which Rancière alludes to Arendt. These passages highlight how those Arendtian concepts that do seem to find their way into Rancière's thought are transformed when displaced from her ontology.

1 The Meaning of Appearances

'Every political philosophy', Arendt tells us, 'faces the alternative of interpreting political experience with categories which owe their origin to the realm of human affairs, or, on the contrary, of claiming priority for philosophic experience and judging all politics in its light.'[15] Arendt believed that traditional philosophy failed to recognize the specificity of politics because it followed the second path, privileging the life of contemplation over that of action. Bikhu Parekh highlights four aspects of Arendt's critique of traditional political philosophy.[16] First, philosophy fails to appreciate the *dignity* of politics. Rather than recognizing action and appearances as intrinsically meaningful, it construes politics as a means to a higher end. Second, philosophy fails to appreciate the *autonomy* of politics. Rather than recognize that political life raises distinct ontological and epistemological issues, it treats political problems as matters of morality or law. Third, traditional philosophy neglects the fundamental character and structure of political *experience* due to its preoccupation with formal features of political life. Formal analysis of concepts makes philosophy inarticulate about political phenomena since it becomes self-contained and divorced from experience. Fourth, traditional philosophy fails to appreciate *action* as the proper object of political philosophy because it treats politics as a matter of ruling. Philosophy's preoccupation with questions concerning the legitimacy of government means that it fails to appreciate how human beings actualize their freedom by participating in public life. Overall, then, traditional philosophy tends to 'derive the political side of life from the necessity which compels the human animal to live together with others ... and it tends to conclude with a theory about the conditions that would best suit the needs of the unfortunate human condition of plurality and best enable the philosopher, at least, to live undisturbed by it.'[17]

Against this tradition Arendt sought to understand politics on its own terms. In her view, philosophy is properly concerned with hermeneutic questions, which originate from existential perplexity, the human need to make sense of experience. Such questions cannot be answered on the basis of knowledge about facts since they entail judgments of worth. Moreover, answers to interpretive questions cannot be judged true or false but only more or less plausible according to the insightfulness of the interpretation they offer.[18] Thus, rather than explain political appearances in terms of a deeper truth that they reveal, she sought to understand the meaning inherent within appearances themselves. Despite her disillusionment with Heidegger's own political errors, Arendt appropriates Heidegger's concept of world in order to understand plurality as the fundamental ontological condition that structures all political experience.[19]

Arendt's insistence on the autonomy of the political as a domain of human experience, distinct from the economic, is crucial to her attempt to develop an authentic mode of political thought. In order to develop a phenomenology of politics, she must assume that those distinctions we make between different kinds of experience (aesthetic, moral, political, economic, etc.) are not simply a matter of convention but reflect objective structures that are part of a universal human condition.[20] To this end, Arendt accords a certain privilege to the political thought of the Greeks who, she claims, were more articulate about political experience than the moderns.[21] For her, concepts should be understood ontologically as distillations of experience, a way of assigning meaning and significance to human affairs. Since the political concepts we have inherited originate in the Greek polis, where they were first articulated without the burden of tradition, returning to the Greeks allows for the recuperation of the fundamental structure of political experience.[22] She derives from Greek political thought an image of the polity as a space of appearance.[23] She contrasts this image of an authentic politics, oriented to being-in-common, to the nihilistic, isolating and, indeed, anti-political politics of modernity that made possible the Nazi death camps.[24]

However, although the language of the Greeks offers an unparalleled insight into political experience, she blames the political philosophies they developed for the displacement and misunderstanding of what she takes to be the proper object of political thought: *action*. In Arendt's view, the fundamental tension between politics and philosophy arises due to the different nature of the experiences of the *vita activa* (active life) and the *vita contemplativa* (life of the mind). Since action is only possible in the company of others, politics is concerned with 'men' in their plurality as *zoon politikon*. It is concerned with winning immortality by appearing before others within the polity, and it entails *doxadzein*, forming an opinion about how the world appears from one's particular perspective within it. In contrast, since thinking always takes place in solitude, traditional philosophy is concerned with 'Man' in his singularity as *animale rationale*. It seeks to discover universal truths and it begins from the experience of *thaumadzein*, speechless wonder at what is from the perspective of transcendent reason. According to Arendt, the philosopher is an 'expert in wondering' and 'in speechless wonder he puts himself outside the political realm where it is precisely speech that makes man a political being'.[25]

In describing the emergence of this tension between philosophy and politics, Arendt presents a 'kind of myth of a philosophical Fall', as Margaret Canovan puts it.[26] In the early Greek polis, action and thought were united in logos. Arendt describes approvingly how Socrates thought that the philosopher's role was to help citizens reveal the truthfulness in their own opinions (*doxa*) rather than to educate them with those truths philosophy had already discovered. For Socrates, *doxa* was 'neither subjective illusion nor arbitrary distortion, but … that to which truth … adhered'.[27] *Doxa* was the formulation of *dokai moi*, 'of what appears to me'.[28] Socrates assumed that the world opens up differently to each citizen and that the commonness (*koinon*) of the world resides in the fact that 'the same world opens up to everyone'.[29] The achievement of philosophical dialogue was the constitution of a common world. In talking about the world that lay between them, the world would become more common to those engaged in philosophical dialogue. In this context, to assert one's opinion also meant to show oneself, to appear within the world, 'to be seen and heard by others', and hence it was a condition of being recognized by others as 'fully human'.[30]

Following the trial and death of Socrates, Arendt argues, an 'abyss opened up between thought and action'.[31] This event 'made Plato despair of polis life' and led him to reject rhetoric, the political art of persuasion, in favour of the 'tyranny of truth'.[32] Consequently, Plato elevated the *vita contemplativa* over *the vita activa*. In contrast to the eternal truths that philosophy sought to discover through reason, the world of politics appeared as contingent, arbitrary, meaningless and potentially dangerous to those who sought the truth. Against the irresponsible opinions of the Athenians, Plato opposed the Ideas. According to Arendt, Plato was the first philosopher to 'use the ideas for political purposes, that is, to introduce absolute standards into the realm of human affairs, where, without such transcending standards everything remains relative'.[33]

Moreover, and following from this, Plato transformed the concept of *arkhê* into the principle of ruling. Arendt points out that the Greeks distinguished between two inter-related modes of action with the words *archein* and *prattein*, which she translates as 'beginning' and 'achieving'. Together these modes of action indicate the contingent and unpredictable quality of a plurality of human beings acting in concert. While action requires an agent to seize the initiative, it is dependent on others joining this enterprise of their own accord in order to see it through.[34] Plato, however, sought to master action from beginning to end according to the model of fabrication. He did so by dividing the polity between those who *know* and command, and those who *do* and follow orders:[35]

> To begin (*archein*) and to act (*prattein*) thus [became] two altogether different activities [since] the beginner has become a ruler ... who 'does not have to act at all (*prattein*), but rules (*archein*) over those who are capable of execution.[36]

Politics was thereby identified with the issue of how to rule effectively while action was reduced to the execution of orders. Since, for Arendt, action is distinguished above all by its initiatory quality (or 'natality'), this amounts to the 'elimination' of action by political philosophy. Plato treated politics as a means to establish social order, to protect the philosopher from the whims of the demos. In treating politics as a means to secure the private freedom necessary to pursue the good life of contemplation, philosophy 'deprived political affairs ... of all dignity of their own'.[37] The consequence of Plato's identification of politics with ruling meant that questions of government, legitimacy and authority came to predominate in political philosophy in place of understanding and interpreting 'action itself'.[38]

2 The Edge of Politics

Given Arendt's anti-Platonism, her disavowal of political philosophy and her desire to understand politics in its own terms, what are we to make of Rancière's claim that Arendt in fact adopts an 'archi-political position', which represses politics by subordinating it to the logic of police?[39] In his essay 'Who is the subject of the rights of man?', Rancière points out that Arendt is able to equate the subject of human rights with a deprived form of life because she characterizes the political sphere as a realm distinct from that of necessity. Stateless people, in Arendt's account, are deprived of the possibility of distinguishing themselves as human within a public realm.[40] As such, they are reduced to their mere biological life within a state of nature, an abject condition beyond oppression. According to Rancière, Agamben radicalizes Arendt's *archi-politics* into a stance of de-politicization.[41] Indeed, he claims, Agamben's view of the camp as the nomos of modernity is:

> the ultimate consequence of Arendt's *archi-political position*, that is, of the attempt to preserve the political from contamination by the private, the social or a-political life. This attempt de-populates the political stage by sweeping aside its always ambiguous actors.[42]

In *Disagreement*, Rancière explains that archi-politics is one of three paradigms through which political philosophy seeks to eliminate politics. According to Rancière, philosophy's hostility towards politics arises not due to its resentment of the plurality and contingency of opinion, but its hatred of democracy. Philosophy is scandalized by the lack of any proper foundation for political community: the fact that every social order and, hence, every principle of legitimate government, ultimately presupposes a radical equality of anyone with everyone. This anarchical foundation of politics is viewed by philosophy as a source of disorder and excess to which 'political philosophy' is a response. Consequently, political philosophy attempts to develop 'an alternative to the unfounded state of politics' by achieving the 'true essence of politics'.[43]

If Rancière accords any special privilege to the Ancient Greek philosophers it is not because they are more articulate than the moderns with regard to the good life of the *bios politicos*, as Arendt thinks.[44] Rather it is because they were the first to encounter the 'secret' of politics that the political community is 'essentially a litigious community'.[45] Classical political theory encounters the 'edge' of politics precisely because it does not seek to avoid questions of the good life but looks for a good upon which the political community should be constituted and, in doing so, 'bumps into' an obstacle: the anarchy of politics; that is, the 'absence of any *archê* meaning any principle leading from the essence of the common to the forms of the community'.[46] This is expressed in terms of the principle of democracy: the qualification according to which the people rule is their 'freedom', but this is really an absence of any specific qualification, which they share with every other citizen. As such, philosophy 'came upon politics as this oddity that disrupts its logic in advance, meaning, properly, a disruption of legitimacy'.[47]

Against the anarchy of politics, political philosophy is founded on the attempt to establish the principles according to which the political community is properly organized. The 'inaugural conceptual act' that philosophy makes is the distinction between the good polity (or Republic) and the various forms of corrupt government.[48] Philosophy suppresses politics in seeking to overcome the various bad forms of government (*politeiaì*) that institutionalize the domination of one class over another by replacing them with the good polity (the *politeia*) in which the true purpose of political community is realized. However, the 'essence' of politics that political philosophy proposes to realize is in fact the opposite of political rationality: it is the logic of police, which is concerned with establishing a distribution of the sensible in which individuals and groups are identified with their position in a social order.[49] Rancière writes:

> The *politieia*, as Plato conceives it, is a community achieving its own principle of interiority in all manifestations of its life. To put it simply, the *politeia* of the philosophers is the exact identity of politics and the police.[50]

In identifying politics with the police, political philosophy disciplines conflict, subordinating agents to their place within a social order. In identifying police with politics, political philosophy imitates politics, opposing an account of the proper origin and end of political community to the anarchic foundation of politics that philosophy first encounters.[51]

Archi-politics, which Rancière associates with Plato, is the project of fully realizing political community according to the fundamental principle for which it exists. It is a form of communitarian rule that subordinates politics by assigning agents to their proper part within the whole. As Luka Arsenjuk puts it, archi-politics is the attempt to 'subsume politics under the logic of a strict and closed distribution of parts, a social space which is homogenously structured and thus leaves no space for politics to emerge'.[52] It effectively assimilates the 'part that has no part' by turning it into a sociological category of people: the artisans or labourers who contribute to the community through their economic function and, consequently, cannot participate in politics simply because they lack the leisure time necessary for politics. Their virtue is temperance, or moderation, which amounts to 'nothing more than their submission to the order according to which they are merely what they are and do merely what they do'.[53]

At first blush, this characterization of archi-politics does not sound at all like Arendt. Indeed, we can easily imagine several Arendtian objections. First, doesn't Arendt precisely aim to understand how individuals transcend their social identity (or 'what-ness') through a struggle for recognition in which the actor is distinguished in his or her singularity (or 'who-ness')?[54] As such, her account of action does not seem at all tied to the social order and the assignation of agents to their proper part within it. Secondly, as we have seen, Arendt explicitly criticizes Plato for identifying *arkhê* with rule and government, forgetting the extent to which *arkhê* entails beginning (*archein*) and is dependent on seeing through an enterprise with others (*prattein*). Since Arendt construes *arkhê* in terms of initiatory action, she takes it to be an uncertain, unpredictable and contingent 'foundation' for politics. Moreover, for Arendt, the animating principle of this kind of action is 'isonomy', which she construes in terms of an equality based on a shared freedom from rule. Is it not the case, then, that she valorizes precisely the kind of politics that an archi-political perspective is supposed to suppress?[55] Thirdly, can her account of the polity as a space of appearances that emerges from the public interaction of a plurality of agents really be reduced to a communitarian image of a homogenous society?[56] For Arendt, polity is a fragile and contingent achievement of praxis, and its unity is not that of sameness (the logic of the social) but a manifold expression of the multiple perspectives that constitute a public sphere. This image hardly seems to fit Rancière's characterization of archi-politics as a project of the complete realization of the community with nothing left over – that is, no excess of representation.[57]

I will return to consider each of these points in the final section of this chapter. Having noted them here, however, and given Arendt's critique of Plato and her sympathetic appropriation of Aristotle, it might seem more plausible to suggest that if Arendt is complicit in the philosophical repression of politics, this is because she adopts a 'parapolitical' position, one which domesticates politics by recasting conflict as always in the service of the unity of the polity. Indeed, James Ingram seems to want to correct Rancière when he observes that this is precisely how Rancière characterizes Arendt.[58] Whereas archi-politics results in the 'total elimination of politics', Rancière tells us, parapolitics 'refuses to pay this price'.[59] While Aristotle follows Plato in identifying political action with the police order, he 'does so from the point of view of the specificity of politics'.[60] While it would be better to have a city in which the virtuous ruled, such a city would not be political for Aristotle since in the polis all citizens partake equally in ruling and being ruled. Aristotle takes this political equality as a given so that the problem for parapolitics is how to reconcile virtuous government with the equality of citizenship. The solution he proposes follows from the recognition that, in order to sustain itself in government, a class must seek to rule on behalf of the common good of the whole. In doing so, 'the party of the rich and the party of the poor will be brought to engage in the same politics'.[61] As Arsenjuk describes it, parapolitics is 'the attempt to reduce political antagonism to mere competition, negotiation, exercise of an agonic procedure'.[62] Class conflict is pressed into the service of political unity by representing the poor as having an equal stake in the shared enterprise of the polity. Elites legitimate their rule by claiming to serve the common good of the whole people, of which they are also a part. In this way, the community contains the demos without suffering from its conflict.[63]

There are certainly elements of this parapolitical perspective in Arendt's work, which Rancière also draws our attention to. Indeed, at times Arendt seems to address the parapolitical problem of how to combine government by the best with the equality of citizenship. She follows Aristotle in recognizing that the artificial equality of the polity distinguishes it from pre-political forms of association, such as the family or tribe based on natural principles of hierarchy. However, she observes, 'the political way of life has never been and never will never be the way of life of the many' even though politics, by definition, always concerns the common good of all citizens.[64] Her solution to the parapolitical problem is for the public sphere to be both open and exclusive.[65] While in principle the public realm is open to all, in practice the *bios politicos* is the preserve of a self-selected elite who are drawn to politics by a love of the world (*amor mundi*) and a 'taste for public freedom', while those who do not care for politics exclude themselves, exercising their right not to participate in government.[66] Against Arendt, Rancière observes approvingly that democratic elections in Ancient Athens were based on the drawing of lots.[67] The role of chance in determining who was to rule was seen to be compatible with the principle that 'good government is the government by those who do not desire to govern'.[68] Moreover, it was a fundamentally political principle because it eroded the 'natural' entitlement to rule based on kinship or wealth: the 'title specific to those who have no more title for governing than they have for being governed'.[69]

Perhaps more significantly, Arendt follows Aristotle in understanding politics in terms of its specificity as a way of life (*bios politicos*) that redeems human existence from the futility of mere biological life (*zoē*). By participating in politics, human beings actualize their freedom and invest the world with meaning. On this basis she differentiates political action as *praxis* (involving public speech and action that is an end in itself) from the instrumentality of work as *poïesis* (involving fabrication or production that is a means to a higher end) and the cyclicality of labour (concerned with sustaining life through toil, reproduction and consumption). However, she departs from Aristotle in understanding political equality not in terms of partaking in ruling and being ruled, but the principle of *isonomy*, which meant both to be free from necessity and 'neither to rule nor to be ruled'.[70] In contrast, Rancière insists that the 'participation in contraries' is the defining feature of a political subject. Indeed, Aristotle's understanding of the citizen as one who partakes in ruling and being ruled 'speaks to us of a being who is at once the agent of an action and the matter upon which that action is exercised'.[71]

For Arendt, as Rancière puts it, 'the order of *praxis* is an order of equals who are in possession of the power of the *archêin*, that is the power to begin anew'.[72] Yet, he insists, Aristotle's paradoxical formulation cannot be resolved by the classical opposition between *poiesis* and *praxis* that Arendt revives. As we have seen, Arendt 'restores' the conceptual link between *arkhêin* and freedom in the principle of natality. Equality is realized through participation in the power of *arkhê*. Rancière argues against this conceptual retrieval, insisting that the logic of *arkhê* is inherently linked to the principle of rule: the meaning of *arkhêin* was to 'walk at the head' so that others must 'necessarily walk behind'. Hence, the 'line between the power of *arkhêin* (i.e. the power to rule), freedom and the *polis*, is not straight but broken'.[73] Political subjectification, he insists, requires a break with the logic of *arkhê*.[74] Arendt can be understood as a parapolitical thinker, then, to the extent that she elides the antagonistic moment of politics, which Rancière thematizes as the way police *wrongs* equality.[75] Consequently, she 'seeks to limit politics, admitting it only in homeopathic doses, containing its spontaneity, uncertainty, and contingency by limiting it to certain actors at certain times and places'.[76]

Yet, since Rancière is a careful reader of Arendt, we should assume that his identification of her *with* Plato, as an archi-political philosopher, is to the point and consistent with his broader critique. As we have seen, he characterizes Arendt in this way because she wants to preserve the political from contamination by the private. The 'opposition between the political and the social', he argues, 'is defined entirely within the frame of political philosophy' and hence 'lies at the heart of the philosophical repression of politics'.[77] Rancière's critique of Arendt was no doubt part of a strategic intervention aimed not only at Arendt herself, but at the uses made of her thought within the particular intellectual milieu in which he was writing. Rancière took issue with the notion of a 'return of the political' and political philosophy in France in the 1980s.[78] Invoking the distinction between the good life (*eu zen*) and mere life (*zen*), some philosophers advocated a recuperation of an authentic politics against the encroachments of the social. This gave rise to a wide debate within philosophy, sociology, economics and political science over whether historical developments had led to a post-political era or had given rise to the possibility of recuperating a more authentic politics. As Rancière comments in an interview with Davide Panagia,

'the return to "political philosophy" in the prose of Ferry, Renaut, and other proponents of what is referred to, on your side of the Atlantic, as "New French Thought" simply identified the political with the state, thereby placing the tradition of political philosophy in the service of the platitudes of a politics of consensus; this occurring all the while under the rubric of wanting to restore and protect the political against the encroachments of the social'.[79]

In returning to Plato, Rancière wants to show how the sociological claim about the end of politics and the philosophical claim about the return of the political 'combine to bring about the same forgetting of politics'.[80] The flipside of Plato's archi-political Republic, he argues, is the invention of a sociological account of democracy against which this ideal community is set. Rather than recognizing democracy as one form of government among others, democracy is redescribed as a 'social phenomena or as the collective effectuation of the properties of a type of man'.[81] According to Rancière[82], contemporary critics who 'contrast the good republic with a dubious democracy' are heirs to the Platonic opposition between the philosophical articulation of the ideal polity and unflattering sociological description of the demos.[83] This finds its expression in philosophy's characteristic 'hatred of democracy', according to which democratic man is represented as unruly and driven by his immediate desires.[84] Indeed, Rancière insists, Arendt's 'critique of "abstract" rights is really a critique of democracy'.[85]

This observation is certainly supported by several passages in *On Revolution* in which Arendt disparagingly equates democracy with the rule of majority opinion and representative cliques. But while Arendt only makes scattered and passing references to democracy in her work, the critique of the social is a consistent theme throughout her work. Arendt deplores what she calls the rise of the social in modernity through which the State becomes concerned with the regulation of economic life. The cost of elevating life as the ultimate end of political organization is that human affairs are deprived of the reality and significance that comes from the world-disclosing activity of praxis. Society is the 'public organization of the life process itself … the form [of living together] in which the fact of mutual dependence for the sake of life and nothing else assumes public significance'.[86] Consequently, she says, the public realm has become dominated by the concern of 'animal laborans' to make life easier and longer.[87] Indeed, Arendt attributes the failure of the French Revolution to the fact that it was overwhelmed by the insatiable needs of the poor so that the aim of the Revolution became 'abundance' rather than 'freedom'.[88]

If Arendt has something in common with Plato, then it is that her philosophical account of the political/republic (as an autonomous mode of being in common through which human beings actualize their freedom) necessarily presupposes a sociology of the social/democracy (as a way of life that is improper because it makes public what ought to remain private, elevating heteronomous needs and interests above the *interesse* of the community). Throughout her work, she contrasts her image of polity as a space of appearance to the sociological reality of modern democracies in which politics is reduced to collective housekeeping, dominated by the concerns of 'animal laborans' who are driven by their immediate needs and desires. In other words, like Plato, Arendt thematizes 'the social' in sociological terms as a realm of natural determination rather than recognizing it as 'a disputed object of politics', a particular distribution of the sensible that is the potential object of politicization.[89]

Rancière takes issue with Arendt for presuming that there is a 'form of life' that is specific to politics since this comes to play a normative function within her work. According to Rancière, the 'notion that politics can be deduced from a specific world of equals of free people, as opposed to a world of lived necessity, takes as its ground precisely the object of its litigation'.[90] In other words, the presupposition of the autonomy of the political, which is necessary to sustain a phenomenological ontology, is question-begging, for it takes as an ontological given what is, in fact, politically contestable. Arendt makes the mistake of trying to derive an account of politics from an understanding of the subject of politics. But this leads to a 'vicious circle' since politics 'comes to be seen as a way of life proper to those who are already destined for it'.[91] Indeed, Rancière writes:

> The canonical distinction between the social and the political is in fact a distinction between those who are regarded as capable of taking care of common problems and the future, and those who are regarded as being unable to think beyond private and immediate concerns.[92]

Arendtian political thought, in this account, represses politics or becomes a form of 'archi-police' in seeking to distinguish, in advance, what counts as properly political action and what amounts to an 'anti-political' politics; namely, the pursuit of particular interests or the satisfaction of needs in the public domain. What it seeks to evacuate from the public domain is precisely what Rancière takes to be politics itself: a struggle over the distribution of public and private, of what is political and what is not, 'displacing the limits of the political by re-enacting the equality of each and all *qua* the vanishing condition of the political'.[93]

Strikingly, Rancière does not consider this to be an idiosyncratic feature of Arendt's work but the vicious circle of political philosophy itself.[94] Moreover, the philosophical repression of politics it leads to has real political effects insofar as it becomes complicit with a police order. With reference to the French polity, Rancière identifies at least three rhetorical effects of Arendtian archi-politics. First, in practice, the Arendtian purification of the public sphere becomes ideological since it surrenders political issues to administration by the State, handing over politics to 'governmental oligarchies enlightened by their experts'.[95] Second, it discounts the universalizability of political claims about working conditions or the satisfaction of needs. Workers on strike, for instance, can be characterized as acting according to their own particular interests rather than considering the public good. As such, it elides the extent to which their actions in fact invoke a *rival* conception of the common in which their claims could be heard as properly political.[96] Third, it deprives the subjects of human rights of political agency. The subject of human rights becomes a 'worldless victim, the ultimate figure of the one excluded from the logos, armed only with a voice expressing a monotonous moan, the moan of naked suffering, which saturation has made inaudible'.[97] Consequently, it legitimizes humanitarian forms of policing. The rights of the rightless are defended by others: they become the right of military intervention.[98] To be sure, Arendt is well aware of the limits of humanitarian rhetoric, noting that the declarations of an emergent human rights movement showed an 'uncanny similarity in language and composition to that of societies for the prevention of cruelty to animals'.[99] Rancière's claim is not, however, that Arendt herself endorses such a form of human rights paternalism, but rather that the rhetorical effect of Arendtian archi-political discourse is to naturalize the capture of human rights within this kind of police logic.[100]

3 The Displacement of Arendtian Political Thought

While couched in distinctive terms, Rancière's critique of Arendt is in many respects a familiar one. Critics of Arendt have long pointed out that she does not allow for any mediation of the antinomy between necessity and freedom that her political ontology presupposes.[101] The opposition between the illumination of the public realm and the obscurity of the private realm does not provide any basis for understanding the dynamic by which the public sphere is enlarged through democratic struggles or privatized by social power. If we accept that politics is fundamentally about politicization, a process of 'denaturalizing' oppressive social relations to reveal them as the contingent effect of social organization, then we are likely to agree with Rancière that Arendt is complicit in the philosophical repression of politics.

While acknowledging this to be a problematic aspect of her thought, however, many sympathetic readers of Arendt nonetheless see important conceptual resources in her work for thematizing an agonistic politics that would be quite close to that advocated by Rancière. In her book *Political Theory and the Displacement of Politics*, for instance, Bonnie Honig recognizes that Arendt can be interpreted either as a 'virtue' theorist (who displaces politics) or as a 'virtù theorist' (who valorizes agonistic politics). It is therefore possible to recuperate Arendt for a radically democratic politics because her 'politics beckons beyond itself to practices of disruption, augmentation and re-founding that surpass the ones she theorizes and circumscribes'.[102] In terms of Honig's distinction, one might say that Rancière's critical reading of Arendt as a virtue theorist is part of an interpretive strategy intended to develop his own thematization of politics from a virtù perspective. But in doing so, he neglects the virtù aspects of Arendt's thought, which we might instead choose to emphasize.

Consequently, sympathetic readers of Arendt (myself included) have been tempted to see in Rancière a way beyond some of the impasses that afflict an Arendtian account of politics.[103] James Ingram, for instance, suggests that Rancière does not arrive at a *radically opposed* account of politics to Arendt, but *radicalizes* Arendt, amending rather than rejecting her account of politics.[104] While Rancière agrees with Arendt that politics is participation as an equal in public affairs, he takes a step back from Arendt's starting point to view politics as the 'struggle to achieve that status'. While Ingram does not seek a synthesis between the two accounts of politics, he suggests that they are complimentary: by understanding politics as a 'struggle to participate in public life', Rancière 'gives Arendtian politics a point and at the same time universalizes it: the point of political action is inclusion and equality'.[105] If the main difference between them is that Arendt conceives politics as a sphere while Rancière views politics as a process, Ingram explains, this difference arises due to their different philosophical backgrounds in phenomenology and Marxism.

Rancière's contemporary relevance is no doubt due, in part, to his contribution to a vein of political theory that Jean-Philippe Deranty characterizes as 'ontology of the political'.[106] This includes Arendt, but also other Heideggerian thinkers such as Nancy, Agamben and Lefort. Rancière's engagement with this phenomenological tradition is always polemical and, as Deranty points out, produces a radical and original position. In this final section, however, I want to suggest that the difference of perspective between Arendt and Rancière that Ingram brilliantly analyses may be more of an obstacle to an accommodation of their respective accounts of politics than he acknowledges. If Rancière does end up using some Arendtian concepts, these are fundamentally transformed when unmoored from Arendt's ontology, which Rancière consistently rejects.

To show this I want to return to the three Arendtian objections that I have already briefly outlined. First, her conception of human agency in terms of the disclosure of the 'who' through a struggle for distinction provides a basis for understanding how actors are able to enact a subject position that is not socially determined. Second, her thematization of *arkhê* in terms of beginning places politics on precisely the kind of anarchic foundation that Rancière thematizes as the equality of anyone with everyone. Third, her understanding of the political in terms of the disclosure of a common world from a plurality of perspectives is only another way of understanding that excess of representation that separates the 'we' invoked in political discourse from a sociologically determined entity. In each case, an Arendtian might suspect, Rancière has actually (albeit, perhaps, unintentionally) taken a concept from Arendt and twisted it to suit his own purpose.

Let us start with the third objection and work backward. In *Disagreement*, Rancière mentions Arendt only once (and then in a half-approving reference to her thesis of the 'banality of evil', which does not concern us here). However, throughout the text there are numerous allusions to Arendtian concepts. For instance, Rancière's thematization of dissensus as 'putting two worlds into one' seems to borrow the idea of 'world' so central to Arendt's phenomenology.[107] Moreover the term 'dissensus' itself alludes to the notion of the 'sensus communis', which Arendt associates with the notion of world disclosure.[108] In both cases, what is important is the aesthetic aspect of politics in the disclosure of the common.

However, in his thematization of dissensus, Rancière resolutely breaks with the idea of the autonomy of the political, which we have seen is fundamental to Arendt's ontology and, indeed, to phenomenological approaches more generally. He insists that there is no such thing as an essence of the political, and he rejects Arendt's understanding of the political in terms of a shared life world.[109] In a key passage in which he refers to Nancy, but might as well be talking about Arendt, he writes:

> Political impropriety is not not belonging: it is belonging twice over: belonging to the world of properties and parts and belonging to the improper community ... Politics ... is not the community of some kind of being-between, of an *interesse* that would impose its originarity on it, the originarity of being-in-common based on the *esse* (being) of the inter (between) or the inter proper to the *esse* ... The inter of the inter *esse* is that of an interruption or an interval. The political community is a community of interruptions, fractures, irregular and local, through which egalitarian logic comes and divides the police community from itself ... Political being together is a being-between: between identities, between worlds ... A political community is not the realization of a common essence or the essence of the common. It is the sharing of what is not given as being in-common.[110]

As we have seen, Arendt turns to Heidegger's concept of world to develop her mode of political thinking, which takes plurality as the ontological condition for action. As Deranty discusses, Rancière twists this notion of world into an ontology that is also an anti-ontology.[111] The putting of two worlds into one means bringing together community and non-community, being and not-being, equality and its absence.[112] Or, in another formulation, it is 'the community based on the conflict over the very existence of something in common between those who have a part and those who have none'.[113]

Following Heidegger, it has now become commonplace to associate politics with the 'ontic' while 'the political' refers to the 'ontological'.[114] If politics refers to struggle over the distribution of the benefits and burdens of political association, the political refers to the background horizon in relation to which politics appears. In Arendt's terms, the political is the disclosure of a common world from the agonistic interplay of plural perspectives brought to bear upon it. In contrast to this twofold distinction, Rancière refers to a 'disjunctive relation between *three* terms' (my emphasis), according to which *the political* is the meeting point of the two heterogenous processes of *politics* and *police*.[115] Politics refers to the process of emancipation based on the verification of an equality of anyone with anyone. Police, in contrast, is a process of government and the parcelling out of roles and identities within a social order. The political is the field for the encounter of these two process (or 'two modes of human being together') in which a wrong is staged or demonstrated: it is the putting of two worlds into one, the community invoked by the part that has no part into the community that is defined by the distribution of the sensible in which politics intervenes.[116]

As such, the political, as Rancière conceives it, has the same quality of an event of disclosure as Arendt accords it.[117] In fact, one might hazard that he provides a way to overcome the impasse between the realm of necessity and the realm of freedom that afflicts Arendtian accounts of politics. Indeed, one might read the police here as just another word for what Arendt conceives of as 'the social'. However, it is important to recognize that for Rancière, police and politics are not different in kind. They are not separate spheres, as the social and the political are for Arendt.[118] For Rancière, police is not 'real' as in the sociology of Arendt's archi-politics but, rather, a symbolic order, a partition of the perceptible. What politics does is insert a rival image of the common within the existing social order, another partition of the perceptible, to produce a 'contentious commonality'.[119] So the concept of world, as Rancière describes it here, loses the quasi-normative status that it acquires in Arendt's account, which allows her to describe some people as being deprived of world and others to be more 'worldly'.[120]

Consider next Rancière's understanding of the anarchic foundation of the political community. Arendt seeks to reclaim the concept of *arkhê* from the tradition of political philosophy. She re-thematizes *arkhê* as beginning (rather than ruling) and restores its relation to *prattein*, as following through.

Moreover, she understands equality as a precondition for action and characterizes this equality as isonomy, which she takes to mean precisely the *absence* of rule. According to Balibar, this principle of isonomy is fundamentally anarchic.[121] As such, the origin of community is to be found in the freedom of a plurality of agents acting in concert. It is the dramatic enactment of this freedom that is the ultimate ground of political institutions, which is re-enacted in moments of civil disobedience. Indeed, certain descriptions that she offers of the public sphere seem to indicate its subaltern or insurgent quality: constituent moments in which the people appear on the political scene.[122] In this account, as Ingram puts it, the common is not homogenous or unified but defined by difference and conflict while promising moments of commonality.[123]

If Rancière seems to follow Arendt in recognizing the anarchical foundation of the polity in a radical equality, he departs from her in thematizing equality in abolitionist terms. In other words, in his view, the meaning of equality can only be determined through the negation of inequality.[124] Equality is a presupposition of an entitlement to participate in politics, which is always enacted in a situation of inequality:

> Nothing is political in itself for the political only happens by means of a principle that does not belong to it: equality. The 'status' of this principle needs to be specified. Equality is not a given that politics presses into service ... it is a mere assumption that needs to be discerned within the practices implementing it.[125]

This explains why Rancière takes issue with Arendt's identification of equality with a shared participation in the power of *arkhê*, insisting, against her, that *arkhê* always also entails commanding.[126] For, in thematizing the anarchic foundation of the polity in terms of the 'wrong' of the social order, Rancière insists on recognizing the antagonistic dimension of constituent moments that Arendtian agonism elides.[127] Contrary to Arendt's[128] claim that politics is only possible where people are neither simply for nor against but only 'with' one another, for Rancière the world-disclosing quality of action is revealed precisely in moments of antagonism.[129] In this account, class struggle is not the 'hidden truth behind appearances' but 'politics itself' – that is, 'politics such as it is always encountered, always in place already, by whoever tries to found the community on its *arkhê*.[130]

Finally, what about Arendt's understanding of the way in which the agent distinguishes herself through action? For Arendt, it is through the struggle for recognition, the striving for distinction in a public sphere, that individual actors reveal who they uniquely and unexchangably are. Arendt's thematization of this process of singularization is attractive to theorists of agonistic politics since it suggests a way to understand how agents are able to transcend oppressive social identities, how action brings about a 're-opening of the terms of our social inter-action'.[131] For Arendt, the 'what' of human existence is part of what we share with nature, those properties of identity and otherness. The 'who' corresponds to natality: it is that ineffable quality of selfhood that transcends the natural world.[132] The disclosure of the singularity of the agent is the existential achievement of action: 'This appearance, as distinguished from mere bodily existence, rests on initiative, but it is an initiative from which no human being can refrain and still be human.'[133] In relation to the natural world of causal determination, the disclosure of the singularity of the agent has a miraculous quality.

Rancière's notion of subjectification might thus seem to build upon Arendt's account of singularization. Indeed, he alludes to Arendt as he develops the concept in *Disagreement*. As in Arendt, the subject of politics does not precede politics but is constituted through action. This disclosure of the agent in the act is the creative aspect of politics. However, Rancière writes:

> A mode of subjectification does not create subjects *ex nihilo*; it creates them by transforming identities defined in the natural order of the allocation of functions and places into instances of experience of a dispute. 'Workers' or 'women' are identities that apparently hold no mystery. But political subjectification forces them out of such obviousness by questioning the relationship between a *who* and a *what* in the apparent redundancy of the positing of an existence.[134]

The above passage suggests that Rancière differentiates his notion of subjectification directly in contrast to Arendt's account of singularization. Subjectification begins through an act of negation or dis-identification and the claiming of an impossible identity within a given context. Rather than understanding agency only in terms of the disclosure of a radically indeterminate subjectivity that is irreducible to the identity ascribed to him or her, the underlying social conditions that determine the embodied experience or 'what' of an agent are taken to be a condition of possibility for his or her effective agency.[135] As such, subjectivization does not simply entail the transcendence of oppressive social identities or 'mere bodily existence', but their transformation. If Rancière shares Arendt's concern with appearances, what he attends to are the ways in which these are regulated, the processes of representation that thwart or co-opt the appearance of subjects in the public realm. As such, subjectivization is always tied up with the struggle to make visible the wrong of the social order.[136]

Arendt and Rancière both want to avoid philosophy's characteristic repression of politics, which arises because philosophy treats politics as a problem of government. Rather than a philosophy of right, therefore, they each turn to aesthetics to understand the conditions of possibility for action and appearance. Working within the tradition of phenomenology, Arendt relies on an ontology that differentiates action into separate domains of experience, each associated with a fundamental aspect of the human condition: life, worldliness and action. The phenomenology of politics that she develops on the basis of this founding presupposition of her theory is evocative, and her concern with political appearances resonates within Rancière's own thematization of politics. Despite Rancière's anti-phenomenological stance, it seems that through his critical engagement with Arendt, Nancy and others, he has inherited some phenomenological concepts.

If Rancière does end up using some Arendtian concepts, however, he unmoors them from her ontology, which he resolutely rejects. Politics for him is not a way of life that we are in danger of forgetting. There is nothing essential about politics that philosophy has repressed, nor is the political an autonomous domain of experience that philosophy has misinterpreted in terms of categories derived from other experiences. Rather, for Rancière, politics is a certain rationality based on the assumption of equality that every social order depends on but seeks to conceal. Philosophy is overtly scandalized by the fact that the legitimacy of every social order ultimately depends on this anarchical foundation. The political is the name given to the appearance of class struggle, which reveals the possibility of social transformation. Consequently, for Rancière, a mode of thinking that would capture the specificity of politics would not start from speechless wonder at human plurality, as Arendt suggests, but would instead take the aporia of dissensus as the starting point of its analyses.[137]

Acknowledgement

This paper was presented at the Centre for Citizenship and Public Policy at the University of Western Sydney in April 2011. Thanks to that audience for their perceptive remarks and to Keith Breen and Jean-Philippe Deranty for their detailed comments on the penultimate draft of the paper.

Chapter 10

The Many Marx of Jacques Rancière

Emmanuel Renault

Any inquiry into Rancière's interpretation of Marx has to tackle several methodological problems. A first one is the choice of the relevant texts. The most famous contribution of Rancière to Marx scholarship is his article in the collective work, edited by Louis Althusser, *Reading Capital*. But his essay, 'The concept of critique and the critique of political economy (from the *Manuscripts of 1844* to *Capital*),'[1] goes back to a time when Rancière was still a student (the essay in fact comes from his master's thesis), a student strongly influenced by his teacher at the Ecole Normale Supérieure, Louis Althusser. Since Rancière only became 'Rancière' after having launched a critical campaign against Althusser in which he explicitly criticized his own contribution to *Reading Capital*, it could seem justified to exclude this early work. I will nevertheless take it into account; otherwise it would be quite difficult to understand the targets and arguments of his Althusser criticism. More generally, the detour by the Althusserian period is fruitful because several features of the later relation to Marx remain conditioned by it.[2]

A second methodological problem is raised by the fact that Rancière's works are characterized by various and contradictory relations to Marx. Starting from an Althusserian interpretation of Marx ('The concept of critique', 1965)[3], Rancière shifted to a defence of a revolutionary Marxism during his Maoist activist period ('On the theory of ideology', 1969;[4] 'How to use *Lire Le Capital*', 1973;[5] *La Leçon d'Althusser*, 1974).[6] He then came to an analysis of the aporias of Marx's discourse (in some of the first articles of the *Révoltes logiques*, 1975–1978)[7], and finally to a harsh criticism of Marx (*The Philosopher and his Poor*, 1983;[8] *Disagreement*, 1995).[9] Since Rancière's thought found its final shape in the 1980s, this harsh criticism could be considered to be the only relation to Marx that deserves consideration. But here again, the stakes and originality of the last readings would be hardly discernible without the detour by the earlier interpretations of Marx.

A third methodological problem concerns the uses of Marx. Even when he turned to criticism, Rancière's reading is grounded in a remarkable knowledge of Marx's works (a fact that is worth noting, since harsh criticism of Marx is usually less informed). It is well known that there are various types of writings in Marx's oeuvre and various periods in the evolution of his thought. Rancière's Althusserian formation makes him perfectly aware of issues linked with such diversity and periodization. There is no doubt that it is in sensitivity to such complex methodological considerations that he refers to the Marxian corpus, but the methodological principles of his readings are far from identical and they are not always made explicit. Reconstructing the various positions attributed to Marx by Rancière, his methodological shifts and the transformations of his own political and philosophical positions in relation to his Marx readings will be the main goal of this article.

A last methodological problem concerns the methodology of reading Rancière himself. Confronted with contradictory relations to and interpretations of Marx, the commentator is condemned to a critical approach. One could then either adopt the teleological point of view of the mature Rancière, running the risk of apology, or conversely, one could take the task of a philological evaluation of his reading of Marx, running the risk of ignoring the specificity of Rancière's problematic. In what follows, I will attempt to follow an alternative path, that of a critique of the mature Rancière by the younger one.

1 Following the First Althusser

Rancière met Althusser as a student of the Ecole Normale Supérieure and, like many others, Althusser's teaching and theoretical radicalism made a strong impression on him. At the end of the 1950s, Althusser had already written some of the articles that would be compiled in the 1965 volume *For Marx*.[10] The years spent by Rancière at the Ecole Normale Supérieure were also those that saw the publication of the remaining pieces of *For Marx*. It is in this context that Althusser decided to organize a seminar on Marx's *Capital* with his students during the university year 1964/1965. Rancière was one of those who participated in this collective endeavour; that is, to read Marx's masterpiece through the lens of Althusser's *For Marx*. As a result, the Althusserian manifesto *Reading Capital* was published in 1965, giving young men such as Etienne Balibar (born in 1942) or Jacques Rancière (born in 1940) their long-lasting philosophical reputations.

Rancière's contribution tackles a strategic problem for the Althusserian reading, that of the status of 'critique' in the 'critique of political economy'. At stake are in fact two crucial theses: first, the rupture of the problematic of *Capital* (1867) with that of the young Marx; and second, the scientific dimension of *Capital*. According to the dialectical interpretations of Marx's economy, as well as to Kantian interpreters such as Della Volpe (explicitly criticized in Rancière's essay), the *critical* dimension of *Capital* reveals a continuity with the writings of the *German-French Annals* (1843–1844) and of the *Parisian Manuscripts* (1844). According to such interpretations, this critical dimension also proves that *Capital* is not (only) intended to be a scientific economy but (also) a philosophical critique of classical economy. Rancière's aim is to refute these readings through a comparison of the problematic of the *Parisian Manuscripts* with that of *Capital*. Considering these manuscripts as a first critique of political economy, he strives to show that their logic is totally heterogeneous to that of *Capital*. He argues that they give a fundamental and autonomous role to a philosophical model of 'critique', whereas for the mature Marx, 'critique' is nothing more than a particular aspect of the scientific enterprise.

At the beginning of the part dealing with the *Parisian Manuscripts*, Rancière highlights that the object of the critique – that is, 'political economy' – is 'located' neither as reality nor as discourse: political economy is only understood as a mirror of economical facts. He then moves to the critical operation itself, pointing out that 'critique' only means the translation of the concepts of political economy into anthropological concepts: 'worker' is replaced by 'human being', 'product' by 'object', 'capital' by 'alienated being' and so on. He then states that since critique is reduced to an interpretation through the idea of alienation (as transformation of the human being into a thing, or inversion between aim and end), there is no transformation of ideology into science but only transformations internal to ideology. Rancière is clearly following and developing the Althusserian reading of the *Parisian Manuscripts* as the culmination of an 'anthropological' and 'humanist' problematic coming from Feuerbach. And if Rancière is deserving of praise here, it is mainly because he gives to Althusser's reading a systematic shape.[11]

The second part of the essay puts weight on the fact that the specificity of Marx's own discourse in *Capital* is no longer labelled 'critique' but 'science'. 'Critique' now only names the difference between Marxist science and the scientific dimension of classical political economy. It is well known that Marx contends that his main difference with Ricardo concerns the relation between value ('value' itself) and its phenomenal forms (forms of 'exchange

value'). Following one of the main lines of *Reading Capital*, that of an interpretation in terms of structural causality, Rancière explains that this relation between value and its manifestations is not grounded in value itself,
but in an 'absent cause': 'the social relations of production'. More challenging is the attempt to apply this interpretative framework to the fetishism
chapter. As Rancière recalls it, in many Marxist interpretations, fetishism is
equated with alienation; and when other interpretations reduce fetishism
to the concept of an illusion through which economic subjects constitute
economic objects, it implies a kind of idealism. It is not possible to enter
here in the complex strategy developed by Rancière in order to give a structuralist interpretation of fetishism, with its detour through the third book
of *Capital* and especially its theory of the sources of income: rent, interest
and wages (the 'Trinity formula' chapter).[12] The main point of the demonstration is that the fetishist illusion is not produced by the relation subject/
object (alienation of subjects in objects, or constitution of objects by subjects), but by the unfolding of the process of production, a process in which
the absence of its structure manifests itself as an illusion of subject (as 'per-
sonification' of the relations of production) and as an illusion of object
(fetishism itself).

There is much that could be said about this contribution of the young
Rancière from the point of view of Marxist scholarship[13]. More interesting
for our concern is to focus on the themes that will soon become the matter
of Rancière's self-criticism. From 1969 to 1974, this self-criticism was mainly
developed through a critique of Althusser. However, in 1973, Rancière also
wrote a systematic criticism of his own former position.[14] The target is the
general logic of the Althusserian interpretation of *Capital* and the way it
characterizes his own contribution. On the one hand, Rancière denounces
the 'falsification' of the Marxian text that made possible its 'scientistic'
interpretation. The main point is that the Althusserian reading deprives the
text of its 'strategic' dimension; that is, its embeddedness in the conflicts of
a political discourse with various powers. Althusser's conception of philosophy as 'theoretical practice' tends to reduce the Marxian text to a problematic which is autonomous from social praxis, and transform it into an
implicit critique of the problematic of the *Parisian Manuscripts*. However,
for a political discourse structured by its critical aims, 'there is', according
to Rancière, 'no *implicit* criticism'.[15] Althusser claims to disclose the scientific problematic of *Capital* and what remains 'unthought' in this book
('symptomatic reading'). He also attempts to distinguish which concepts
belong to this problematic (what is 'produced' by the theoretical practice
of Marx) and what remains 'terms' without notions (such as alienation)

and signs of the 'lack of awareness' of his own theoretical practice.[16] In Rancière's view, this is nothing other than denying the 'speech function' that is the critical and political dimension of *Capital* by displacing it into 'the space of commentary'.[17]

On the other hand, Rancière undermines the thesis of the discontinuity between 1844 and 1867. He rejects his former structural interpretation of fetishism according to which 'the manifestation/dissimulation of relations of production, which reduces the economic object to a phantom and the subject to the functioning of an illusion, constitutes a positive refutation of any talk about alienation'.[18] First, he considers as false and politically misleading the interpretation that 'reduces bourgeois and workers to [the] same status as *agents of production*, inevitably mystified by their practice as agents':[19] the whole movement of *Capital* Book One is that of a dissolution of the illusions of circulation in the reality of production, and the fact that illusions vanish in the 'capitalist lair' points to the epistemological dimension of the class struggle that deserves consideration.[20] Moreover, it is not by accident that the fetishism chapter is the place where Marx introduced the description of the communist society, a description that is intertwined with 'the dreams of struggling proletarians'.[21]

Second, Rancière argues that there is continuity between the *Parisian Manuscripts* and *Capital*: 'The "ideological" discourse of the *Manuscripts* and the "scientific" discourse of *Capital* reflect the same theoretical principle: the principle which posits that *the constitution of an object and the constitution of its illusion* are one and the same process.'[22] There are indeed differences between the two problematics, but instead of a *shift* in problematics, these differences result from Marx's attempt to overcome the political shortcomings of the first conception of ideology (that of *The German Ideology*) as a separation of ideas (of *ideologues*) from social life. After the defeat of 1848, Marx became aware that the proletariat was not free from ideology and participates as the other classes do in the illusions of political representation. Here would be located 'the political knot which is precisely what defines the *position of science*. In *Capital*, this is the position whose essential aim is to replace the mechanism of ideology at the heart of reality itself, a mechanism which *The German Ideology* has located only in its petty-bourgeois margin.'[23] As a consequence of this genetic reinterpretation of fetishism and of its politicizing, the relation between science and critique is also totally recast: 'The position of science is thus located by the very moment which poses the critical discourse.'[24] These few quotes suffice to suggest the increasing philological complexity and the very substantial transformations that Rancière's readings of Marx are undergoing.

2 After Althusserianism: Death on the Barricades

In 'On the theory of ideology' and *Althusser's Lesson*, the mode of argumentation is not so much oriented towards Marx scholarship as it is towards the political shortcomings of Althusser's philosophical and political positions. Instead of only denouncing the Althusserian reading of Marx, Rancière suggests an alternative interpretation that deserves special consideration.

Before 1968, Rancière was already one of the Althusserians who broke with the Communist party to which Althusser remained loyal. This rejection of 'revisionism' (according to the Maoist terminology) constituted a first political break soon followed by a theoretical one after the revolts of May–June 1968. Some of the early statements in Rancière's *Althusser's Lesson* express perfectly, although retrospectively, the crux of the matter: 'The Marxism that we learnt under Althusser was a philosophy of order. All its principles were taking us away from the movement of revolt that was shaking the bourgeois order'[25]; 'Althusserianism died on the barricades of May, and with it many ideas from the past.'[26]

The first step in the criticism of Althusser is an article for an Argentinian collection of essays. Written in 1969 and published in 1970, 'On the theory of ideology' develops a theoretical and political position strongly influenced by Rancière's activism in the French Maoist movement.[27] *Althusser's Lesson*, where 'On the theory of ideology' is reproduced in appendix,[28] is written in the context of the fall of Maoist organizations and of the spreading out of the struggles, and it already belongs to the transition to another era.[29] In the context of a return to party politics, and notably to the Communist party, and to what he understood to be a new denial of May 1968 by Althusser in his *Reply to John Lewis* (1973),[30] Rancière develops a more systematic criticism of Althusserianism now considered in its two versions: that of the first Althusser (before 1967), and that of his rejection of his former 'theoriticism', especially in his *Reply to John Lewis*. In both these texts, Rancière writes in full adhesion to Marxism. What is at stake is still the defence of a certain type of Marxism against others.

The explicit aim of 'On the theory of ideology' is to explain that there is an internal link between the Althusserian reading of Marx on the one hand, and Althusser's revisionism and the difficult relations with the revolts of 1968 on the other. According to Rancière, this link is located in the conception of ideology.[31] Hence, the political stake of the discussion about ideology is twofold. On the one hand, the issue is that of the status of academic knowledge: should it be justified by the authority of science, or on the contrary, could the 1968 insurgency against the University and its specific network of powers be considered as legitimate? On the other hand, what is at stake is the status of ideology and struggles against ideology in communist regimes such as the USSR or China in the context of the cultural revolution: whereas the 'revisionist' position assumes that the 'socialist regime' means the 'end of classes', and therefore the end of ideology, on the contrary, the cultural revolution shows that 'the socialist revolution requires a struggle against the many forms of bourgeois ideology that maintain themselves after political power has been taken over.'[32] Inspired by the student revolt of the French in 1968, as well as by the Chinese Cultural Revolution, and attempting to defend them as well as their French leftist sequels, Rancière criticizes Althusser's concept of ideology as being cut off from class struggles and the reality of power relations.

In his texts of the 1960s (things will change in the mid 1970s with the essay 'Ideology and state apparatus'),[33] Althusser defines ideology as the expression and dissimulation of the social structure, and contends that its function is to promote social cohesion. The political consequences of this definition of ideology by the structure reveal its theoretical shortcomings: (1) leftist struggles against effects of exploitation are criticized since they touch only the effects of the structure and not the structure as such; (2) the persistence of ideology in socialist societies is only a structural effect and has nothing to do with class struggle; and (3) political struggle has to be directed by the knowledge of the hidden structure which only the party and Marxist science could provide. In Rancière's view, this conception of ideology is no longer Marxist and has to be criticized for that very reason. In Marx, the notion of 'structure' could mean nothing but 'relation of productions'; that is, class relations. Ideological dissimulation could not mean dissimulation of the 'relations of production' (a self-criticism of Rancière's former interpretation of fetishism), but of their 'antagonistic dimension'.[34] It is in the sociological tradition of Durkheim that ideology could be conceived of as a system of representations promoting social cohesion, but not in the Marxist tradition, where it is always referred to class struggle.

When Althusser captures the link between ideology and class struggle, it is 'under a fantastic, fetishized form, as class struggle between ideology (as the weapon of the dominating class) and science (as the weapon of the dominated class)'.[35] Therefore, Althusser misses the significance of conflicts within ideology, as well as the relation between science and power. Following Rancière, ideology is, above all, the discourse of a class in struggle against another. For example, it is impossible to speak of a 'humanist ideology' in general, as Althusser does, since humanism can either be the discourse of power (through a denial of class divisions) or a protest discourse.[36] In relation to the Althusserian opposition between ideology and science, Rancière suggests that it relies upon a misunderstanding of the idea of 'scientific socialism'. Instead of following Marx and the idea that a given scientific knowledge is a tool for the emancipation of the proletariat, Althusser grants science in itself the status of a revolutionary power. Rancière argues that there is much evidence that 'normal science' participates in the production and reproduction of ideology, via institutions such as schools and universities.[37] Here again, it clearly appears that the theoretical marginalization of class struggles and of power relations are intertwined.

According to Rancière, who follows Foucault on this point, as well as recent developments in the sociology of the sciences, ideology should be redefined as a mode of appropriation of knowledge in given relations of powers:[38]

> Knowledge is a system whose contents cannot be thought independently of the forms of their appropriation (acquisition, transmission, control, utilization). This system is the ideological domination of a class. It is not " science" or " ideology " ... In that system are articulated the class appropriation of science and the ideology of the dominating class. The distinction (*partage*) science/ideology hides a knot which in turn expresses the ideological domination of a class.[39]

The political consequence of the denial of power relations within the order of knowledge is that Althusser legitimizes the hierarchy of knowledge that ensures the authority of his professorial discourse.

Even if Rancière attempts to introduce the Foucauldian and sociological themes (which are also 'leftist' themes) of relations between power and knowledge and of the social construction of sciences in Marxism,[40] he presents his own discourse not as one among many Marxisms, but as the only way of maintaining the revolutionary core of Marx's writings. In 1969, Rancière apparently believes that there is a 'true' Marx and that he is undoubtedly the Marx of 'revolutionary Marxism'.[41] The Marx that Rancière favours at that time is the one of the *Theses on Feuerbach*, in which the primacy of praxis, and the unity of theory of praxis, are brought to the fore. But this is only one among many interpretations of the *Theses on Feuerbach*. For instance, 'praxis' could be equated either with 'revolutionary praxis' or with 'production', and the unity of theory and praxis could be equated either with auto-emancipation and education of the educators, or with the direction of political praxis by science. In total contradiction with what he contends in 1969, the mature Rancière will assume the second of these alternatives. In his later readings, the *Theses on Feuerbach* are interpreted in the opposite way: Marx is rejected; his concept of praxis is now read as asserting the primacy of production rather than revolutionary praxis, and the sovereignty of science replaces self-emancipation and the education of educators.

In Rancière's 1974 work *Althusser's Lesson*, the core of Marx's thought is still identified with class struggle, revolutionary praxis, self-emancipation and the education of the educators. Nevertheless, the relation to Althusser changes, as do the references to Marx and to Marxism. Whereas in 1969, the target was Althusser's theoreticism, the target now is Althusser's self-criticism of his former theoreticism. According to Althusser, the mistake of his former position was to reduce philosophy to a science of science, whereas philosophy has to be conceived of as a way of 'taking side (*prise de parti*)', as a representation of class struggles in the sciences and a representation of the sciences in class struggles. Rancière strives to show that the first position had a real political content, adjusted to the situation of de-Stalinization, but that the second one is no more than an attempt to save the first one in a context where it has lost all its critical power. Basically, the definition of philosophy as class struggle in theory would mean either an 'imaginary politics' relying upon the denial of the real politics of the cultural revolution of 1968 and its following,[42] or a discursive 'police': the scientific police of intellectuals of the Communist party in their post-1968 struggle against leftism, and of the leading intellectuals within what Rancière terms 'authoritarian leftism'.[43] I will not enter here into the details of the analysis of Rancière's criticism of Althusserianism, nor in the deconstruction of his confrontation with John Lewis. Rather, I will focus on the new relation to Marx that appears in this book.

At first glance, the book appears simply to deepen the themes of the 1969 article. Marx is still the Marx of the *Theses on Feuerbach*, these very *Theses* that 'Louis Althusser continues to find so enigmatic'.[44] The latter are interpreted along the same lines, but are associated in a more developed way with a new reading of the *Parisian Manuscripts*, in a way that expresses more clearly the Maoist inspiration. It is highly significant that it is in the framework of this Marxist interpretation that themes emerge for the first time which will later be articulated by Rancière on their own.

Relying upon the *Parisian Manuscripts* and the *Theses on Feuerbach*, Rancière points out that the primacy of revolutionary praxis means the primacy of the question of the transformation of the world, and that it requires an exit out of philosophy (whereas Althusser, conversely, tries to 'save philosophy', and his own social position with it).[45] He explains that the very idea of revolutionary praxis is associated with a major break with Feuerbach: the historicization of his humanism (whereas Althusser is forced to attribute historicization to Feuerbach in order to unify Marx with him).[46] He also shows that for Marx, history is made by human praxis as such, and this practical contact with history is also the origin of the knowledge of history (whereas Althusser states that the masses do not have any contact with history and that the knowledge of history is independent of practice).[47] He highlights that the primacy of class struggle is intertwined with the project of a self-emancipation of the proletariat, which means that the proletariat has the power to transform the world by its own means (whereas Althusser believes in its impotence, and in the omnipotence of the bourgeoisie)[48], and that it is able to construct his own revolutionary consciousness (whereas Althusser, following Kautsky, believes that true consciousness is to be introduced in the proletariat by intellectuals).[49] It is in this context that what could be labelled Rancière's own voice can be heard for the first time. Mao is presented as the origin of the new idea of the 'competence of the masses'. Indeed, this idea is formulated on 'the field occupied by the *Theses on Feuerbach*, namely that of a new intelligence forged in struggle and wrested from the exploiters'.[50] When Rancière comments on Mao in the following terms: 'it is the oppressed that are intelligent and it is from their intelligence that the weapons of their liberation arise',[51] his intention is only to explain a fundamental insight of the *Theses on Feuerbach*. In the writings of the mature Rancière, the very same terms will be used independently, without any reference to their Maoist and Marxist origins, indeed, in the framework of a critique of Marx.

In 1974, the critique of the Althusserian conception of ideology was another element of continuity. Rancière recalls that for Althusser: (1) false ideas (ideological illusions) stem from praxis (in direct contradiction with Marx and Mao);[52] (2) that his definition of ideology as general subjection excludes that a class struggle could develop in ideology (making self-emancipation impossible);[53] and (3) that the relation between ideology, power and the disciplines is totally missed.[54] When Rancière highlights that 'the separation between the worker and the "intellectual powers of production"' is what 'Marx designates as the core of bourgeois ideological oppression', he finds in Marx what he will later develop against Marx; namely, the idea that emancipation is, above all, intellectual emancipation.[55]

Besides this deepening of his earlier insights, there are, however, significant shifts in comparison with 'On the theory of ideology'. The notes introduced in the French translation of this article (in 1973), which are reproduced in the Appendix, propose some rectifications. Rancière no longer believes that Leninist-Marxism expresses the 'proletarian ideology', nor that this latter notion should be understood in a sociological sense (that is, in reference to a sociological definition of class): 'Proletarian ideology is neither the catalogue of workers' ideas or virtues, nor the body of "proletarian" doctrines; it is a production line stopped, an authority no longer respected, a system of division between working posts that has been abolished.'[56] Rancière now reduces the meaning of the classical opposition between 'bourgeois ideology' and 'proletarian ideology' to a difference in the mode of production of knowledge: 'bourgeois ideology is a system of power relation reproduced everyday by the ideological state apparatuses of the bourgeois state; proletarian ideology is a system of power relations established by the struggle of the proletariat and the other dominated classes against all forms of bourgeois domination and exploitation.'[57] Here, in this first anti-sociological drive, the voice of the future Rancière is identifiable, but this voice is still considered to be a genuinely Marxist one. What is also interesting to note is the significance given to the sensible and poetic ᵈimension of class struggle as proletarian struggle, which is identified as 'the invention, through a thousand small gestures, of a new world'.[58]

Rancière's relation to Marxism is undoubtedly less dogmatic than in 1965 or 1969. Even if Rancière is still trying to prove that Althusser is in contradiction with Marx, he makes it clear from the beginning that the situation of Marxism itself, and of scholarly Marxism especially, is at stake.[59] Furthermore, he highlights that there is neither 'true' Marxism nor 'deviation' 'there is no such thing as pure Marxism … Marxist discourse has always been twisted by social practice: twisted by the discourses and practices of revolt … twisted at other places by the disciplines and the discourse of power.'[60] There is not one but many Marx; this convincing remark is a powerful reply to all attempts to liquidate Marx: those attempts made at that time by all the former leftists whom Rancière criticizes, but also the attempt made by the mature Rancière himself. There is not one but many Marx, and from a retrospective point of view, one might consider that one of them, the one of *Althusser's Lesson*, is largely compatible with the political philosophy of the late Rancière.

3 Marx and Proletarian Discourse

The journal *Révoltes logiques* (1975–1981) launched by Rancière and other former members of the Maoist movement, belonged to the period of post-Maoist leftism. Its political project was clearly to defend the post-1968 leftism through self-criticism, and notably through a critique of the nature and functions of the reference to 'workers' in activist discourse. The 1976 book (co-edited with Alain Faure) *La Parole ouvrière* represents a similar project. As Rancière plainly states in a recent post-script, this project had a direct link with Marx: 'My career in Marxist science had started ten years earlier, with an analysis of the theses in the 1844 *Manuscripts*. Now I decided to look at things from the opposite side: namely, from the side of those whose thoughts and struggles the young Marx translated in his sovereign dialectic.'[61] In a period where the criticisms of Marxism were flourishing, 'the problem was not to denounce the illusions or the crimes of Marxism, but to study the ways in which it had encountered, or missed, been faithful or unfaithful, to the traditions and the struggles of workshops, or of the Republican militants and the rebelling workers.'[62] With this double shift towards the analysis of discourses and towards history, a research program was set up which was already sketched in *Althusser's Lesson*. In this last book, it was pointed out, against Althusser, that ideological struggles are not struggles between words (for instance: 'human being' versus 'masses') but between discourses of power giving opposite political meanings to the same words.[63] For instance, it was shown that in the workers' movement, the reference to the 'human being' was a 'motto to shift the gaze from workers' practices to practical ways of appropriating the means of production; from the independence of the workers to the autonomy of producers.[64] Therefore, the hypothesis had emerged according to which Marx's criticism of humanism (in *The German Ideology*) was directed against philosophical uses of the notion of 'human being', whereas the return of 'human being' after 1848 was intended to bridge the gap between theoretical critique and the discourse of emancipation formulated by workers.[65] A new way of reading Marx was then articulated:

> there is not *one* Marxist conceptuality that would have to be extracted from ideological clothing or bourgeois invasions, but rather, several conceptualities. Not one single logic of *Capital*, but different discursive strategies each corresponding to different problems, echoing in different ways the discourses in which classes think themselves by confronting the opponent's discourse: the science of classical economists or the workers' protests; the philosophers' discourse or the reports by *fabrique* inspectors, and so on.[66]

It is worth noticing that, against Althusser, Rancière was therefore interpreting *Capital* itself as a text where Marx was trying to introduce in his scientific discourse the claim that will be later considered so fundamental in the

1980s and 1990s; namely, that the workers want not only to be workers, but also 'human beings', in all of the dimensions that the category entails.[67]

In the first issue of *Les Révoltes logiques* (1975), Rancière describes the 'specificity of the Marxian discourse', that of the modern model of the 'revolutionary intellectual' invented by Marx, in the following terms: 'A type of discourse unheard of by comparison with Plato's or Colbert's; a system of reasons organized in reference to the knowledge of the elites and simultaneously one that claims to be identical to the live consciousness of those who are excluded from knowledge; discourse of the proletariat, which constantly makes of the latter a subject out of an object.'[68] In 1975, Rancière is clearly considering Marx's discourse as a model of critical discourse, from which it is politically impossible to escape. At the same time, a first distance with Marx appears which is linked again to the heterogeneity of workers' discourses, expectations and political claims. As regards their location in the social space of legitimate knowledge, intellectuals are obliged to struggle against the powers that structure their critical discourses, but cannot overcome them. Therefore, they have to renounce the dream of being something more than a critical representation of those they stand for. In a later article from 1978, Deleuze and Foucault's discussion about 'Intellectuals and power', is presented as an illustration of the leftist version of this dream, and criticized for this very reason.[69] Moreover, the forms of knowledge of those who are excluded from the social space of legitimate knowledge are themselves structured by specific power relations, and by conflicts among themselves, so that they themselves contain their own, autonomous epistemological and political dynamics.[70]

To be sure, there is no trace left of any dogmatism in this new image of Marx: the Marx reference is now taken as multiple with respect to the content of his writings, and as aporetic with respect to the form of his discourse. But what is at stake is still a defence of Marx against some of his new critics, a defence of Marx whose discourse is explicitly opposed to that of Plato. This defence is possible because the aporias of his discourse seem to be impossible to overcome (and certainly not in the Deuleuzian-Foucaldian way), and because the Marxist tradition seems rich and flexible enough to help find a political discourse appropriate to the new political context. Here again, it might seem that this reading of Marx undermines in advance the future Rancièrian campaign launched against him. The idea that Marx is interesting for his very aporias and contradictions reduces all global criticism to one-sidedness. To give an example, one might wonder if the later Rancière has not stressed the critique of the intellectual claim to stand for the workers by forgetting the other side of the coin; namely, that consciousness from below is also embedded in power relations and can never be totally self-sufficient.

Even if they could provide arguments against the future Rancière, *Les Révoltes logiques* helps to disclose what is at stake in the reversal of this defence of Marx into criticism. The key to this reversal may lie not so much in the reconstruction of the meaning of Marx's writings as such, than in the self-criticism towards the strategic project that Rancière now sees as the cause behind the failure of his former leftist activism. According to him, one should acknowledge the gap between, on the one hand, a project of social transformation through the political organization of revolts and conquest of State power, and, on the other hand, 'the feeling of the unbearable and the forms taken by its refusal, for the worker or the Cronstadt sailor, which obey a logic that is not a logic seeking to replace white power by red power at the top of power'.[71]

4 Marx Against Craftsmen and Communists

However, the future relation to Marx is also explained by a political shift in the historical context of the aftermath of the post-1968 leftism. As appears clearly in the volumes of 1978 (in the seventh issue of *Les Révoltes logiques* and in the special issue published on the ten-year anniversary of 1968), a double trend deeply modifies the political landscape. On the one hand, the new centrality of the Communist and Socialist parties, and the new references to the working class, lead to the conclusion that the Marxist logic of class politics can be a means for political conservatism. One the other hand, the emergence of the 'autonomous movement' is associated with a criticism of the centrality of the working class, of all political representation and of 'work'. After 1978, the criticism of class politics belongs to the program of *Les Révoltes logiques*. In Rancière's writings, it will be charged not only for simplifying the heterogeneity of the proletarian claims (as in the former period), but also for identifying them with their alienated identity and for criticizing them as soon as they try to become something other than workers. Increasingly, Marx is presented as the best illustration of these two political shortcomings.

In *The Nights of Labour* (1981), Rancière sets up his original conception of emancipation as intellectual emancipation, and as the refusal by the workers themselves of their definition by work. In *The Philosopher and his Poor* (1983), this new conception of emancipation and the refusal of work are explicitly turned against Plato, Marx and Bourdieu: all of them are accused of assuming that the poor are not able to achieve their own emancipation and should not try to lose their social identity; that is, their social way of living and thinking as defined by their productive activities. In the long chapter devoted to Marx (more than a hundred pages), Rancière develops spectacular inversions of his former interpretations. There is no room left for aporia, for hermeneutic caution and attention to the specificity of a discourse. Tensions in Marx's writings are reduced to self-contradictions; the relations of science with workers' aspirations and their political claims are reduced to nothing; and most of the criticism rests upon a psychological analysis and sociological typification of Marx's tastes and expectations. Marx is portrayed as a bourgeois with classical tastes that led him to feel contempt for any mixing of work and art; as an intellectual representative of the bourgeoisie's hope in the substitution of industry for craftsmanship; as a self-conscious upper-class intellectual who dismisses the idiot workers that belong to the same party as him but are unable to understand his writings.

What is most disturbing for a reader familiar with his former texts is that Rancière takes for granted some interpretations of Marx that his previous work had systematically undermined. The issues of production, of philosophy, of science and of ideological illusion provide good illustrations of this point. The first inversion is that of revolutionary praxis into production. Whereas the *Theses on Feuerbach* were previously considered to be the centre of Marx's thought, this centre is now located in *The German Ideology* and the *Communist Manifesto* and in the paradigm of production.[72] This paradigm is also considered as the principle of the *Theses on Feuerbach*, since 'praxis' is now read as 'production' instead of 'revolutionary praxis' or 'class struggle'.[73] In a way, with this shift from 'revolutionary praxis' to 'production', Rancière is coming back to his first, Althusserian, interpretation of Marx, according to which the truth of Marx's position is not in the primacy of the notions of 'work' (in *Parisian Manuscripts*) or 'praxis' (in the *Theses on Feuerbach*), but in the structuring power of the 'relations of production' (in *Capital*). Crucial for Rancière's critique is now precisely the opposition between 'work', associated by him with 'workers'and 'craftsmen' on the one hand, and 'production', associated with 'industry' and 'proletariat' on the other hand. From *The German Ideology* to *Capital*, Marx is now said to have developed a long-lasting polemic against the Proudhonian valorization of work that led him to reject all the worker struggles waged against the de-skilling of work through fragmentation and mechanization. Whereas Rancière highlighted the criticism made in *Capital* of the separation between workers and intellectual powers of production, Marx is now identified with the modernist hope that the industrial transformation of work is good in itself, since the contradictions inherent to capitalist production are the only revolutionary force.

Interpreted from the point of view of the paradigm of production, the critique of philosophy obviously loses all its meaning. Whereas the idea of a critique of philosophy was defining of the specific situation of the revolutionary intellectual when it was interpreted from the point of view of the relations between knowledge and power, it is now reduced to the crude materialism that sees production everywhere and in philosophy its poorest and most illusory form. Curiously enough, Rancière associates this conception of philosophy to an implicit Marxian thesis according to which the worker should reduce his or her being to the being of proletarian suffering: 'There is no longer any philosophical order from which the shoemaker could be excluded. But neither is there one to which he could gain access … The absence of a time to do something other than one's work might have become the absence of a place where something else but the illusion of the trade could be produced.'[74] At this point in his argumentation, Rancière develops the idea that for the communist workers of the time, being communist meant participating in political and philosophical discussions instead of being mere workers. Indeed, Rancière quotes the page of the *Parisian Manuscripts* where Marx praises the Parisian workers for their passionate involvement in intellectual discussions and for the 'need of society' that their activism creates.[75] Rancière's point, however, is that in the theory (and in the psychology) of the old Marx, there is no room left for such an appraisal and for the possibility of 'being communist before communism'.[76] For Marx, Rancière now argues, workers' activism would be justified only when they struggle against their suffering as proletarian, and never when they strive to become artists or philosophers. Here again, Althusserianism is taking its revenge: the critique of philosophy has lost its political meaning (disconnected from power, it is now supposed to be only an indication of the state of the relations of production); and the humanist critique and claims of the workers (wanting to be a 'human being and not only a worker') are now said to be totally absent from *Capital*, despite all that was said against such interpretations in the 1970s.

The very ideas of science and ideological illusions are also interpreted in a way that amounts to a return to Althusser, though admittedly with a major difference: instead of being presented as incompatible with Marx, these conceptions of science and ideological illusion are now considered as revealing the fundamental flaws in Marx's thought. From the *Theses on Feuerbach* to *Capital*, Marx is now said to have been convinced that

(1) workers are condemned to illusions, (2) that they are totally impotent and that only the Bourgeoisie has the power to transform society, and (3) that nothing else but science could emancipate the proletariat.[77] No less one-sided is the claim that for Marx, the main function of *Capital* is to take refuge in theory at an age where workers, as well as history, are disappointing, and to wait for the men that deserve this science to finally come.[78]

The Marx chapter in *The Philosopher and his Poor* is built on two major operations. The first is a selective and teleological reading of Marx's evolution: what is taken into consideration is only what is supposed to lead to the scientist and bourgeois conception attributed to *Capital*. The second is a transformation of tensions and aporias into self-contradictions. The most interesting example of this second operation concerns the relation of critique and demystification. Marx's intention is clearly to produce a theoretical critique of capitalism, but the method he employs to achieve his goal – that of demystification – is, for him, nothing but the disclosing of existing reality. In Rancière's view, intention and method stand in direct contradiction: 'the ethics of demystification is that of conservation. The ethics of critical science is destruction.'[79] For Rancière, the tension between critique and demystification is nothing more than a contradiction the solution to which is the rejection of critique as demystification. It is interesting to note that in a recent article,[80] Rancière makes a step beyond this point: the contradiction between critique and demystification would belong to the essence of the 'critical thought' as such, and consequently, 'critical thought' itself, and not only its Marxist forms, should be rejected.

This new polemical attitude towards Marx is not only due to a political shift. Since *The Nights of Labour*, a deepening of Rancière's anti-sociological drives is at play (although his criticism of Marx is, paradoxically, quite sociological). Behind Marx, Bourdieu is targeted. Instead of being conceived of (like before) in its relations with the idea of class struggle, the Marxian explanation of communist politics in terms of class position is identified with a sociological reduction of political action to social being.[81] This criticism of Marx is plainly coherent with the idea that emancipation is above all an attempt to get rid of social identities produced by relations of domination. But what exactly should be concluded from this definition of emancipation if claims of emancipation are also the resistance of workers against social suffering and de-skilling of work and attempts to make their social condition visible (as *La Parole ouvrière* had argued), and if emancipation struggles are confronted with power relations between classes that produce specific relations to values and knowledge inside struggle itself (as the articles of *Les Révoltes logiques* had shown)? *The Philosopher and his Poor* develops a convincing demonstration of the aporias of the project of class politics, but it also leads to the removal of all reference to class domination and class struggles in emancipatory politics. The baby has been thrown out with the bathwater.

5 Marx as Political Philosopher

The defence of philosophy and the critique of sociology developed in *The Philosopher and his Poor* was the sign of a new inversion. In the 1970s, in the struggle against the powers pervading his or her discourse, the critical intellectual was called upon to question disciplinary boundaries. But after his historical incursions in social history, Rancière went back to the classical space of philosophical discourse and to its genealogies: Plato, Marx and Sartre in *The Philosopher and his Poor*; Plato, Aristotle, Hobbes, Rousseau and Marx in Chapter 3 of *Disagreement* (1995).

In this last book, Marx is caught in a new theoretical apparatus, a purely philosophical one. The target of the book is no more sociology and the sociologization of politics, but the so-called 'return of political philosophy'; that is, the rebirth of normative philosophical investigations about justice, rights and democracy, and especially its consensus versions associated with the names of Rawls and Habermas. Beyond contemporary philosophy, it is the very contradiction between political philosophy itself and politics that is at stake. When Rancière criticizes the new philosophical ambition, it is not for its claim to restore the political against its sociologization at the age of the fall of Marxism. He only charges it with the philosophical error that goes back to the old project of submitting politics to a 'principle' (*archè*), whereas true politics – that is, democracy – is precisely the bracketing of social order in the name of equality.

In *Disagreement*, the presence of Marx is twofold. Rancière uses many Marxian arguments and formulas while locating Marx within his genealogy of the illusions of political philosophy. The mode of argumentation underpinning his critique of the contemporary renewal of political philosophy clearly sounds Marxian. In his introduction, Rancière highlights the fact that the return of political philosophy is contemporary with the withdrawal of the political. He argues that this connection discloses the contradiction between politics and political philosophy. This echoes one of the main themes of Marx's writings in the *German-French Annals*: political philosophy in its purest form (that is, in its Hegelian form) is nothing more than the alienated expression of political alienation (that is, of abstract, illusory, untrue politics).

Even the project of political philosophy is defined in the terms of the young Marx. Just as Marx had criticized the young-Hegelians for believing that true politics should proceed from a realization of philosophy, Rancière identifies political philosophy as an attempt to realize the essence of philosophy (that is, the philosophical description of a social order grounded on a principle). And just as Marx explained that philosophy could not be realized without being suppressed, Rancière defines the very project of political philosophy as a project of 'realization-suppression of politics'.[82] The Marxian way to achieve this 'realization-suppression' of politics would be precisely 'the realization-suppression of philosophy itself'.[83]

According to Rancière, there are three possible ways to develop this paradoxical project. The first is 'archi-politics'; that is, the construction of a society in total conformity with the philosophical principle (Plato and his 'republican' heirs). The second is 'para-politics'; that is, the attempts to prevent any social trend that could destroy the social order (Aristotle and all the liberal defenders of civil peace). According to the third scenario, the 'meta-politics' of Marx, politics is not conceived of as the realization of justice but as absolute injustice, and the truth of this injustice is located in the social organization. Rancière refers to 'On the Jewish question' as the perfect illustration of a critical operation disclosing the gap between the principles of the political discourse and the social reality that contradicts them; and he states that this critical operation led Marx to an oscillation between hope in a 'true' politics and a nihilism identifying all politics as an illusion.[84] The Marxian notions of 'class struggle' and of 'ideology' would also express this oscillation.[85] Here again, the tension is reduced to self-contradiction, since for Rancière true politics is the participation in the political space of those who are excluded from it. Against Marx, he points out that political illusions should not be demystified, but considered as the means of emancipation: for instance, workers have to claim the political rights that are already recognized but for bourgeoisie alone, women for political and social rights that are already recognized but for men alone.[86] If, however, the Marxian opposition between political emancipation and human or social emancipation points to the double meaning of the political sphere which can function both as an illusion and as a promise, as Rancière suggests perfectly, where precisely does the contradiction with Marx lie? Why, exactly, could the demystification of political illusions not be a means towards the realization of political promises? We already know the answer: demystification is incompatible with emancipation, because the dominated have the competence to understand their domination, and because one should acknowledge that emancipation means rupture with social identities, whereas the demystification of politics means reduction of politics to society.

At the end of this journey, Rancière seems to have returned to a Sartrian philosophy of absolute freedom where everybody can free themselves from their social fate, a philosophy of political freedom grounded in the communist principle of equality rearticulated in the epistemological (that is, Althusserian?) and Maoist terms of the 'equal competence of everybody'. There is no doubt that on these grounds, Marx's writings could have nothing more than a place in philosophical genealogies, despite their betrayal of philosophy. Nevertheless, even if on the surface nothing more than erudition and phraseology are preserved from Rancière's former Marxism, as we have seen the main lines of his thought were elaborated in this now denied past.

Chapter 11

Work in the Writings of Jacques Rancière

Jean-Philippe Deranty

This chapter studies the changing ways in which issues of work are discussed throughout Rancière's writings. Four key moments can be delineated in Rancière's writings that relate to the work question: an early structuralist moment, in which work offers no meaningful reference; a leftist moment, where work by contrast is the central reference; a moment of hesitancy, where workers remain the key subjects of politics but the work reference is rejected; and a mature period where all traces of earlier 'workerism' seem to have disappeared.

The journey that the category of work traces throughout Rancière's oeuvre thus seems to be easily retraced as a story of ebb and flow. Against this appearance, I would like to show that Rancière's relationship to the work reference is in fact much more complex. Attention to the letter of Rancière's texts shows that the question of work continues to cast a long shadow in his later writings. The apparent abandon of work as the ground of politics is only superficial. One can in fact continue to identify important remainders of the earlier work references even in the mature writings.

Demonstrating the continuing underlying presence of work in the thought of Rancière serves not just exegetical purposes. Rancière's research into the 'archive of the proletarian dream' in the 1970s was second to none in terms of its empirical wealth and conceptual sophistication. He was one of the foremost thinkers of the labour movement. His apparent withdrawal from labour studies in the 1980s, after the publication of *The Nights of Labour*, could appear to be just as emblematic. But if it can be shown that the key concepts and arguments of his later, more famous books on democracy and aesthetics, were in fact spawned in the study of the workers' movement and of working cultures, then a more general point starts to emerge out of the exegetical study – namely, that the apparent disappearance of work from the intellectual centre stage is only an illusion, and that work continues to be a core category of political thinking and social criticism.

1 Conceptual and Critical Dimensions of Work: Work and Labour

Work functions as a key conceptual operator in critical social and political philosophy on the basis of two separate sets of considerations. These dimensions are related in many ways, but they point to different aspects of work.[1] Inasmuch as they lean on the reference to work, Rancière's political writings and his writings in social criticism also point back to these two dimensions: the first relates to work as an individual activity, and the second to work as a socially defined activity. Let us first briefly delineate the conceptual and associated critical meanings of these two dimensions, as it is an essential condition for the clarity of the discussions that follow.

Work is, first of all, a type of individual activity. This view of work, as individual *working*, entails what we might call 'ergonomic' dimensions. It refers to the intelligent, bodily and mental, activity of a subject confronted with specific tasks and constraints, as a result of his or her inclusion in the productive order.

This primary, 'praxeological' sense of work, initially defined from the perspective of the subjective experience of the working agent, also entails specific cultural and social dimensions: the particular cultures of trades and crafts, bound by the sharing of bodily and discursive forms of knowledge and experience; and the social bodies that arise on the basis of such shared forms of knowledge and experience – corporations, social-professional groupings, guilds and so on. The French word '*métier*' captures these interrelated senses of a specialized activity that anchors specific life-worlds.

The critical counterpart of this praxeological view of work is, first of all, the critique of alienation; that is, the denunciation of what happens to human features when the working activity is pathological, either because the latter is dysfunctional in its very ergonomic aspects, in terms of concrete working conditions, or because of the organization that frames it, the type of work supervision, the cadences imposed on the worker and so on. However, the social-cultural meanings of the '*métier*' also point to other critical categories. Social and political criticism can, first of all, target the denial or exploitation of workers' collective knowledge. A famous example of this kind of criticism is the 'de-skilling' thesis that was popular in the late 1970s.[2] Alternatively, the emphasis can be put on the specific socialization that occurs by belonging to a *métier*. The critical counterpart here is the identification of forms of exclusion or marginalization of particular groups on the basis of their occupation and activities.

This latter form of work-based criticism provides a good transition towards the second broad set of dimensions of work; namely, work as a social activity. Work can be a core reference for critical social and political philosophy as the key principle behind the social division of labour, and as a result of this, as the main factor explaining the hierarchical aspect of the political structure. Critique of work here is critique of the hierarchies that are put in place on the basis of the division of labour, in particular the distinction between intellectual and manual labour. These divisions and hierarchies obviously intersect with the cultural and social dimensions of the working activity just discussed, yet they are different. The differences become obvious when viewed from the individual worker's perspective: whereas in the first instance, it is the contempt of the cultural and social validity of a given professional life-world that is at stake, in the second, it is the status within the social order as a whole, based on one's position in the hierarchy of occupations. In the first, the core content at stake is professional culture; in the second it is social standing, and attached to that, social and political rights. Of course the discriminations suffered as a result of belonging to a particular *métier*, and those suffered as a result of one's low social standing, usually intersect substantially. However, they can still be distinguished in terms of the element that provides the basis for discrimination (a concrete form of activity in the first case; a social position in the second).

For Rancière, as for any critical thinker interested in these issues, there is an inherent tension between the two broad dimensions that have just been distinguished. The most general, critical purpose underlying Rancière's work throughout is the critique of domination and the development of a political philosophy based on the struggle against social domination. Since a key structure of social life responsible for domination is the division of labour, the work issue is central in Rancière's thinking right from the start. This focus, however, is premised on the possible conflation of the ergonomic/cultural sense, with the social sense of work. As a result, there is a constant fluctuation in Rancière's writings, between moments where the second dimension more or less coincides with the first, versus other moments where the two are held apart; indeed, the second dimension, taken to its radical conclusion, leads to a rejection of the ergonomic/professional reference. The moment where the two dimensions are held together corresponds to the early proletarian writings. The moment where the two dimensions are held apart corresponds to the established political philosophy of the mature Rancière. However, even in the latter writings, work can be shown to continue to operate in the background in a number of ways. Rancière can never quite detach himself from the reference to work, even in its material sense.

2 Work in the Early, Althusserian Period

It is important to look at the fate of work in Rancière's contribution to *Reading Capital*, when the structuralist assumptions were still unquestioned, because the structuralist methodology leaves a lasting mark on Rancière's thinking, so much so that it continues to produce some effects in the later work, despite its official rejection.

The structuralist reading of Marx propounded in 1965 rejects any meaningful reference to work taken in the individual, 'ergonomic' sense. This structuralist reading takes as its unquestioned premise the Althusserian assumption that the true scientific nature of Marx's analysis of capitalistic economy emerges only slowly, in *Capital* and the mature writings, and even there, only in patchy, ambiguous form. In these writings, so the famous claim goes, Marx gradually comes to define and articulate the specificity of his scientific discourse, in opposition to everyday perception and bourgeois, or ideological, forms of theory. Rather than taking its objects as being naturally given, or assuming that their modes of interaction can be reconstructed through the analysis of basic units, scientific knowledge is based on the presupposition that these objects are defined and relate to one another on the basis of the functions they fulfil within that structure. The structure produces its objects, regulates the ways in which they interact and determines the forms in which they appear to perception and ordinary thought. It is only on the condition of seeing capitalism as a formation functioning on the basis of specific relations of production that one is able not only to characterize all the key factors involved in capitalism (living and dead labour, value, production, class struggle and so on), but also understand why they come to be understood the way they are by 'inverted' forms of consciousness. The structuralist reading is functionalist: it believes that elements of reality owe their being and their mode of interaction with other elements from the functions they fulfil; and the functional order of the structure is itself captured in a general 'formation'.

From this perspective, a number of key assumptions behind the 'praxeological' understanding of work are no longer tenable. First of all, it is a mistake to interpret social reality from the perspective of the subject. The underlying premise of such an approach, whose philosophical methodology would be formulated in phenomenological terms, is that objectivity depends on human intentionality (or *praxis* for the young Marx) for its meaning. This vision is at odds with the 'real movement' of capitalism, in which subjects are only 'carriers' of social structural meanings, and the core 'content of the subject function' is 'being mystified'.[3] Material analysis is premised on the radical separation between reality as it appears to social agents, and the real movement unfolding behind their backs. Similarly, the notion of 'experience' points only to surface phenomena, it is antithetical to a proper scientific position.[4] As a result, alienation means something completely different in Marx's 'true' scientific writings, and in the early writings. In the latter, it was an anthropological notion signifying the loss of humanity's essence through the perversion of work, itself understood as an essential medium for humanity's self-constitution. Instead, a structuralist theory of alienation reinterprets the notion as, so to say, alienation of the structure itself: the result of a highly mediated process – for instance, interest-bearing capital, appears as a 'thing' whose processual nature has disappeared. Accordingly, as Rancière writes, 'in this movement, the worker and the capitalist play no part. The worker features here only as "*support*" for the relation of wage labour production, not as a subject in which the process would originate. The mechanism of *Entfremdung* does not concern him.'[5]

Combined with this rejection of work as a category of experience, the values and social bonds growing out of working life-worlds have just as little significance. However, even the general social sense of work, work as principle behind the division of labour, loses all relevance. The political theory entailed by the structuralist reading is only concerned with capitalists and workers inasmuch as the latter respectively embody the two conceptual poles of the unequal relation of production that is capitalistic value-extraction. The theory of domination and of political struggle that ensues cannot, in principle, refer to any form of social experience, notably to experiences of denial of equality, dignity, esteem or rights. On an objectivistic interpretation well represented in the Marxist tradition, political struggle and its theory must be annexed to the development of the forces of production, and their antagonism with relations of production. By contrast, on a reading rejecting such objectivism, one that is well represented by Althusser, the proletarian movement is led by the party, which helps it define its proper direction. Party intellectuals, armed with Marxist science, determine which trends in social reality correspond to the 'real movement' of capitalistic forces, as opposed to the surface effects. The combined forces of party practice and Marxist theory indicate its real class interests to a proletariat structurally inclined to misperceive them as a result of the system's ideological apparatus. In this framework, work operates only as an explanatory structural element, but its subjective, cultural and sociological dimensions are irrelevant.

3 Work in the Workerist Writings

The radicalization of certain Marxist forces in the late 1960s destroyed these structuralist certitudes.[6] The echoes of the Chinese revolution abroad, at home the growing discontent among the youth and the radicalization of workers' actions throughout the 1960s, the immense hope raised by the explosion of May 1968 and the ambiguous role of the Communist party in these events – all this combined to withdraw all credibility from the dogmatic vision of a Marxist science dictating to mystified masses the ways to their emancipation. Like many in his generation, Rancière embraced the Maoist motto of the primacy of the experience of oppression. Right from the start, he articulated it in terms of 'the intelligence of the oppressed'; 'the oppressed are the intelligent ones, and the weapons for their liberation come from their intelligence'; or, 'the intelligent understanding of class struggle, as well as of production, does not belong to the specialists.'[7] From the perspective opened up by these fundamental axioms, in an important article from 1969, and then more amply in *Althusser's Lesson* in 1974, Rancière launched a scathing attack on Althusserian Marxism, completely overturning the position he had taken as a young disciple ten years earlier.

The key axiom of the 'intelligence of the oppressed' refers to the 'intelligence', that is, the understanding and capacity to discursively articulate the experiences of oppression and the possibilities of emancipation. Against the haughty structuralist attitude assuming the theorist is there to enlighten and guide mystified subjects, the new perspective argues exactly the opposite: the oppressed do not need anyone else to tell them what their oppression consists of, or how they should attempt to reject it. As a result, it is the theorist, rather, who can learn from the oppressed – and, indeed, not from their pathos, but from their discourse and action – about the causes and structures of domination, and the ways to combat these. With this, the characteristic features of Rancière's social and political thought are already in place: trust in the actions and discourse of those who fight against injustice on the basis of their own experiences of it; hermeneutic humility towards their actions and voices.

The fresh perspective leads to a new reading of Marx. Marx is an example to follow and his texts continue to represent the core reference, no longer on the grounds of his having uncovered a revolutionary new 'scientific' standpoint for the study of history and society, but for his having attempted in the most sustained way to integrate the actions and discourses of the struggling workers of his time in a systematic whole:

> Marx might have ridiculed the clumsy theoretical tools (*la quincaillerie théorique*) of Proudhon, or the syncretic conceptions of the Parisian militants. But the terms in which he thought the aim to reach were no different than those of these "artisans": communism, workers' emancipation, abolition of the wage relation, free association of workers.[8]

This revolutionizes the reading of *Capital*, which must still be taken as a model, but for reasons totally opposed to those propounded by Althusser:

> there is not one logic of *Capital*, but several logics, several discursive strategies corresponding to different problems, and echoing in different ways the discourses in which classes think themselves or oppose adverse discourses: the science of classical economists or the workers' protests, the discourse of philosophers or the reports by the inspectors of fabrics, and so on.[9]

Philosophical analysis is thereby redefined in its aims and methods. Rather than constructing a functional system a priori, its task is to reconstruct the scope and clarify the meanings of given forms of discourse and real modes of action, by replacing them in their particular contexts and identifying their stakes. All the while, this social hermeneutic needs to operate on the double assumption of class antagonism and the 'equality of intelligences', as the Jacotot study will call it.

On the basis of these new methodological principles, and following the example of Marx as it is now read, we understand the deep logic behind Rancière's sustained work of archival research in this decade, the product of which can be read in the collections of proletarian writings he edited[10], and his articles in the journal of *Les Révoltes logiques* collective.[11] Proletarian science is to grow at the intersection of philosophy and history: its role is to reconstruct the conceptual and political significance of real struggles for emancipation.

This historical hermeneutic of the struggles of the oppressed, and Marx's lesson, both point to the fact that work now has to be taken as the central category. It is the factor around which class antagonism revolves as well as the principle of emancipation: 'the point from which the mystification of the commodity must be thought and the functioning of the capitalistic system understood is the aspiration that is carried by workers' struggle: the association of those "free producers", those "human beings freely associated" whose social relations and relations to their objects will all be "simple and transparent".'[12] In this period, Rancière's position is classically one that can be called 'workerist'; that is, a position in social and political philosophy that makes work the fundamental basis for both criticism and programmatic assertions, and of the 'workers' the carriers of emancipation:

> (The workers) (*les ouvriers*) speak to be recognized as more than just the power of numbers or the strength of many arms, or as people who know how to handle tools and guns: they speak to show that they can speak the just and the reasonable, that they should be allowed to take place in society not because they are the strongest, but because this place is in accordance with justice and history. Their voices are not the cries coming out of the suffering lows of society, but the voice of an intelligence that is also the world's new principle: work.[13]

A key feature of the workerist perspective is that the two dimensions of work (as individual activity and as division of labour) are tightly welded together.

The social dimension of work is an easy one to mobilize for a critique of social domination and a theory of political struggle predicated upon it. The proletarian status brings with it a series of denials of rights and freedoms, a multifaceted denial of equality, as a result of its position in the social hierarchy: the denial of basic health and well-being through inhuman working conditions and poverty; denial of education; denial of political rights; denial of rights granted to other social groups, such as the right to assemble, to organize one's material interests, to access the courts to defend one's interests. Such systematic mistreatment is a direct product of the workers' position in the relations of production. From a historical point of view, as Rancière discovered through his historiographical research, it is on the basis of this social dimension of work that the classical republican opposition to despotism and tyranny was appropriated in many workers' writings in the early stages of the labour movement, and reinterpreted in class terms: the masters are no longer the tyrants of the old regime, but the bourgeois masters, their armies and police.[14] The principles underpinning the workers' claims, however, remain principally the same: liberty and equality.

The specificity of the 'workerist' position, however, is that such classical critique of injustice is internally linked to demands related to the 'ergonomic' and cultural sides of work. The link between the two sides is at first justified negatively, inasmuch as both sides designate a common evil, workers' 'dispossession': 'the idea of proletarian revolution is in fact inexorably contemporaneous to the discourses of this workers' avant-garde who thinks and acts, not to prepare a future where proletarians would inherit the large capitalistic industry premised upon the dispossession of their labour and intelligence, but rather, *in order precisely to halt the logic of such dispossession.*'[15] The republican struggle against political disenfranchisement is continuous with the concrete struggles waged *against* alienation and exploitation in and through work. As a result, the struggles revolving around working conditions or forms of work organization, or indeed those forms of reflection and collective action concerned with alternative modes of distribution or social protection – all the 'thick', concrete and manifold reality of the world of work is, from the workerist perspective, part and parcel of the movement of emancipation.

Indeed, the necessity for the theorist to show hermeneutic humility in his or her approach to the reality of struggling workers entails that he or she must be attentive to the specificities of particular industries and professions. The history of the labour movement reconstructed on the premise of 'the intelligence of the oppressed', must 'take into account the diversity of workers' experiences, the differentiated perceptions of work, tools, the boss, the bourgeoisie or the working class according to the different work processes, and according to the practices of solidarity, struggle or negotiation specific to each corporation. These different practices give a different tonality to the dreams of the shoemakers, the collective discussions of the tailors, the industrial thought of the typographers, or the organizational thought of the mechanics.[16] In brief, taking seriously the two axioms that work is the principle of the new world and the oppressed are intelligent demands of the theorist an entomological attention to all the aspects of the world of work, down to its technical and 'ergonomic', as well as its social-professional, cultural and 'corporatist' details. All these aspects, it is important to stress once more, are studied for the very purpose of establishing a proper theory of emancipation.

As is evident in this analysis, the negative justification of the link between social domination and domination in and through work is easily turned around and issues in a positive principle of justification. In programmatic, political terms, this link is captured in the notion of 'association', which designates simultaneously a form of economic solidarity, political equality and productive reciprocity. In short, this link designates an organization of production that also entails a more humane form of interaction. The ideal of an association of free producers designates a society of equal rights and free citizens and a non-alienating, non-exploitative organization of production.

4 *Nights of Labour:* Ambiguities of Workers' Emancipation

This patient research culminates in the extraordinary book that is *The Nights of Labour*. At this point in Rancière's intellectual journey, however, the two sides of work appear to come apart: hermeneutic attention to the real content of proletarian discourses demonstrates that the way to emancipation actually leads away from the material and cultural realities of work.[17]

The more one studies the real discourses and practices of workers at the inception of the labour movement, the more the latter appear to escape predetermined images of the proletarian as a figure of oppression and as a carrier of full emancipation. But if faithfulness to the reality of the working class is the fundamental methodological axiom, then these contradictory features of proletarian reality have to be taken seriously, they cannot be rejected out of hand as ideological obfuscations, outdated subjective and social positions, or as illusions created by the machinations of disciplinary power. Somehow, one must reconcile the idea that the working classes are the true witness to real domination and therefore the chosen agents of real emancipation, with all the aspects of their discourses which evade predetermined theoretical constructions. The following passage, from the introduction to *The Nights of Labour*, captures well the logic of this transformation in Rancière's methodology. The passage is one among several backward glances in which Rancière has justified the second major shift in his work. This one is particularly significant as it opens the very book in which a decade of sustained archival research is consigned and analysed:

at first we weren't surprised that this search for a deeply hidden truth had to traverse so much chattering; that the search for proletarian authenticity encountered so many simulacra: so many professions of faith imitating politicians' speeches, so many verses imitating the great poets, so many moral declamations aligned onto bourgeois norms, so many representations that seemed to be so many screens that had to be scratched to let truth shine through'. But then, 'when one does proceed to scrape the varnish off those too civilized savages and those too bourgeois proletarian labourers, there comes a moment when one asks oneself: is it possible that the quest for the true word compels us to shush so many people? What exactly is the meaning of this evasion that tends to disqualify the verbiage of every truly spoken speech in favour of the mute eloquence of the one who is not heard?[18]

Once one realizes how flawed it is to search for a true working class experience by actually denying the relevance and authenticity of the real working class voices, the methodological conclusion is clear and amounts to the second great shift in Rancière's work: instead of attempting to find the voices and expressions that would be somehow typical of the working class experience, one has to take seriously precisely those voices which seem at first, on a dogmatic or superficial understanding, to miss or lead away from it: 'go back in the company of those whom I had come across first: those who were travelling the road in the opposite direction, deserting what was said to be their culture and their truth to go toward our shadows: those workers whose … dissonant voices create dissonance in the duet of mute (proletarian) truth and the contrite illusion (of the intellectual).'[19] In other words, the truth about proletarian speech is to be found precisely in those real proletarian voices who sought to escape their proletarian fate.

What these voices show, according to the post-workerist Rancière, is that the hopes for emancipation were actually not expressed in reference to substantial norms or values that would have been anchored in the material or cultural realities of work. The dream of full freedom was in fact consistently disconnected from the concrete reality of work and its alleged values and norms.

There are two ways, however, to understand this severing of the link between the rejection of domination (and thereby of work as factor of domination), and the values and representations of professional life-worlds. The first is simply to insist on the fact that the first kind of demands could be made in absence of any reference to the second. This appears most explicitly in the fact that the proletarian writers usually articulated their arguments in reference to the discourses of (class) others.

In particular, it was the writings of bourgeois philosophers, poets and novelists, Rancière argues at the beginning of the book, that raised the consciousness of the proletarian writers about the injustice of this world: 'in the moments when the real world wavers and seems to reel into mere appearance, more than in the slow accumulation of day-to-day experiences'.[20] This is why, Rancière concludes, 'Those other worlds, which supposedly anaesthetize the sufferings of the workers can actually be the thing that sharpens their awareness of such suffering.'[21]

Rather than trying to trace neat ideological divides between forms of expression, one must take seriously the ways in which the proletarian writers read and appropriated the bourgeois writers of their times: what the proletarian needs in order to denounce the system's injustice, 'is not the knowledge of exploitation' as that is just too obvious to them to be worth dwelling on. Rather, what they were after was 'a knowledge of self that reveals to them beings dedicated to something else besides exploitation: a revelation of self that comes circuitously by way of the secrets of others'.[22] That is, romantic descriptions of emotional torment and unhappy passions, when read from the perspective of one's dominated position in the productive order, harbour more subversive power than scientific critiques of political economy.

The abandon of the positive reference to work as professional culture and social identifier means that it is now solely the sharing of a position of domination – in other words, a *negative* common denominator, which defines the class of those who, as the later political writings will say, 'have no part'. The concept of class becomes equivocal, a purely negative and relational concept, grounded in no specific form of experience, be it the experience of particular professional activities, or a specific social experience: 'being always in the process of taking shape could be a permanent characteristic of the working class. At every stage it might look like a transit point, so that the eye of the expert gets lost in trying to differentiate the true proletarian labourer from the belated artisan or the disqualified member of the tertiary sector.'[23]

The only positive principle that remains is the demand for freedom and equality. This is precisely what the writings of the proletarian writers demonstrate at length. The tailors' strikes of 1833 or the writings of the typography workers all show that what matters to the workers is a form of 'proletarian dignity at odds with those forms of dignity that would be grounded in physical expenditure or manual skill'.[24] Dignity, respect and recognition as equal social partners are what workers truly demand.[25]

Indeed, the last quote points to a second way in which the social dimension of work (domination through the division of labour) is severed from the first (work as experience and activity). Here, work as experience and culture is not just made absent, but is explicitly rejected as such. The experience of domination at work is not only a social experience, the experience of one's lower status or, indeed, of one's absence of status in the social hierarchy – it is also a bodily experience, the bodily experience of social domination, we might say, the experience of having to suffer in one's flesh the fact of being exploited for the sole benefit and enjoyment of others. In this respect, work does matter, and matters as experience, individual and collective, but this time as a negative reference, as something to be absolutely avoided. In the workers' literature, this is the theme of work as a form of torture and of the workplace as a modern equivalent of hell. A whole chapter of *The Nights of Labour* (Chapter 3, which follows a remarkable phenomenological diary by the carpenter-philosopher Gauny of a day's work) is dedicated precisely to denouncing the perniciousness of any positive reference to the necessity of work, which ignores the suffering entailed in 'the necessity to have to work in order to live'.[26] Here, work is not only no longer relevant as a norm or principle; rather, it becomes a negative value in its own right, the 'hell' from which workers aspire to be freed, not just an affront to freedom but an affront to human needs.[27]

Finally, the last two parts of the book demonstrate the impossibility, experienced in practice by the utopian communities founded by the disciples of Saint-Simon, of marrying the legal, political demands of workers, of full equality and freedom, with the dream of the association of free producers. In these failed utopias is revealed, time and again, through multiple concrete experiences, the irreducibility of the two sides of work.

5 Abandon of Work After *The Night of Labour*?

Rancière's later political writings could easily be read as completing the movement of dissociation between the two sides of work. On that reading, the nineteenth-century struggles of the labour movement continue to matter, but only as *examples* of moments in which the axiom of equality was asserted and tested. Other examples can be taken, which illustrate the point just as much, notably feminist struggles.[28] The other side of work, however, the 'ergonomic' side, with its professional-cultural dimensions, which gives specific and substantial content to the struggles of the labour movement, and in particular sustains the ideal of the 'association', that side is now irrelevant. Indeed, any insistence on that aspect of work would seem to lead to what the mature thought of Rancière identifies as the most serious obstacle to democratic equality – namely, the essentialization of political agents, the attempt to ground political action in socially or culturally defined identity. The decisive encounters with the proletarian writers – especially Gauny and the teacher of the people, Jacotot – led, by a process of generalization, to Rancière's famous definition of politics: true politics begins when sociological destiny is transcended. Whenever ways of doing, ways of being and ways of saying are assumed to be attuned to one another, the order of the police is at play, and politics begin precisely with attempts, practical and discursive, to challenge and disrupt it. From the perspective of this dialectic of the police and politics, any reference to shared experiences of dominated work or to a professionally defined form of collective life as grounds of politics would appear to perform precisely the kind of essentializing and sociologizing of political action Rancière has so vehemently rejected in so many of his writings.

However, I would like to suggest that there is an alternative way to understand the place of work in Rancière's later writings. This alternative reading comes into view once the more famous political and aesthetic writings of the last two decades are considered against the background of Rancière's earlier 'periods'. Such 'genetic' perspective shows that the mature model accommodates conceptual features gleaned throughout Rancière's 'periods', thereby pointing to a complex, underlying continuity in his oeuvre, despite the significant, self-consciously described methodological shifts the latter has undergone over the decades. Rancière's oeuvre appears to have been built through a complex process of sedimentation, where positive elements are retained as established principles, while negative elements account for the more spectacular shifts. The early structuralist period left a suspicion towards any phenomenological perspective, in the technical sense of that term, which has remained constant. We can read Rancière's insistence on politics as a process of subjectivation rather than as an expression of identity as a late mark of that suspicion. Or his insistence on what we could term the 'stochastic' aspect of politics, the fact that it is rare and unpredictable, that also can be read as a way of maintaining a structuralist insight (free agency as constrained by the structures in which it is to unfold), even after the scientism of that position has been abandoned.[29] The 'workerist' period bequeathed the 'intelligence of the oppressed', the notion that is without the doubt the defining one for Rancière's thinking, explaining in particular why his attention was drawn to the figure of Jacotot, the peculiarity of his understanding of equality, or the emphasis on speech and voice for the practical implementation of that equality. Similarly, the gradual distance taken towards the associative model functions as a key (if negative) principle: the historical examples of the proletarian writers demonstrate a general truth about politics; namely, that it is waged as the attempt to escape the denial of freedom and equality entailed in the different forms of social destiny.

In the context of this process of conceptual sedimentation, the place of work appears to be central, but in a peculiar sense. Work continues to produce massive effects even after it has officially left the stage, or rather has been demoted from its status as the main character. Or to put it another way: like a trace indirectly (or negatively) denotes the thing that produced it even after that thing is no longer present, the more explicit features of the political and aesthetic models of the recent writings all point to work as their source. The reading of Rancière's oeuvre suggested above interprets his evolution, leading from the work paradigm to the abandon of work, as a process of *generalization*: from the specific historical experiences of workers in the early stages of the labour movement, Rancière extracted notions and theses that can now be detached from their historical origin without altering their sense. The alternative reading that I am suggesting argues by contrast: the political and aesthetic theses defended by Rancière today point to work as their secret source; the conceptual and historical origin cannot be ignored without altering the understanding of these theses. In other words, I am questioning what we mean when we say that the worker movements are for Rancière's later politics (and indeed, to some extent, for his aesthetics) *examples* of general political (and aesthetic) principles. What do we mean by examples? Just mere illustrations, such that others could just as well have been taken? Or examples that are so influential as to become paradigms, references that directly inform the principle they illustrate?

To defend this alternative exegetical hypothesis, it is possible to point to substantive textual parallels between the earlier, 'proletarian' writings, and the later, better-known writings of political thinking.

To begin with, there is the pivotal role of *The Nights of Labour* in the evolution of Rancière's thinking. The book brings to a theoretical close the decade of historiographical research preceding it, drawing on and presenting the incredibly rich scholarship into the early labour movement amassed by Rancière; but it also contains *in nuce* many of the themes developed at length in later texts. Precisely, however, this pivotal role speaks in favour of the interpretation of work as the vanishing mediator: from the perspective of *The Nights of Labour*, the famous definitions of politics presented in *Disagreement* often look like direct extrapolations from the study of proletarian writers.

In turn, a careful reading of that key text shows that the workers' movement provides the guiding thread of Rancière's famous definition of emancipation and political action. If it is just an illustration, it is one that appears at almost every stage of the book's overall argumentation – indeed, it is one that lends some of its key terms and references to a number of central analyses.[30]

In the initial pages, Rancière draws from the discussion of the hidden contradiction in Plato's and Aristotle's seminal analyses his famous definition of politics as 'part of those who have no part'. The identity of the *demos* defined in this way is very explicit; it is synonymous with the workers: 'any one of these speaking bodies destined to the anonymity of work or repro-duction ... anyone old artisan or shopkeeper whatsoever is counted in this party to the city that calls itself the people, as taking part in the affairs of the city as such.'[31] Or: 'It is in the name of the wrong (*tort*) done to it by the other parts (*parties*) that the people can identify with the whole community. Whoever has no part – the poor of the Ancient world, the third estate, or the modern proletariat – cannot in fact have any part other than all or nothing.'[32]

After the twisted ontology underlying politics has been unveiled, a key historical reference is introduced. That reference runs throughout *Disagree-ment*. It begins as a discussion of the critical adaptation of a famous Titus-Livy passage from the history of Rome, by the nineteenth-century writer Pierre-Simon Ballanche, in the context of the 1830 revolution in France, which marked the birth of the modern labour movement in that country. In his critical adaptation of the classical reference, the journalist uses the debate between patricians and plebeians as a foil to discuss the equality of proletarians and bourgeoisie. Later in the book, the reference is comple-mented by the reference to strikes and worker petitions immediately follow-ing the 1830 revolution.[33] Close attention to Rancière's text shows that the historical reference functions as much more than just a mere illustration. In a characteristic use of indirect style, Rancière's recounting and analysis of the historical references move seamlessly into conceptual analyses of key political notions. In particular, the manifests surrounding the tailors' strikes of 1833 become literally paradigmatic (not just illustrative) of the 'litiga-tion' (*litige*), around which politics revolves.[34]

In the chapter that follows, dedicated to the different modes in which political philosophy, in its ancient or modern forms, misses the radical, egalitarian core of politics established earlier – the proletarian movement once again represents a core example. Here, Rancière explicitly calls the 'proletarian' and the 'worker' (*ouvrier*) 'the privileged names' of political subjectivation.[35]

Finally, in the penultimate chapter, Rancière's analysis of the rise of xeno-phobia in consensual societies centres on the disappearance of the worker status as a political status: 'today's "immigrant" is first of all a worker who has lost his second name, who has lost the political form of his identity and alterity.'[36] Once again, the key assumption is that work and proletarian sta-tus were key operators of egalitarian politics. Rancière explicitly claims that the demise of work coincides with the demise of democratic politics.

Underneath the famous analyses of *Disagreement* thus runs the assumption that the proletarian movement has been the paradigmatic form of true egalitarian politics. Workers' struggles have given the best incarnation of the '*tiers peuple*', that *demos* that is 'at odds with itself' in the sense that it demonstrates its legal and political equality in the very places where the latter is supposed to be essentially denied.

From the perspective of our focus on work, this notion of '*tiers peuple*' is crucial. The *demos* of true, egalitarian democracy is '*tiers*' in that it is placed between two other views of the people – between the sovereign *demos* discussed by classical political philosophy and referred to in the classical declarations of rights, and the working people discussed both by Marxist critiques of formal democracy and by sociology. The key argument that the neologism of '*tiers peuple*' captures is the following: the democratic, universalistic power harboured by 'the people' is situated nowhere else than in the social reality of the working people. But in order to avoid any abstraction or essentialization, the two aspects must be held together. It is equally an abstraction to refer only to the ideal, sovereign people of democratic theory, as it is to refer only to the people at work. The *demos* is the carrier of true egalitarian democracy precisely when it performs 'demonstrations' of equality in the very immanence of social life – in other words, from the point of view of the division of labour. Such demonstrations, however, are not the expression of some essential, sociological or cultural qualities, but they claim universal equality precisely from their specific social position.

This argument is crucial for us because it shows how abstract it is in the end to distinguish too sharply between the two dimensions of work. The privileged name of the *demos* is the proletarians or the workers, because that social position is, *par excellence,* one which entails invisibility, having 'no part'. However, this should not be understood merely in terms of structures of domination and hierarchical status. The most concrete dimensions of the working condition (the workplace, working conditions, working collectives) matter just as much as status and hierarchy, since, as has just been said, they are the very place and issues at stake in political 'demonstrations'. The point of egalitarian demonstrations is to make visible rightful claims for equality in the places where such claims appear to be either irrelevant or impossible. The places and concrete issues are therefore just as necessary as the structure of domination for the performance of democratic claims and actions. In other words, even the 'thick' dimensions of the world of work continue to play a role in Rancière's later thinking. They do so, however, no longer, as in the workerist period, in a positive sense, as a cultural ground of politics and as providing a substantive ideal (the 'association'), but simply as the locus *par excellence* in which real democratic struggles take place. We could say that work, taken in a thick sense (as culture and experience) is the negative ground of politics for Rancière: without reference to it, the interpretation of political struggle risks remaining abstract; but the reference to it cannot be in any sense positive, lest the movement is sociologized, essentialized and thereby depoliticized. More precisely, we should say that work is *a* ground of politics for Rancière, if the ground of choice. Other struggles present the same dialectic of particularity in terms of the experience of domination and universality, as regards political claims: notably, feminist struggles.

If the evolution of Rancière's thinking consisted solely in the gradual abandoning of work as experience and culture, and the parallel emphasis on work as vector of domination, it would be difficult to explain how his theory of democracy would differ from liberal and republican theories. His emphasis on freedom and equality as the driving values of the workers' movement, and his insistence on legal and constitutional advances to entrench these values,[37] could easily make him sound like a liberal political philosopher. To emphasize only the 'struggle against domination' aspect of his democratic theory – more particularly, inasmuch as domination is based in people's position in the division of labour – would make him look like another republican theorist. Indeed, it would become difficult to see how his emphasis on the demonstration of equality through discourse, wrested away from the social destiny mostly represented by work, would substantially differ from Arendt's own political theory.[38] Rather, the originality of Rancière's political thought stems from the complex logic he establishes between social life and political claims: to avoid being abstract, politics must be grounded in social life; politics and police are intrinsically and reciprocally related; and yet, social life does not 'explain' politics. This vision of politics grew out of the study of the labour movement, and as many texts post-1995 demonstrate, the world of work has long continued to represent the paradigmatic example of such politics.

Chapter 12

Work, Identity, Subject

Jacques Rancière

Jean-Philippe Deranty has chosen to focus on an underlying, polymorphic motif in my work, rather than discuss the validity of my theses on politics, emancipation or the regimes of the arts. The choice of such an angle makes sense within the debates around what has been called *French Thought*. For it is a characteristic generally attributed to it – either as a virtue or a flaw – that it asks not so much about the truth or falsity of particular claims. Rather, it asks in what ways these claims can be asserted; that is, these claims are the result of which specific interventions in the distribution of possibilities. This reminds one, of course, of the famous claim by Bergson that a philosophical system is only ever the development of a fundamental intuition. In the case of my writings, one cannot speak of a system. What one finds instead is an apparently disordered mix of various interventions on topics as distant from one another as Plato's Republic, the strikes of the taylor-workers (*ouvriers-tailleurs*) in the 1830s, Schiller's aesthetic education, the troubles of Emma Bovary, Godard's *Histories of Cinema* or the rise of consensus in so-called democratic states. With such diverse topics, the issue is not so much to discover a central intuition, but rather to select a guiding thread that runs through the stages and domains of an entire body of work, or indeed a touchstone capable of revealing the constant themes, the bifurcations and transformations of a thought. The issue of 'work' is certainly a notion that runs through my oeuvre, from my contribution to *Reading Capital*, to the discussion of the forms of contemporary political art in *The Emancipated Spectator*. Jean-Philippe Deranty has remarked correctly that the arguments of the taylors,[1] the secession of the plebeians on the Aventine[2] and the forms of dis-identification of the night proletarians (*les prolétaires de la nuit*) were all at the heart of political subjectivation as presented in *Disagreement*. And he has shown that they were present not only as illustrations of theory, but as operating a shift in the very mode of theorizing. One can only concur with his appraisal. But one must also ask *what exactly* defines this consistent thread. I have never tried to do a philosophy of work, nor presented a unified concept of work as object of my analyses. One can give work a central position only by showing that it is at the centre of a constellation of notions whose coherence is problematic: my contribution to *Reading Capital* opposed an idea of production to all the visions of production as arising from a working subject; conversely *The Nights of Labour* attempts to transform the name 'proletarian' into a subject of experience that cannot be identified to any productive process. This gap within the notion itself is confirmed by the gap between a language that distinguishes between *work* and *labour*, and a language that does not. In this respect, the gap between the two titles of the same book is significant: *La Nuit des Prolétaires* and *The Nights of Labour*. The English editor thought that an implicit play on words (the *knights of labour*) was a good way to render the ambivalence of the French '*nuit*', which rejects the metaphor of the night as misery, in order to emphasize the positive reversal of the order of time. He probably did not know that the French title had been chosen in reference to *La Nuit des Rois*, the French translation of Shakespeare's *Twelfth Night*.

All this is to say that work is indeed at the centre of my writings, but as the centre of tensions between contradictory logics, as an object well suited to the staging of these tensions and well suited also to the analysis of the parts that the worker (*le travailleur*), the labourer (*l'ouvrier*) and the proletarian (*le prolétaire*) can play on this stage. Talking of a part means that some process of doubling (*dédoublement*) occurs, and I had renamed my doctorate dedicated to the formation of proletarian thinking in France: 'The proletarian and his double'. Who plays the part of the subject who incarnates, represents or symbolizes work: that is the way in which, in the end, the 'question of work' has presented itself for me. It is also the way in which I have been able to address that monstrous question that has always terrorized me in the same measure as my contemporaries made it paramount: the 'theory of the subject'. This explains why I have only ever addressed it but from the side, through a specific aspect; namely, the relationship between subject and identity. This critique of identity is in fact the most recurrent theme running through my work, as a constant polemical stake. That critique has expressed itself through the adoption of systems of thought that were opposed, and has taken shape in forms that were sometimes contradictory. It is, however, the thread that links interventions that differ in relation to their objects or the moments in which they took place, or indeed those opposed in their very organizing principles. Jean-Philippe Deranty shows that it is already present in my contribution to *Reading Capital*, in which the theme of the alienation of the working subject was rejected in favour of the theme of the agent as 'carrier' of the relations of capitalist production. However, I was not born Althusserian. I had found the very same concern expressed in the philosophy of the author who was the main target of the structuralist attack in general, and of the Althusserian attack in particular; that is, Jean-Paul Sartre. My own rejection of identitarian fixations (*fixations identitaires*) was first satisfied in Sartrian freedom, its rejections of fixed identities, and the opposition it establishes to Being of doing things and making oneself (*l'opposition du faire et du se faire à l'être*). Indeed, this was the initial grid through which I first read the writings of the young Marx and adhered to the critique of alienation as the critique of a subjectivity expelled from itself and attached to an alien identity. For me, the discovery of Althusser meant an inversion of perspective. Sartrian praxis became the ultimate figure of the Cartesian cogito, and alienation became the myth of a subjective wealth extorted from the workers in order to create the objective wealth at the hands of Capital. The critique of identity then took the shape of the primacy of structure over the subject, and therefore of the relations of production over the worker. Importantly, such devaluing of the figure of the worker was paralleled by a valorization of the theoretician as a producer of concepts. Importantly also, it is not this vision of the theoretician as producer which was the essential aspect of my adherence to Althusserianism, but rather the critique of the thematic of dispossession. It is precisely this very critique which later took me away from the Althusserian logic, for there are several ways of understanding that critique. To the humanist compassion for the suffering of the alienated worker, one can oppose the formative virtues of big industry and the proletarian discipline guided by the science of the relations of production. This was the implicit basis upon which the Althusserian critique of 'humanism' and 'the subject' was conducted. But one can also find in that critique, as I did later on, the assertion of the always present possession by those who are allegedly dispossessed, or of a competence which can always be actualized, by the incompetent.

Between these two interpretations, there occurred the twofold lesson I received in the years following my intervention at the seminar on *Capital*. First, I started a thesis on the concept of the human being in Feuerbach, which, to begin with, was based on the Althusserian genealogy of humanism. Although this research remained incomplete, it showed me at least that the genealogy of 'the human being' was infinitely more complex than appeared in the structuralist dogma, while reinforcing my intolerance towards all the concrete philosophies of the flesh and blood individual.

Let's say that it took me away at the same time from structuralism and phenomenology. The second lesson, of course, is that of May 1968, and the political sequence that the event triggered. In May 1968, the whole problematic of alienation and dis-alienation, which Althusserianism had thrown in the bin of old ideologies, resurfaced and showed its capacity to mobilize. The Marxist scientific rigour, which Althusser had implicitly opposed to the monopoly of the 'workers' party', showed itself to be in fact supporting this monopoly. It supported the identitarian vision, which equated the workers' movement and the party of the working class, Marxist science and the doctrinal heritage of the workers' party.

The programme at the time was to undo the knot tying together the science of the relations of production to the monistic vision of the working class and the concept of the party as a twofold incarnation of science and class. Such undoing could be achieved in several, potentially contradictory, ways. To the knot class/party/science, it could oppose another kind of substantialist identification of class and its thinking. In this case, the notion of work is central, as the core identifying element of class and the core constitutive element of its thought. But the undoing of the conceptual knot could also oppose to this first solution a performative conception where class is defined through the manifestos and forms of action in which the latter asserts its opposition to the existing order. In that case, work is no longer the substantial activity that constitutes the class and nourishes its thinking; it is but one of the names of the dissensual stage upon which it asserts itself. In this case, the worker as subjective figure defines work as polemical relation, rather than the positive materiality of work defining the formative culture of the class of workers. This also implies that this subject exists only in the construction of this polemical relation.

However, in the political and theoretical sequence opened by the explosion of May 1968, such an opposition was not so easy to see, and the critical rejections of Althusserian scientism and the positivism of the 'party of the working class' often mixed up the two logics. To criticize the theory that saw the dominated as being necessarily stuck in 'ideology' naturally led to an emphasis on the positive nature of the 'possessions', values and knowledge of the workers criticized by Marxist science. The 'history lesson' which forms a chapter of *Althusser's Lesson* thus developed the analysis of *Reading Capital* the other way around.[3] The latter sought to deconstruct the 'humanist' theme of 'the loss of the worker in his production'. The new critique asserted against it the reality of capitalistic dispossession of the workers' control over their work, and showed the extent to which the 'humanist' reference to their human dignity had always been at the heart of workers' struggles. In doing so, however, it brought together two different forms of identity: on the one hand, the identity of the class of work which claims, as the street poet said, that 'the worker's true name is humanity', and opposes producing man to the idle who, as the same song said, 'will have to make his bed somewhere else'. This identity of man and the worker referred to the counter-figure which had asserted itself strongly as the very figure of the working class, before being dethroned by Marxist science and party: the figure incarnated by worker associations and later revolutionary union-ism. From this point of view, the negativity of revolutionary subjective action is grounded in the positivity of the working class' substantial culture. How-ever, on the other hand, the 'history lesson' emphasized not so much this substantiality of work, but rather its linguistic set up, which, in order to highlight this substantiality of work, shifts established positions and appro-priates when needed the language of the enemy in order to create the col-ective in the name of which it speaks, as well as to give it its full name and ways to express itself. *La Parole Ouvrière*, a collection of workers' writings published after *Althusser's Lesson*, centres on these language games, most eminently represented by the 'Banquet of Socialist Workers' of 1848,[4] in which the expounders of the scandalous doctrine praise the bourgeoisie's sacred values of order, work and property, which they redefine for their own purposes and in their own ways. My analysis was clearly directed against Althusserianism and more broadly against the model of ideological strug-gle in which the latter took place: that is, a model that naturalizes words by attributing them to the vocabulary of a class and which denounces, as a result, as the product of ideological capture any borrowing from the vocab-ulary of the other classes. By contrast with this, my analysis defined ideo-logical and political struggle as a struggle for the appropriation and the redirecting of words. It did so perhaps at the price of replacing the mean-ingless struggle between two vocabularies with a struggle between two uses of language, always capable of being referred to two separate worlds: the established culture of the leisurely class and the fluid, performative culture of the working class.

In order to escape this struggle between competing identities, it was not sufficient to emphasize the performative dimension of identitarian con-struction. It was necessary also to unveil a gap at the heart of this performa-tivity, to rethink the very opposition of work and leisure out of the material points where they come together and come apart. *The Nights of Labour* took one such point as its object. The impetus behind the book was given by a letter written by a Saint-Simonian worker to another worker in which he tells about a Sunday in May spent with two colleagues walking through the countryside, talking metaphysics and doing propaganda among other workers that they had met during their trip along the water. In this letter, the propagation of the idea of emancipation coincides with the appropriation of leisure. The day of rest in which the forces and the courage of workers is supposed to be restored hides something very different, indeed its opposite: namely, the conquest of leisure as the sensible mode of those who are not subjected to the necessity of working. *The Nights of Labour* proposes no theory of the subject or of subjectivation. Rather, it is wholly dedicated to the paradoxical relationship between the constitution of the discourse of the collective working subject, and what makes the latter's enunciation possible. That is, the constitution of a network of individuals whose capacity to produce the statements of the working collective rests upon a radical separation with the forms of being-worker (*l'être-ouvrier*): the traumatic experience of entering the world of work; the discovery of ideal forms of enjoyment normally reserved for those who are not subjected to the constraint of work; the effort to distance oneself from the language and ways of being linked to the working condition; the control of one's gaze or the freedom to think retrieved from working time; time wrested from the night and from sleep for the purpose of individual transformation and collective *oeuvre*. Work, then, can no longer represent the substance of an identity. It now appears as what I would later call an object of dissensus (a way of sharing/dividing the sensible – *une forme de partage du sensible*). On the one hand, it is a material condition implying specific forms of sensible experience – relations to time, space, to ways of doing, seeing and being seen, speaking and being named – that are simultaneously ways of being relegated or symbolically excluded. On the other hand, work is the subject of a quarrel, a collective power asserted against this relegation or exclusion, both as the specific characteristic of a group and as the principle behind a different organization of the community. *The Nights of Labour* stretched to the limit the link between these two poles: between the individual experience of what is unbearable in work, and the construction of glorious – or even improbable – collective figures of work and the worker. Between the two extremes of dis-identification and reincorporation, it left no room for a positive conception of the subject. In short, one might say that my work on the workers' archives presented as disjointed the two levels of a possible theory of subjectivation. On the one hand, in *La Parole Ouvrière*, polemical scenes of collective workers' expressions, which revealed the latter's identity by correcting or hijacking the discourses of masters and governments. On the other hand, in *The Nights of Labour,* experiences of radical dis-identification towards an imposed being-worker, which all those attempts to realize the army of work or the republic of workers necessarily betrayed. Somehow the idea of dis-identification was getting in the way of the idea of subjectivation. It led to seeing any positive figure of the worker as a figure of identification, which would give substantial and positive appearance to the original verdict of relegation pronounced by Plato: the worker is the person who can do nothing else but 'their own business'. *The Philosopher and his Poor* traced this relegation in the double Marxist figure of the producer and the proletarian combatant, in Sartre's dialectic and in the analysis of reproduction and distinction in Bourdieu. *The Ignorant Schoolmaster* detached the idea of emancipation from all substantialist visions of a collective subject. Emancipation appeared there as the always singular act by which an individual declared him- or herself capable, and declared any other capable, of exercising a capacity belonging to all. This notion of exercising a shared capacity was supposed to give figure in both positive and non-substantial ways to what appeared previously only in the negative form of dis-identification. Looking at it retrospectively, that was like another piece of the jigsaw puzzle. The idea of intellectual emancipation identified the ability of anyone to perform an identical type of work with a linguistic performance that has nothing substantial or identitarian left in it. It could thus relate the experience of dis-identification to the formation of a collective capacity of enunciation. But it is not sufficient that all the pieces of the puzzle exist for the general outline in which they could fit together to exist itself. For that outline to appear, one must in fact take the pieces out of the ensembles in which they function. And so Jacotot's idea of emancipation only asserted the radicality of the principle of egalitarian presupposition by adding the following corollary: it is individuals alone who can emancipate themselves, as society as such maintains itself solely through multiple bonds created by the inegalitarian presupposition. Similarly, just as much as the analysis of workers' dis-identification was sufficient to criticize the identities indefinitely reproduced by worker organizations and social sciences, the scandal of intellectual emancipation was sufficient to object both to those who claimed to give equality to the children of the people through instruction and to those who intended to do it by adjusting instruction to their cultural background. The issues of the subject, his or her identity and capacity were basically still addressed on the basis of the same critique of the Marxist tradition under its twofold aspect: the substantialist positing of the working class as historical subject and the scientist assertion concerning the illusions of the agents of production and the necessity of Marxist science in dispelling that illusion. The pieces of a theory of the political subject did not fit together yet because such a theory was not yet my concern.

It became so as a result of an impetus coming from elsewhere: namely, the rearrangement of political practice and political thinking in the wake of the tumults and hopes of the 1960s and 1970s. This period, as is well known, was marked, in the so-called Western world, by a general recess not only of revolutionary perspectives, but also of social-democratic movements. In the Anglo-American world, this translated into the brutal assertion of the primacy of the law of the market and of State reason; whereas in France, and a few other European countries, a softer version took hold; namely, consensus. This latter can be understood not only as the tendency for government parties to align themselves more closely to one another, but also as the rise of a vision of politics as a realistic response to a host of non-equivocal data concerning a community whose parts can be precisely numbered and whose problems can be objectively defined. A specific feature of the French situation in this respect was that this quest for a neutral account of the political was accompanied by two phenomena that betrayed its hidden tensions: on the one hand, a rich philosophical literature justifying the official realism through an abundance of reference to the grand tradition of politics as the search for the common good; on the other hand, the spectacular rise of a racist and xenophobic far-right which reawakened forms of radical alterity that the consensual doctrine was supposed to have buried. I was asked then by some to contribute to shedding light on this unusual situation. I tried to thematize this odd triangle of consensus, the return to the Greeks and the return of racism. These were the circumstances in which I was led to give a new, systematic significance to the salient moments of my journey through the figures of work and being-worker. The current situation demanded to think anew the figure of the people as subject of politics, to think the gap between the political *dèmos* and the identitarian *ethnos*. In order to do that, it was also necessary to show the gap between the *demos* and the population as managed by the consensual governments. In order to conduct this task, I proposed to rethink the *demos* through two essential traits, both borrowed, as it were, from the working figures I had once studied. The first trait is the *demos*' polemical nature, manifested in the construction of an original discursive stage (*scène de parole*). The non-authorized discursive stage where the taylor-workers invited themselves as they invited the masters who did not recognize this stage took on a new meaning when it was confronted with the inaugural scene in Aristotle where human *logos* debating the just is opposed to animal *phônè* expressing displeasure. The conflicts around the appropriation of words could be shown to rely upon a more fundamental conflict around the very conditions in which some beings could be recognized as speaking beings. This first trait is related to the second, which concerns the supplementary nature of *dèmos*, its status as a non-counted intervening element in the general count of the parts of society. The Platonic dictum to stick to one's own business and nothing else defined no longer simply the fate reserved for the worker and refused by him. The 'nothing else' also defined in the negative the actions of those who act where they should not be. Such a polemical definition borrowed from the philosopher who was the enemy of democracy could be shown to correspond to a structural determination of the democratic people such as Cleisthenes' reform in Athens had constituted it: namely, the abstract people, made up of territorial entities separated from one another. Democracy could then be conceptualized as the necessarily polemical action of those who are where they 'are' not, where they 'cannot' be. The same terms that used to define the impossible separation between the workers and being-worker could now define the wrong that constitutes the democratic people as the one that should not be on the public discursive stage, as well as the transgressive act through which that people asserts its presence, where there is no room for it, and asserts its speech where it does not count as a speaking being. Dis-identification could now define positively the public intervention of a non-identitarian people-subject (*peuple-sujet*): a people no longer identifiable with the social body nor reducible to an electoral body. All that was needed was to add a third term to the definition of the *dèmos*; namely, to link the 'supplementarity' of the people to its polemical self-assertion by highlighting the capacity of incompetents, that same 'equal intelligence' which Jacotot's intellectual emancipation assumed to exist in anyone. And so the previously disjointed terms of militant performativity, the experience of dis-identification and the definition of an equal capacity could now be united. This made it possible to define a conception of political subjectivation whose structural elements could be found in Ancient democracy – in the thought of its very enemies – but whose dynamics could only be truly shown in the modern forms of workers' emancipation. The ' workers' movement could then become the political subject *par excellence*. It could be that because it was the movement which questioned the very opposition between the social world of work and the political world of property and leisure. This means also that 'work', as well as 'the social', appeared clearly as divided entities. I refer here to the analyses of metapolitics in *Disagreement*: the social is presented there as the place where an exemplary tension occurs between opposites.[5] On the one hand, 'the social' is the signifier for the forms of subjectivation that enable the worker to exist as a political subject distinct from a sociological entity. On the other hand, it is supposed to embody the truth of the social body by dissipating political illusion and asking workers to identify with the reality of this truth. Work appears as a privileged example of dissensus where police identification, political subjectivation and its metapolitical reincorporation endlessly clash.

This threefold structure of politics can also be defined as an aesthetic structure. And it is clear that it is also in *The Nights of Labour* that the matrix for my work in 'aesthetics' has to be sought, notably in the description of a day's piece work by the carpenter Gauny, and more specifically of the disjunction between his arms, occupied to servile activity, and his gaze escaping through the window to take possession of a perspective better than that of the owners of the neighbouring houses.[6] This matrix-image was for me naturally associated to some of the formative images and concepts of the very idea of aesthetics: Shaftesbury's meditation upon the shepherd who, from the top of the headland, can catch a better sight of the ocean's horizon than the doge on his Bucentaur;[7] Kant's analysis about aesthetic appreciation of the shape of a palace, to be distinguished both from expert appreciation of its being well adapted to its function, and from the moral judgement regarding the ostentatious taste for luxury among the rich;[8] the triangular relation between the pleasant, the good and the beautiful in Kant,[9] or between formal, sensible and play impulse in Schiller.[10] I also highlighted the political significance of this structure in *The Philosopher and his Poor*, in reference notably to an amazing text by Baudelaire, written at the time of the 1848 revolution as a preface to the songs of the poet-worker Pierre Dupont, in which Baudelaire underlined the 'infinite taste of the *République*' as manifested in this *Song of the Workers*, in which is asserted the capacity of the workers to 'understand the beauty of palaces and parks', and, as a result, 'the art of being happy'.[11] In this case, once more, the reference was critical at first. At that time, I was especially concerned to refute Bourdieu's analyses in *La Distinction*, by emphasizing the subversive value of 'disinterest' for the worker, where Bourdieu saw only a supreme denegation of class realities. In *The Emancipated Spectator*, by contrast, I insisted upon the sense of the operation of subjectivation performed in descriptions, by recalling the fact that Gauny's text had appeared in June 1848 in a journal titled *The Workers' Warning Bell* (*Le Tocsin des travailleurs*), and that the separation of the disinterested aesthetic gaze from the workers' arms was the condition that made possible a 'voice of the workers'. The constitution of a specific 'aesthetic' sphere thus appears as an essential moment in the modern idea of equality. It is the place where the categories, classifications, oppositions and hierarchies, which inscribe the forms of domination within

the very structures of perception and sensory experience, are first questioned: form and matter, nature and culture, appearance and truth, activity
and passivity, the vulgar and the refined, work and leisure, play and serious
activity. I tried to show how this questioning, which defines the very idea of
a sphere of aesthetic experience, opened up three possible interpretations:
an interpretation, which brings together all of its possible effects inside an
autonomous sphere of art; a second, opposite interpretation which sees this
idea of aesthetic experience usher in the realization/abolition of art in the
creation of the forms of a new life-world; and, finally, a third interpretation,
which takes into account the phenomenon of aesthetic suspension and
understands it in terms of the dis-identification of social positions and the
reconfiguration of the spheres of experience. It would be possible to show
how 'work' is thus fragmented into three different figures. There is, first of
all, the exemplary nature of artist work, as separate from the everydayness
of work as social relation. In the nineteenth century, such an interpretation
– from Flaubert to Mallarmé to Rodin – privileges the heroic figure of the
artist as a model of a worker whose absolute demands contrast with the
proletarian work aiming merely for remuneration. In the twentieth century,
the same interpretation is present in more a subtle fashion in the modernist
vision that opposes the material (sensible) resisting texture of the autonomous artwork to the mercantile aestheticization of everyday life. Secondly,
there is, on the one hand, the opposite project attempting to establish an
identity between art practices and the production of objects; and on the
other hand, the forms of the life-world, a project at the heart of futurist and
constructivist avant-gardes of the young USSR. Thirdly and finally, taking
more diverse and less spectacular paths, there is the separation at the heart
of the working activity itself, and the discovery of new forms of life which
create a new life-world and working subjectivities different from the working and popular identities of the old order.

This is not the place to develop this analysis any further. I would just like to
point out in conclusion the tension which for me remains inherent in the
relation between aesthetics and politics. This tension relates less to the status
of work than to that of willed action. At the heart of aesthetic experience lies
the abolition of a whole set of oppositions that used to structure the sharing/
dividing of the sensible: activity/passivity, work/leisure, play/seriousness.
The old order was based on a rule that granted the same men the privileges
of gratuitous leisure and of true action that aims only for its own perfection.
Leisure, Aristotle said, is not a break between two periods of work; leisure is
the condition of those who are free from its constraints. And true action is
action that carries its end in itself, not the action that is a means for an exter-

nal end. Rousseau's *rêverie*, Kant's finality without end, Schiller's play impulse, all signal the abolition of this division of the world into two kinds of sensible humanity. And such abolition has practical counterparts in the forms of emancipation through which the workers declare themselves inhabitants of the same sensible world as the poets. This, however, means that emancipation at its heart entails the acquisition of the most precious of goods that the men of action had so far kept to themselves; that is, the power to do nothing and to want to do nothing. A few months after the popular revolution of July 1830, Stendhal's *Scarlet and Black* appeared in Paris. This is the story of a plebeian who has used all possible strategies to climb the social ladder and who discovers, while waiting for death in jail, the true secret of happiness, which is to do nothing and to no longer want anything. The lesson is not just valid for the individualistic artist; it is also true for the rise of the class of workers in the new society. The following year, the Saint-Simonians who had gone to recruit shock workers for their industrial armies only encounter dreamers who find nothing better to express their adherence to the new faith than this formula, by one of them: 'When I think about the beauties of Saint-Simonism, my hand stops. Some, like Sartre, have attributed the theme of the nothingness of action, developed by Flaubert's generation, to the reaction of a bourgeoisie terrified by the workers' insurrection of June 1848.[12] But the pleasure to do nothing, the pleasure to erase now the old separations between activity and passivity, between work and leisure, this was already at the heart of the assertion of the worker's reign. And we could interpret the Marxist theses about the necessity to wait for the development of the productive forces, as a necessary preamble to any revolutionary action, as a way still of translating in the terms of science and strategy this suspension at the heart of emancipatory practice. The function of these strategic theses is to hide the fundamental tension within emancipation between the promises of the reign of work, and the vertigo attached to the experience of leisure. It is clear also why such theses had to be accompanied by another thesis: the thesis which attributes the lateness of the movement to the illusions of the agents of production, and gives to science the task of correcting them endlessly. 'You shall only come out of the cave if you enter it first': that, in effect, is science's command to the emancipated workers. From that point on, it was obviously possible to put in place the theoretical mechanism (*le dispositif*) erasing the tension of work in an order of production that is both the truth principle and the principle of illusion. It is this very mechanism I encountered in Althusserianism and in the opposition between the scientific production of concepts and the illusions of the agents of production. It is this mechanism whose genealogy I have attempted to make.

Notes

Chapter 1

[1] Rancière, J. (2004), *The Politics of Aesthetics: The Distribution of the Sensible*. Trans. G. Rockhill, London: Continuum, p. 12. See also, Rancière, J. (1999), *Disagreement: Politics and Philosophy*. Trans. J. Rose, Minneapolis: University of Minnesota Press, pp. 124–125 and Rancière, J. (2000), *Le Partage du sensible: Esthétique et Politique*. Paris: La Fabrique éditions, p. 12.

[2] Rancière, J. (1991), *The Ignorant Schoolmaster: Five Lessons in Intellectual Emancipation*. Trans. K. Ross, Stanford: Stanford University Press, pp. 72–73.

[3] Ibid., p. 72. Emphasis added.

[4] Ibid., p. 136. See also the discussion regarding the necessary separation between intelligence and the will so that a 'pure relationship of will to will had been established between master and student: a relationship wherein the master's domination resulted in an entirely liberated relationship between the intelligence of the student and that of the book – the intelligence of the book that was also the thing in common, the egalitarian intellectual link between master and student', ibid., p. 13.

[5] Ibid., p. 72.

[6] Ibid., p. 136.

[7] Badiou argues that there is a 'correspondence, quite perceptible in all of Rancière's work, of a negative certainty and a suspense of the prescription, or of the conclusion. For him it is a question, at best, of fixing a peg, or a skilfully constructed paradox, on the general incline of premature conclusions. His books are neither conclusions nor directives, but *arrest clauses*.' Badiou, A. (2005), *Metapolitics*. Trans. J. Barker, London and New York: Verso, p. 111, his emphasis. See also Lachaud, Y. (1997), 'Les pauvres et leur philosophie', *Critique*, 601–602, pp. 421–445.

[8] Rancière, J. and Hallward, P. (2003), 'Politics and aesthetics: an interview', *Angelaki*, 8 (2), 191–211, p. 208.

[9] Rancière, *Ignorant Schoolmaster*, p. 73.

[10] Rancière and Hallward 'Politics and aesthetics: an interview', pp. 208–209. Cf. Rancière, J. (2005), 'L'héritage difficile de Michel Foucault', in J. Rancière, *Chroniques des temps consensuels*. Paris: Éditions du Seuil, 183–9, p. 189.

[11] See Rancière, 'Work, Identity, Subject', this volume.

[12] We are indebted to the excellent study by Renaud Pasquier on Rancière's 'politics of reading'. However, this study does not sufficiently highlight the practical, agentive aspect of Rancière's politics of reading, the way in which it mobilises a politics of writing. See Pasquier, R. (2004), 'Politiques de la lecture', *Labyrinthes*, 17 (1), 33–63.

[13] See Badiou, *Metapolitics*, for a critical discussion of this point: 'Rancière never refutes anyone for this would establish the master's authority. Refutation establishes heritage, succession. In the great anti-philosophical tradition, Rancière wants instead to discredit the master by showing that his position suggests representations whose arrangement is fallacious. And the fact that it is fallacious is established precisely through the local positions of the non-mastery of the dominated who contradict, at each and every moment, the guarantees of the master's existence.' p. 109.

[14] Rancière, J. (2004), *The Flesh of Words: The Politics of Writing*. Trans. C. Mandell, Stanford: Stanford University Press, p. 50. Translation amended.

[15] Ibid., p. 53. Translation amended.

[16] Here we can cite the central role of the 'sentence-image' and of the 'montage' metaphor in his later aesthetic writings. See, for instance, on the 'sentence-image', Rancière, J. (2007), *The Future of the Image*. Trans. G. Elliot, London: Verso, p. 45; and on the use of an extra-cinematic sense of 'montage' to discuss the function of jarring conjunctions that thereby bear meaning, ibid., p. 56.

[17] See Nicolas Bourriaud's response to Rancière's account of Bourriaud's relational aesthetics in Bourriaud, N. (2009), 'Precarious constructions: answer to Jacques Rancière on art and politics', *Open*, 17, 20–40.

[18] See Rancière, *The Future of the Image*, p. 38.

[19] See in particular Rancière, J. (1974), *La Leçon d'Althusser*. Paris: Gallimard, p. 132.

Chapter 2

[1] Perkins, V. F. (1993), *Film as Film: Understanding and Judging Movies*. New York: De Capo Press, p. 17; (first edition 1972).

[2] Ibid., pp. 12–13.

[3] Ibid., p. 24.

[4] I chose Wollen's essay because, apart from its sheer aptness, Godard's cinema matters to the history of cinema. For a useful analogous essay that takes the writings of Roland Barthes (Barthes, R. [1977], 'The third meaning: research notes on some Eisenstein stills', in trans. S. Heath, (ed.), *Image-Music-Text*. New York: Hill and Wang) and Stephen Heath (Heath, S. [1975], 'Film and system: terms of analysis part I', *Screen*, 16 [1], 7–77) as its point of departure, see Thompson, K. (1999), 'The concept of cinematic excess', in L. Braudy and M. Cohen (eds), *Film Theory and Criticism: Introductory Readings* (fifth edn). New York: Oxford University Press, pp. 487–98. The Wollen essay is most readily accessible at: Wollen, P. (1999), 'Godard and counter cinema: *vent d'est*', in L. Braudy and M. Cohen (eds), *Film Theory and Criticism: Introductory Readings* (fifth edn). New York: Oxford University Press, pp. 499–507. Although Wollen is theorizing Godard's practice, I will routinely treat the theory as Godard's own.

[5] Wollen, 'Godard and counter cinema', p. 499.

[6] Montage means to release the image from its immersion in narrative plenitude, bestowing on it the indigence and dignity of the fragment. However, this

oversimplifies the stakes: in its method of decomposition and recomposition montage still generates a narrative order, only now it is one in which the force of narration trumps narrative order, hence potentially emptying the image of whatever semantic independence it might have possessed. No matter how brilliant a montage arrangement is, in its distrust of the authority of the image it cannot avoid becoming an expression of subjectivity, a triumph of the will.

[7] Wollen, 'Godard and counter cinema', p. 500.

[8] Ibid., p. 499.

[9] Ibid., p. 500.

[10] Ibid., p. 506.

[11] Cavell, S. (1979), *The World Viewed, Enlarged Edition*. Cambridge, MA: Harvard University Press, p. 103 (italics removed).

[12] Montage was originally intended as a direct answer to this question.

[13] Wollen, 'Godard and counter cinema', p. 499.

[14] Some think that it is too easily available; a charge that can answered simply by acknowledging that Godard's critique of Hollywood, even if, as I think, significantly false, is not for all that empty or inappropriate. Cinephobia marks a site of disappointment, resentment and betrayal. We battle about the arts because they seem to possess a field of experience and claiming that is unintelligible from the perspective of their apparently marginal position in social reproduction, and their patent practical purposelessness. Rancière's conception of the politics of aesthetics as the shadow of the aesthetics of politics begins, at least, to explain that disorienting sense of art's form of significance.

[15] Adam Gies helpfully urged the clarification of the last three sentences on me.

[16] Rancière, J. (2004), *The Politics of Aesthetics: The Distribution of the Sensible*. Trans. G. Rockhill, New York: Continuum, p. 23.

[17] Rancière, J. (2009), *Aesthetics and its Discontents*. Trans. S. Corcoran, Malden, MA: Polity, pp. 30–31. As I will argue below, I take Rancière's gesture of reading the protocols of the aesthetic regime as primarily or fundamentally lodged against the norms of the representative regime to lead to a distortion and undermining of the critical force of the aesthetic regime.

[18] Ibid., p. 5.

[19] On several occasions, Rancière instances Hegel's defence of Dutch realist art in this regard. For example, see Rancière, J. (2007), *The Future of the Image*. Trans. G. Elliot, New York and London: Verso, pp. 76–7. See also Bernstein, J. M. (1997), 'Against voluptuous bodies: of satiation without happiness', *New Left Review*, I/225.

[20] Bois, Y. A. and Krauss, R. E. (1997), *Formless: A User's Guide*. New York: Zone Books, p. 15.

[21] Rancière, *Aesthetics and its Discontents*, p. 11.

[22] Rancière, *The Future of the Image*, pp. 13–14.

[23] Proust, M. (1932), *Remembrance of Things Past: Volume Two*. Trans. C. K. Scott Moncrieff, New York: Random House, p. 509.

[24] Goncourt, E. and Goncourt, J. (1981), *French Eighteenth-Century Painters*. Trans. R. Ironside, Oxford: Phaidon, p. 117, quoted in Rancière, *The Future of the Image*, p. 80.

[25] Rancière, *The Future of the Image*, p. 14; the thought is repeated in Rancière, J. (2006), *Film Fables*. Trans. E. Battista, Oxford: Berg, p. 8.

[26] Rancière, *The Politics of Aesthetics*, p. 24; italics mine – JMB.

[27] Hunt, L. (2007), *Inventing Human Rights*. New York: Norton, Chp. 1.

[28] Rancière, *Film Fables*, p. 1.

[29] Ibid., p. 2

[30] Bazin, A. (1967), 'The ontology of the photographic image', in *What is Cinema? Vol. 1*. Trans. H. Gray, Berkeley: University of California Press, p. 13.

[31] Rancière, *The Politics of Aesthetics*, p. 23.

[32] Bazin, 'The ontology of the photographic image', p. 15.

[33] Rancière, *Film Fables*, p. 3.

[34] Ibid., p. 10.

[35] Ibid., p. 11.

[36] Ibid.

[37] Ibid., p. 58.

[38] Rancière, *The Politics of Aesthetics*, pp. 38–9; first italics mine – JMB.

[39] Rancière, *Film Fables*, p. 58.

[40] Henrich, D. (1992), *Aesthetic Judgement and the Moral Image of the World: Studies in Kant*. Stanford, CA: Stanford University Press.

[41] Wood, M. (1989), *America in the Movies*. New York: Columbia University Press, p. 128.

[42] In Bratu Hansen, M. (1997), 'Introduction', in S. Kracauer, *Theory of Film: The Redemption of Physical Reality*. Princeton: Princeton University Press. Miriam Bratu Hansen argues that Kracauer 'understood cinema as an alternative public sphere – alternative to both bourgeois institutions of art, education, and culture and the traditional arenas of politics – a discursive horizon through which, however compromised, something like an actual democratization of culture seems to be taking shape' (p. xi). The conversation between Kracauer and Rancière over cinema and democratization, which Rancière locates more profoundly in the novel, is one for another occasion.

[43] In stating the matter this way, I am following the lead of Kristin Thompson; see Thompson, 'The concept of cinematic excess', op. cit.

[44] This is why the 'Indian' question continues to gnaw at American consciousness, and why, furthermore, the incremental shift from the image of 'the melting pot' to that of the 'salad bowl' comes to mark a significant shift in the nature of the experiment.

[45] Marrati, P. (2008), 'A lost everyday: Deleuze and Cavell on Hollywood', in P. Marrati, *Gilles Deleuze: Cinema and Philosophy*. Trans. A. Hartz, Baltimore: The Johns Hopkins University Press, p. 102. Marrati's compelling Appendix is the antecedent to this section of my essay. Her Deleuze is strongly proximate – for whom cinematographic realism possesses two defining features: milieus (*environments*) and behaviors – to my Rancière.

[46] Rancière, *Film Fables*, p. 122.

[47] Sontag, S. (2001), 'A century of cinema', in S. Sontag, *Where the Stress Falls: Essays*. New York: Farrar, Straus and Giroux, p. 118.

Chapter 3

[1] I would like to thank Alison Ross, Mick Carter and Toni Ross for their comments on earlier drafts of this essay, and Genevieve Duche for her work translating the dialogue and voice-over of *Histoire(s)*.

[2] Godard, J. L. (1988–1998), *Histoire(s) du cinema*. Gaumont.

[3] Rancière, J. (2006), *Film Fables*. Trans. E. Battista, Oxford: Berg; Rancière, J. (2007), *The Future of the Image*. Trans. G. Elliot, London: Verso.

[4] Rosenbaum, J. (2009), 'Trailer for Godard's *Histoire(s) du Cinéma*', (accessed 17 February 2011) http://www.jonathanrosenbaum.com/?p = 15760 (revised January 2009). Originally published (1997) in *Trafic*, 21, Printemps.

[5] Rancière, 'Prologue', *Film Fables*, p. 5.

[6] Chapter 1(a) 'Toutes les histoires' ['All the (Hi)stories'] (1988), 51 minutes; Chapter 1(b) 'Une Histoire seule' ['A Single (Hi)story'] (1989), 42 minutes; Chapter 2(a) 'Seul le cinéma' ['Only Cinema'] (1997), 26 minutes; Chapter 2(b) 'Fatale beauté' ['Deadly Beauty'] (1997), 28 minutes; Chapter 3(a) 'La Monnaie de l'absolu' ['The coin of the Absolute'] (1998), 27 minutes; Chapter 3(b) 'Une Vague Nouvelle' ['A New Wave'] (1998), 27 minutes; Chapter 4(a) 'Le Contrôle de l'univers' ['The Control of the Universe'] (1998), 27 minutes; Chapter 4(b) 'Les Signes parmi nous' ['The Signs Amoung Us'] (1998), 38 minutes. Regarding Chapter 3(a), the title recalls Malraux, A. (c.1949), *Psychologie d'art: La Monnaie de l'absolu*. Paris: Albert Skira.

[7] Godard, J. L. and Ishaghpour, Y. (2005), *Cinema: The Archaeology of Film and the Memory of a Century*. Trans. J. Howe, Oxford and New York: Berg, p. 78.

[8] Ibid., p. 5.

[9] Godard and Ishaghpour, *Cinema*.

[10] Guy Debord describes the situationist practice of the *dérive* as a 'technique of rapid passage through varied ambiences'. While the *dérive* is not unlike a conventional stroll in engaging the curiosity of the disinterested yet active spectator, this disposition is mandatory in the case of the *dériviste*, who abandons the trappings of her everyday existence (work, leisure, relationships) in order to open up to the dynamic interactivity of her immediate environs. The psychogeographical research of the *dériviste* involves observance of the way that microclimates, contours and currents, fixed points and vortexes, neighbourhood identities, centres of administration, and so on encourage and discourage admissions and discharges from particular spaces. Debord, G. (2006), 'Theory of the dérive,' in K. Knabb (ed. and trans.), *Situationist International Anthology* (revised edn). Berkeley: Bureau of Public Secrets. First published in France as Debord, G. (1958), 'Théorie de la dérive', *Internationale Situationniste*, 2 (December). Rancière has also observed the similarity between the nature of displacement in Godard's practice of producing films comprised of collages of heterogeneous elements and the *dérive*. Rancière, *The Future of the Image*, pp. 61, 63.

[11] Rancière, 'A fable without a moral: Godard, cinema, (hi)stories', *Film Fables*, p. 180.

[12] Ibid., pp. 171–187.

[13] Rancière, J. (2004), *The Politics of Aesthetics: The Distribution of the Sensible*. Trans. G. Rockhill, London: Continuum, p. 13.

[14] Ibid., p. 85

[15] Ibid., pp. 20–21.

[16] Ibid., p. 21.

[17] Ibid., Rancière's emphasis.

[18] Rancière says: "The representative primacy of action over characters or of narration over description, the hierarchy of genres according to the dignity of their subject matter, and the very primacy of the art of speaking, of speech in actuality, all of these elements figure into an analogy with a fully hierarchical vision of the community" (Ibid., p. 22).

[19] Rancière, *The Future of the Image*, p. 38.

[20] Ibid., p. 39.

[21] Ibid., p. 23.

[22] The aesthetic is also a *realm* upon which distributions of the sensible impact. The aesthetic realm encompasses aesthetic practices that Rancière describes as 'forms of visibility that disclose artistic practices, the place they occupy, what they "do" or "make" from the standpoint of what is common to the community'. Rancière, *The Politics of Aesthetics*, p. 13.

[23] Ibid., p. 81.

[24] Rancière, *The Future of the Image*, p. 39.

[25] Rancière, 'Prologue: A thwarted fable', *Film Fables*, p. 2.

[26] Ibid., my emphasis.

[27] Ibid., pp. 4–5

[28] Ibid., p. 5.

[29] Ibid.

[30] Ibid., p. 6.

[31] Ibid., p. 4.

[32] Ibid., p. 15.

[33] Ibid., p. 19.

[34] Rancière shows other connections that Godard makes between cinema and the pictorial tradition by discussing how the work articulates with the painting of Cezanne, Rembrandt and Giotto and the art theory of Élie Faure.

[35] Rancière, 'A fable without a moral', *Film Fables*, p. 179.

[36] Ibid., p. 174.

[37] Rancière, *The Future of the Image*, p. 38.

[38] Rancière, 'Prologue', *Film Fables*, pp. 8, 2.

[39] Rancière, 'A fable without a moral', *Film Fables*, p. 175.

[40] Ibid.

[41] In his second engagement with *Histoire(s)*, Rancière's argument suggests that images such as these will be understood as operations of a dialectical montage.

[42] Rancière, 'A fable without a moral', *Film Fables*, p. 181.

[43] Ibid.

[44] Here he simply contrasts the metamorphic poetics of pure presence that derive from associative and interexpressive relationships, which he calls 'anti-montage' and 'fusional montage', with the poetics of metaphorical montage whose

dialogical power is that of association and metaphor (ibid., pp. 178–181). And when he analyses metaphorical montage he stresses the 'rigorous connection' between images (ibid., p. 183).

[45] Rancière, 'Prologue', *Film Fables*, p. 8.

[46] Rancière, 'A fable without a moral', *Film Fables*, p. 183.

[47] Ibid., p. 186.

[48] Godard, J. L. (1956), 'Montage, mon beau souci', *Cahiers du cinéma* 65, 30–31. The essay was republished in English as Godard, J. L. (1986) 'Montage my fine care,' in T. Milne (ed.), *Godard on Godard*. Trans. T. Milne, Cambridge, MA: Da Capo Press. pp. 31–41.

[49] Benjamin, W. (1972), 'A short history of photography', *Screen*, 13 (Spring), 5–26, p. 7 (first published 1931).

[50] Bazin, A. (1967), 'The ontology of the photographic image', in *What is Cinema?* Vol. 1. Trans. H. Gray, Berkeley: University of California Press, p. 15.

[51] Ibid., p. 13.

[52] Cavell, S. (1971) *The World Viewed*. Cambridge: Harvard University Press, p. 23.

[53] Godard, 'Montage, mon beau souci', pp. 30–31.

[54] See Hedges, I. (1993), 'Jean-Luc Godard's *Hail Mary*: Cinema's "Virgin Birth"', in C. Warren and M. Locke (eds), *Jean-Luc Godard's Hail Mary: Women and the Sacred in Film*. Carbondale and Edwardsville: Southern Illinois University Press, pp. 61–66.

[55] He explains how direction/*mise en scène* involves foreseeing in space while montage is a temporal foreseeing, in other words, a clairvoyance: '[s]uppose you notice a young girl in the street who attracts you. You hesitate to follow her. A quarter of a second. How to convey this hesitation? *Mise en scène* will answer the question "How shall I approach her?" But in order to render explicit the other question, "Am I going to love her?", you are forced to bestow importance on the quarter of a second during which the two questions are born'. Godard, 'Montage my fine care', p. 39.

[56] In the English translation of Godard's essay, montage, rather than *mise en scène*, expresses 'the life of an idea or its sudden emergence in the course of a story' whenever 'within a shot when a shock effect demands to take the place of an arabesque, each time between one scene and another when the inner continuity of the film enjoins with a change of shot the superimposition of the description of a character on that of the plot'. Godard, 'Montage my fine care', p. 39. In 'Montage, mon beau souci' it reads 'Quand? Sans jeu de mot, chaque fois que la situation l'exige, qu'à l'intérieur du plan un effet de choc demande à prendre la place d'une arabesque, que d'une scène à l'autre la continuité profonde du film impose avec le changement de plan de superposer la description d'un caractère à celle de l'intrigue' (p. 30). Perhaps a better translation would be: 'When? Each time that the situation requires it, when within a shot a shock effect claims the place of ornamental style, when from one scene to another the deep continuity of the film imposed with the change of shot superimposes the description of a character on to the description of the plot'.

[57] Godard, 'Montage my fine care', p. 39.

[58] Ibid. At the outset of this essay Godard not only places *mise en scène* and montage in opposition to each other, but also directing and editing: 'If direction is a look, montage is a heart-beat. To foresee is the characteristic of both: but what one seeks to foresee is space, the other seeks in time'.

59 'It is, in effect to bring out the soul under the spirit, the passion behind the intrigue, to make the heart prevail over the intelligence by destroying the notion of space in favour of that of time'. Ibid.

60 Lacan, J. (1979) *The Four Fundamental Concepts of Psycho-Analysis.* J. A. Miller (ed.), Trans. A. Sheridan, Harmondsworth: Penguin Books, pp. 73–74.

61 Perhaps this accounts for Godard's emphasis on the technological specificity of the cinematograph, wherein a single machine (the camera) does not see what it gives to be seen (by means of the projector).

62 In this regard, Rancière notes in the 'Prologue': 'Cinema, in the double power of the conscious eye of the director and the unconscious eye of the camera, is the perfect embodiment of Schelling's and Hegel's argument that the identity of conscious and unconscious is the very principle of art'. *Film Fables*, p. 9.

63 Rancière, 'A fable without a moral', p. 179, Rancière's emphasis.

64 Ibid., p. 175.

65 Ibid.

66 Ibid., p. 178.

67 Ibid., p. 179.

68 It is accounted for in his mention of Schlegel's 'progressive universal poetry": a poetry of metamorphosis that not only transforms the elements of ancient poems into fragments that can be combined into new poems, but also ensures that the speeches and images of art are interchangeable with the speeches and images of common experience'. Ibid., p. 178.

69 Rancière, *The Future of the Image*, p. 48.

70 He is also contemplating the significance of an art exhibition entitled *Sans commune mesure* held in three different art institutions in France in 2002 and curated by Régis Durand.

71 Rancière, *The Future of the Image*, p. 39.

72 Ibid., pp. 37–38.

73 Ibid., p. 55.

74 Ibid., p. 56.

75 Ibid., p. 57.

76 Ibid.

77 Huret, J. (1994) 'Interview with Stéphane Mallarmé (1891)', in H. Dorra (ed.), *Symbolist Art Theories: A Critical Anthology*. Berkeley: University of California Press, p. 141.

78 Rancière, *The Future of the Image*, p. 56.

79 Ibid., p. 57.

80 Ibid., p. 62.

81 Ibid., p. 67.

Chapter 4

1 I would like to thank Alison Ross and Todd May for their helpful comments on the paper.

2 Rancière, J. (1994), *The Names of History: On the Poetics of Knowledge*. Trans. H. Melehy, Minneapolis: University of Minnesota Press, pp. 9, 41. Originally

published as Rancière, J. (1992), *Les Noms de l'histoire: Essai de poétique du savoir.*
Paris: Seuil, pp. 23–24, 88. The book remains Rancière's major contribution to
the philosophy of history. Ever since, reaching across social and political theory to
literature, Rancière has provided an account of a redistribution of social justice,
which, however, neither supersedes nor denies but further elaborates thoughts
which are central to *The Names of History.* For this reason, in what follows I will be
referring to and discussing mostly this work.

[3] See, for example: Febvre, L. (1943), 'Parole, matière première de l'histoire',
Annales d'histoire sociale, 15, 89–91, p. 91; Braudel, F. (1958) 'Histoire et sciences
sociales: la longue durée.' *Annales E.S.C.,* 13 (4), 725–753, (reprinted in: F. Braudel [1969], *Écrits sur l'histoire.* Paris: Flammarion, pp. 41–83).

[4] Le Roy Ladurie, E. (1975), *Montaillou, village Occitan: de 1294 à 1324.* Paris: Gallimard. This includes a detailed history of local habits, institutions and families.

[5] Nora, P. (ed.) (1996–1998), *Realms of Memory* (3 vols.). Trans. A. Goldhammer,
L. D. Kritzman (ed.), New York: Columbia University Press.

[6] Rancière, *The Names of History,* p. 7

[7] Rancière, *The Names of History,* pp. 6–7, 66–67, 76, 88, et passim.

[8] Ibid., 41

[9] Ibid., pp. 42–60; Rancière, *Les Noms de l'histoire,* pp. 89–124.

[10] Rancière, *The Names of History,* p. 42 sqq.

[11] Barthes, R. (1995), *Michelet.* Paris: Seuil (first edition 1954).

[12] Rancière, *The Names of History,* p. 43.

[13] France 'n'aura jamais qu'un seul nom, inexplicable, et qui est son vrai nom
éternel: la Révolution.' Michelet, J. (1846), 'Préface', *Le Peuple.* p. xxxv. Cited in
R. Barthes, *Michelet,* p. 63.

[14] Another example of the Michelet Romanticism as subject-, literature- and pro-
gression-oriented: 'We progress from one ideal to a more complex ideal ... also
in individual existence: I pass from my individual self to my literary self, which
intensifies the world as beauty, then to my moral self, which absorbs the world as
benevolence, so that it may purify itself through resignation.' Michelet, J. (1984),
Mother Death: The Journal of Jules Michelet, 1815–1850. Trans. E. K. Kaplan (ed.),
Amherst: The University of Massachusetts Press, p. 58.

[15] Rancière, *The Names of History,* p. 43.

[16] Ibid., p.51.

[17] Michelet, J. (1861), *La Mer.* II 2, p. 111. Cited in R. Barthes, *Michelet,* p. 37.

[18] Michelet, J. (1967), *History of the French Revolution.* In G. Wright (ed.), trans.
C. Cocks, Chicago: The University of Chicago Press, p. 80 (31 January 1847).
Cf. Michelet's description of the Père-Lachaise cemetery: 'Those leafless trees,
the white stones that rise up on all sides, everything seemed bare to me, sad
and harsh, despite the softening hues of a half-shadow.' Michelet, *Mother Death,*
p. 61.

[19] Rancière, *The Names of History,* pp. 98–99.

[20] Ibid., p. 57.

[21] Ibid., p. 58.

[22] Barthes, *Michelet,* p. 66.

[23] Rancière, *The Names of History,* p. 48; cf. p. 99.

[24] Ibid., p. 41.

[25] Braudel, F. (1976), *The Mediterranean and the Mediterranean World in the Age of Philip II* (Vols. I–II). Trans. S. Reynolds, New York: Harper & Row, pp. 1234–1237. In French, Braudel, F. (1949), *La Méditerranée et le mondeméditerranéen à l'époque de Philippe II*. Paris: Colin (Revised edn 1966). The king's death 'was not a great event in Mediterranean history', because a historian for Braudel should reflect on 'the distance separating biographical history from the history of structures, and even more from the history of geographical areas'. Braudel, *The Mediterranean*, p. 1237.

[26] Rancière, *The Names of History*, p. 10; Rancière, *Les Noms de l'histoire*, p. 25.

[27] Rancière, *The Names of History*, p. 11; Rancière, *Les Noms de l'histoire*, p. 27.

[28] See: Kantorowicz, E. H. (1997), *The King's Two Bodies: A Study in Medieval Political Theology*. Princeton: Princeton University Press, p. 13, et passim; (First published 1957).

[29] Rancière, *The Names of History*, p. 24.

[30] Ibid., p. 12, cf. p. 16.

[31] Ibid., p. 86.

[32] Ibid., p. 87.

[33] See Confucius (2003), *Analects, with Selections from Traditional Commentaries*. Trans. E. Slingerland, Indianapolis: Hackett.

[34] Rancière, *The Names of History*, p. 19.

[35] Ibid., pp. 22–23; Rancière, *Les Noms de l'histoire*, pp. 50–52.

[36] Rancière, *The Names of History*, p. 42.

[37] Ibid., p. 23.

[38] Ibid., p. 88; Rancière, *Les Noms de l'histoire*, p. 177.

[39] Rancière, *The Names of History*, p. 90.

[40] Ibid., p. 91; Rancière, *Les Noms de l'histoire*, p. 183

[41] Rancière, *The Names of History*, p. 17.

[42] Ibid., p. 22; Rancière, *Les Noms de l'histoire*, p. 49.

[43] Rancière, *The Names of History*, p. 76.

[44] Ibid., pp. 81–82; Braudel, 'Histoire et sciences sociales'.

[45] Rancière, J. (2003), *The Philosopher and His Poor*. Trans. J. Drury, C. Oyster, A. Parker (ed.), Durham: Duke University Press, p. 93; originally published as: Rancière, J. (1983) *Le Philosophe et ses Pauvres*. Paris: Fayard.

[46] Rancière, *The Names of History*, p. 63.

[47] Ibid., p. 46; Rancière, *Les Noms de l'histoire*, p. 97.

[48] Barthes. *Michelet*, p. 65: 'Les racines de la vérité historique, ce sont les documents comme voix, non comme témoins.'

[49] Rancière. *The Philosopher and His Poor*, p. 74.

[50] Rancière, *The Names of History*, pp. 25–30.

[51] *Annals* I, 16–18, see Tacitus (1931), *Histories, Books 4–5. Annals, Books 1–3*. Trans. C. H. Moore and J. Jackson, Cambridge (Mass.) London: Harvard University Press.

[52] Rancière, *The Names of History*, p. 28.

[53] According to Rancière, this is what Babel does in telling the story of the *Red Cavalry*; Rancière, *The Names of History*, pp. 52–53. However, Babel uses the modernistic technique of writing in order to suspend and supersede both the 'illiterate' and 'literate' ways of those who speak around and during the revolutionary event. Lev Lunts uses similar devices to redescribe the Exodus in his 'In the

Desert'. See Lunts, L. (1998), 'In the Desert [V pustyne]', In *The Serapion Brothers: Anthology*. Moscow: Shkola-Press, pp. 399–404.

[54] Collingwood, R. G. (1994), *The Idea of History: With Lectures 1926–1928* (revised edn). W. J. Van Der Dussen (ed.), Oxford: Oxford University Press, p. 205 sqq.

[55] Rancière, *The Names of History*, p. 46.

[56] Ibid., p. 100.

[57] Ibid., p. 92; Rancière, *Les Noms de l'histoire*, p. 185.

[58] Jonas, H. (1984), *The Imperative of Responsibility: In Search of an Ethics for the Technological Age*. Trans. H. Jonas with D. Herr, Chicago: The University of Chicago Press.

[59] See: Rancière, J. (1995), *On the Shores of Politics*. Trans. L. Heron, London: Verso, pp. 63–92. Originally published as: Rancière, J. (1992), *Aux Bords du Politique*. Paris: Osiris. ('The Community of Equals'). The non-exclusive universal community of the equals is suspected to be a 'great all-devouring Whole'; Rancière, *On the Shores of Politics*, p. 65.

[60] Rancière, *The Names of History*, p. 63; Rancière, *Les Noms de l'histoire*, p. 129.

[61] Rancière, *The Names of History*, p. 91.

[62] Ibid., p. 8.

White, H. (1994), 'Foreword', in J. Rancière. *The Names of History*, p. xii.

[64] Rancière, *The Names of History*, p. 52.

[65] Rancière, J. (2007), *Politique de la littérature*. Paris: Galilée, p. 88.

[66] Rancière, *The Names of History*, p. 101.

[67] Ibid., p. 89; Rancière, *Les Noms de l'histoire*, p. 180. Thus, the main question for Rancière is to define historicity (une historicité) with reference to 'the possibility that subjects in general would make a history – and of the forms of writing that account for them by inscribing them in the genre of a narrative and the figure of truth'; Rancière, *The Names of History*, p. 98; Rancière, *Les Noms de l'histoire*, p. 198.

[68] Rancière, *The Names of History*, p. 101; Rancière, *Les Noms de l'histoire*, pp. 203–204.

[69] Rancière, *The Names of History*, p. 90.

[70] Ibid., p. 56; Rancière, *Les Noms de l'histoire*, p. 117.

[71] Scholles, R. (1974), *Structuralism in Literature: An Introduction*. New Haven and London: Yale University Press, p. 47.

[72] See: Propp, V. (1968), *Morphology of the Folk Tale*. L. A. Wagner (ed.), trans. L. Scott, Austin: University of Texas Press.

[73] Jakobson, R. (1980), 'Two aspects of language and two types of aphasic disturbances', in R. Jakobson and M. Halle, *Fundamentals of Language*. The Hague: Mouton, pp. 90–96; (First published 1956) ('The metaphoric and metonymic poles').

[74] Rancière, *The Names of History*, pp. 56, 99.

[75] Ibid., pp. 99–100.

[76] Aristotle, 'Poetics 1451a19; 1455b15–16; 1456a12; 1459b26–28'. See Kassel, R. (ed.) (1965), *Aristotlis de arte poetica liber*. Oxford: Clarendon.

[77] The convenient beginnings and endings to Homer are added by later poets (e.g. in the *Cypria*). See: Bernabé, B. (ed.) (1987), *Poetae et epici Graeci. Testimonia et fragmenta. Pars I*. Leipzig: Teubner, pp. 36–64; and also: West, M. L. (ed.) (2003),

Greek Epic Fragments: From the Seventh to the Fifth Centuries B.C. Trans. M. L. West, Cambridge, Mass.: Harvard University Press.

[78] Jacoby, F. (1956), 'Hekataios', in F. Jacoby, *Griechische Historiker*. Stuttgart: Alfred Druckenmüller Verlag, pp. 185–237. Cf. Aelian (1866), *Claudii Aeliani Varia Historia* (Vol. II). R. Hercher (ed.), Leipzig: Teubner, XIII, 20; Cicero (1928), *De re publica. De legibus* [*On the Republic. On the Laws*]. Trans. C. W. Keyes, Cambridge (Mass.) London: Harvard University Press, I, 1, 5. Of Hecataeus' two major works, *Periēgēsis* and *Genealogiai*, around 400 fragments are preserved. See: Hecataeus (1954), *Hecatei Milesii Fragmenta*. G. Nenci (ed.), Firenze: La Nuova Italia.

[79] Rancière, *The Names of History*, p. 47.

[80] Ibid., p. 96; Rancière, *Les Noms de l'histoire*, p. 193.

[81] Rancière, *The Names of History*, p. 86.

[82] For a comparison of literary and historical discourses, see: Todorov, T. (1981), 'Les catégories du récit litteraire', in *L'Analyse structurale du récit*. Paris: Seuil, 131–157, esp. pp. 134–138.

[83] Nikulin, D. (2008), 'Memory and history', *Idealistic Studies*, 38 (1/2), 75–90.

Chapter 5

[1] In *The Names of History*, Rancière identifies the distinctive voice of the conditional that underpins the history of Michelet. Michelet uses the conditional to give his images of the silent, mute subjects of history a logical structure: 'The only one who speaks is *the only one who would be able to speak*. The silent voice of the conditional is that which can come back to us only through the tombstone or the cries of the rocks: a voice without paper, a meaning indelibly inscribed in things, which one may read, which one *would be able* to read endlessly in the materiality of the objects of everyday life.' Rancière, J. (1994), *The Names of History: On the Poetics of Knowledge*. Trans. H. Melehy, Minneapolis: University of Minnesota Press, p. 57, his emphasis.

[2] One of the important features of Hegel's position on Romanticism is the explanation it provides of the lessening function of beauty as a criterion of fine art in the modern world. This situation arises for Hegel once art is no longer a venue for the presentation of the Absolute. In contrast, Rancière attempts to describe a pincer movement in which the loss of representation as a cogent normative practice of value able to determine topic and technique, on one side, together with an expansion of the field of aesthetic relevance itself on the other, show art to be a porous category. I have discussed this topic in more detail in Ross, A. (2007), 'The aesthetic anomaly: art, politics and criticism in recent European philosophy (from Adorno to Rancière)', *Theory@buffalo*, http://wings.buffalo.edu/theory/archive/t@b11.html, 11, 97–121.

[3] This is the position that Rancière outlines in his paper: Rancière, J. (2002), 'The aesthetic revolution and its outcomes: emplotments of autonomy and heteronomy', *New Left Review*, 14 (March/April), 133–151.

[4] See, for instance, the discussion in Rancière, J. (2007), *The Future of the Image*. Trans. G. Elliot, London: Verso, p. 89, which disputes the 'nihilistic' interpretation of Hegel's thesis regarding the 'end of art'.

[5] See J. M. Bernstein's 'Movies as the great democratic art form of the modern world (notes on Rancière)', this collection; see also, for a recent discussion of Hegel, Rancière, J. (2010), 'The aesthetic heterotopia', *Philosophy Today*, 54, pp. 15–25

[6] Hegel, G. W. F. (1993), *Introductory Lectures on Aesthetics*. Trans. B. Bosanquet and M. Inwood (ed.), London: Penguin, pp. 92–3.

[7] As Heidegger comments: 'Hegel never wished to deny the possibility that also in the future individual works of art would originate and be esteemed. The fact of such individual works, which exist as works only for the enjoyment of a few sectors of the population, does not speak against Hegel but for him. It is proof that art has lost its power to be the absolute, has lost its absolute power. On the basis of such loss the position of art and the kind of knowledge concerning it are defined for the nineteenth century'. Heidegger, M. (1981), *Nietzsche: Volume 1, 'The Will to Power as Art'*. Trans. D. Farrell Krell, London: Routledge, p. 85.

[8] Hegel, *Introductory Lectures on Aesthetics*, p. 96. This description of poetry provides a condensed version of Hegel's story of Spirit as the search for a ground in external material, until the inadequacy of such grounding leads to the self-grounding of spirit, which as self-grounding no longer needs the mediation of material forms. See Hegel, G. W. F. (1998), *Aesthetics: Lectures on Fine Art* (Volume 1). Trans. T. M. Knox, Oxford: Clarendon Press, especially pp. 79–81 and pp. 100–105.

[9] Hegel, *Aesthetics: Lectures on Fine Art*, pp. 594–5. The vocabulary of the unhappy consciousness belongs more straightforwardly to his discussion of symbolic art. Rancière praises the way that Hegel identifies the perpetual time lag between ways of life and their identification as 'art': 'Art lives so long as it expresses a thought unclear to itself in a matter that resists it. It lives inasmuch as it is something else than art, that is a belief and a way of life'. Rancière, 'The aesthetic revolution and its outcomes', pp. 133–151, 141. See also his approving comments on Hegel's before the fact riposte to the purism of modernism in Rancière, *The Future of the Image*, p. 89. It is from Hegel that the terms of the modernist debate regarding the exploration of the potential of material media and techniques are derived. The question of media and techniques arises once the purpose of art as the presentation of the absolute is lost. Rancière argues that Hegel's position is in fact at odds with modernist dogma. In keeping with the central place that 'words' have in his thinking, he points out that the modernist framing of art is a description in words. It does not make sense to reduce painting, for instance, to pigment on a surface. The surface of the image does not fit the purism of modernism because the image 'is not wordless, [it] is not without "interpretations" that pictorialize it ... When the surface is no longer split in two, when it is nothing more than a site for the projection of pigments, Hegel taught, there is no longer any art' (Rancière, *The Future of the Image*, p. 89). The life of art requires that art be something other than art. On the other hand, it is precisely this position that renders Hegel's 'spirit of forms' an inverted image of the aesthetic revolution: Hegel cancels the promise of the aesthetic revolution for a new life because he attempts to contain what Rancière views as the general features of aesthetic experience within artworks alone. It is clear that art is something other than art for Rancière because of the essential role that 'words' play not just in poeticizing the prosaic in literature, but in describing constellations of meaning in cinema and

painting. There are a number of problems that this focus on words introduces for Rancière's discussion of cinema. I have discussed some of them in Ross, A. (2009), 'The aesthetic fable: cinema in Jacques Rancière's "Aesthetic Politics"', *SubStance*, 38 (1), 128–151.

[10] Rancière, J. (2004), *The Flesh of Words: The Politics of Writing*. Trans. C. Mandell, Stanford: Stanford University Press, p. 5. Incidentally, this is the post-Kantian Idealist and Romantic legacy which Rancière also detects in Badiou: 'the Platonism of the aesthetic age ... lets the Idea come forth as passage within the sensible and lets art be its witness. It depends on the aesthetic identification of the Idea with the double difference that obtains both between thought and itself and between the sensible and itself, one which determines the passage of the Infinite within the finite'. Rancière, J. (2004), 'Aesthetics, inaesthetics, anti-aesthetics', in P. Hallward (ed.), *Think Again: Alain Badiou and the Future of Philosophy*. London: Continuum, p. 223.

[11] Rancière discusses Hegel's aesthetics in some detail in Rancière, J. (1998), *La Parole muette, Essai sur les contradictions de la littérature*. Paris: Hachette Littératures, pp. 62–69; and Rancière, J. (2001), *L'Inconscient esthétique*. Paris: Galilée, pp. 63–5. The latter book also discusses succinctly what is involved in the idea of 'mute speech', pp 33–43.

[12] Rancière, *The Future of the Image*, p. 89.

[13] Rancière, 'The aesthetic revolution and its outcomes', p. 137.

[14] Rancière, 'The aesthetic heterotopia', p. 24.

[15] Rancière, 'The aesthetic revolution and its outcomes', p. 142.

[16] He writes: '...the word Aesthetics, taken literally, is not wholly satisfactory, since "Aesthetics" means, more precisely, the science of sensation, of feeling ... We will ... let the word "Aesthetics" stand; as a mere name it is a matter of indifference to us, and besides it has meanwhile passed over into common speech. As a name then it may be retained, but the proper expression for our science is *Philosophy of Art* and, more definitely, *Philosophy of Fine Art*.' Hegel, *Aesthetics: Lectures on Fine Art*, p. 1.

[17] See, on this point, Jacques Rancière's *La Parole muette* and *The Flesh of Words*. This position draws on the ambiguity of Plato's position in which the book is 'at once silent and too loquacious' (Rancière, J. [1991], *The Ignorant Schoolmaster: Five Lessons in Intellectual Emancipation*. Trans. K. Ross, Stanford: Stanford University Press, p. 38). In his *Phaedrus* Plato compares the 'solemn silence' of writing to the mute presence of a 'painting'. In the same breath he objects to the way that 'once it is written, every composition trundles about everywhere in the same way, in the presence both of those who know about the subject and of those who have nothing at all to do with it', and he insists that this democracy of the written word requires 'its father to help it; for it is incapable of either defending or helping itself'; see Plato, (2005) *Phaedrus*. Trans. C. Rowe, London: Penguin, p. 63, 275d1-e5. See Rancière's discussion of the innovation that occurs when the communication between the master and student is not mediated by a master-explicator but instead falls on the common link of the book: the book is that 'egalitarian link between master and student' (Rancière, *The Ignorant Schoolmaster*, p. 13).

[18] See Rancière's discussion of this point in Rancière, J. (2008), 'Why Emma Bovary had to be killed', *Critical Inquiry*, 34 (2), pp. 233–248.

19 Rancière, 'Why Emma Bovary had to be killed', p. 242.

20 Rancière, *The Flesh of Words*, p. 153.

21 Rancière, J. (1999), *Disagreement: Politics and Philosophy*. Trans. J. Rose. Minneapolis: University of Minnesota Press, p. 60.

22 This version of Rancière's reformulation of Aristotle occurs in Rancière, J. (2004), *The Politics of Aesthetics: The Distribution of the Sensible*. Trans. G. Rockhill, London: Continuum, p. 39. It is significant that the formulation he gives of this position in *Disagreement: Politics and Philosophy*, qualifies that it is '*modern* man' who is 'a political animal because he is a literary animal' (my emphasis). Rancière, *Disagreement: Politics and Philosophy*, p. 37. It should also be noted that this reformulation recalls Michel Foucault's statement in the first volume of his *History of Sexuality*: 'For millennia, man remained what he was for Aristotle: a living animal with the additional capacity for a political existence; modern man is an animal whose politics places his existence as a living being in question'. Foucault, M. (1990), *The History of Sexuality: An Introduction* (Volume 1). Trans. R. Hurley, New York: Vintage Books, p. 143. See my comments on Foucault in the conclusion to this paper.

23 The 'singular relationship between literature, philosophy and politics' involves this promise of passage between 'words' and 'worlds'. Deleuze, for instance, sees words opening the door of 'a people still to come'; Rancière, *The Flesh of Words*, p. 4.

24 The reference to the 'account' made of speech occurs in Rancière, *Disagreement: Politics and Philosophy*, in particular, pp. 22–23, 40 and 82.

25 In Rancière, J. (2004), 'The politics of literature', *SubStance*, 33 (1), 10–24, he writes: 'so-called interpretations are political to the extent that they are reconfigurations of the visibility of a common world', p. 23.

26 Rancière, *The Politics of Aesthetics*, p. 65.

27 In her introduction to her translation of *The Ignorant Schoolmaster*, Kristin Ross presents Rancière's narrating of Jacotot's discovery of the 'equality of intelligences', after Jacotot's own use of the story device, as 'one of the concrete acts or practices that verifies equality'. This is because 'storytelling' is 'an act that presumes in its interlocutor an equality of intelligence rather than an inequality of knowledge', p. xxii. See also Rancière's presentation of Jacotot's method as a 'story', Rancière, *The Ignorant Schoolmaster*, p. 22. In the case of Rancière's treatment of Hegel we can say that the 'story' motif is used in a more classical sense as a way of lessening the hold of a particular account of modernity. The corollary is that, used this way, the story motif is also a way of qualifying Rancière's competing account as 'probable' rather than certain in all its particulars. See on this point, Rancière's discussion of his style in Rancière, J. and Hallward, P. (2003), 'Politics and aesthetics: an interview', *Angelaki*, 8 (2), 191–211, p. 208.

28 Rancière, 'The aesthetic revolution and its outcomes', p. 142.

29 Ibid.

30 Ibid.

31 Ibid., p. 141.

32 Ibid., p. 145.

33 Rancière, 'The politics of literature', p. 20.

34 The principle of the so-called realistic novel is 'not reproducing facts as they are, as critics claimed. It was displaying the so-called world of *prosaic* activities as

a huge *poem* – a huge fabric of signs and traces, of obscure signs that had to be displayed, unfolded and deciphered'. It is a new conception of meaning that renders characters intelligible not through their ends and will, but 'through the clothes they wear, the stones of their houses or the wallpaper of their rooms'. Rancière, 'The politics of literature', pp. 18–19, my emphasis.

[35] Badiou, A. (2005), *Metapolitics*. Trans. J. Barker, London and New York: Verso, p. 107: He writes: '[t]he site for Rancière's enterprise is not internal to a system [*dispositif*] of knowledge ... For the point at issue is *never* (my emphasis – AR) being a member, *ex officio*, of any particular academic community, whilst consistently drawing on textual positivities.'

[36] See Foucault, M. (1988), *Politics Philosophy Culture: Interviews and Other Writings 1977–1984*. L. D. Kritzmann (ed.), trans. A. Sheridan et al, London: Routledge, p. 310.

[37] See Rancière, J. (2005), 'Literary misunderstanding', *Paragraph*, 28 (2), 91–103. In this essay he distinguishes literature, which works on the disincorporation of meaning in 'individual units', from politics, which works on 'the whole', p. 99.

Chapter 6

[1] Rancière, J. (1991), *The Ignorant Schoolmaster: Five Lessons in Intellectual Emancipation*. Trans. K. Ross, Stanford: Stanford University Press.

[2] Bingham, C. and Biesta, G. (2010), *Jacques Rancière: Education, Truth, Emancipation*. London: Continuum.

[3] Pelletier, C. (2009), 'Education, equality and emancipation: Rancière's critique of Bourdieu and the question of performativity', *Discourse: Studies in the Cultural Politics of Education*, 30(2), 137–150; and Pelletier, C. (2009a), 'Rancière and the poetics of the social sciences', *International Journal of Research & Method in Education*, 32 (3), 267–284.

[4] A very different way of conceptualizing Rancière's 'untimeliness' is the argument that his work touches on issues characteristic of feminist interventions in education over the last twenty years, particularly feminist ethnography in education. This is not a criticism of his work but rather of the attention which a male French/ continental philosopher manages to garner, in contrast to the ongoing work of feminist women researchers. In order to avoid reinscribing this dynamic, and also to examine how Rancière's writing might become a resource within feminist debates, I have, in previous work, explored the continuities and discontinuities between Rancière's writing and feminist writing. This exploration could go much further, particularly, I think, with regard to ideas of method and discipline. My focus in this chapter is on some more negative responses to Rancière's ideas in education.

[5] Ross, K. (1991) 'Introduction', in J. Rancière, *The Ignorant Schoolmaster: Five Lessons in Intellectual Emancipation*. Stanford: Stanford University Press.

[6] Lave, J. and Wenger, E. (1991), *Situated Learning: Legitimate Peripheral Participation*. Cambridge: Cambridge University Press; Lave, J. and Wenger, E. (1996),

'Practice, person, social world', in H. Daniels (ed.), *An introduction to Vygotsky*. London: Routledge.

[7] Rancière, *The Ignorant Schoolmaster*, p. 65

[8] Ibid., p. 50.

[9] Ibid., p. 56.

[10] Vygotsky quoted in Derry, J. (2004), 'The unity of intellect and will: Vygotsky and Spinoza', *Educational Review*, 56 (2), 113–120.

[11] Derry, 'The unity of intellect and will'.

[12] It is worth noting that the distinction between spontaneous and scientific concepts has been dropped by more recent socio-cultural theory, notably Lave and Wenger, and been replaced by the opposition between 'legitimate peripheral participation' and 'full participation': in other words, a distinction between types of concepts has been replaced by one between types of positions within a collectivity.

[13] Rancière, *The Ignorant Schoolmaster*, p. 32.

[14] Ibid., p. 66.

[15] Ibid., pp. 66–67.

[16] Power, N. (2009), 'Axiomatic equality: Rancière and the politics of contemporary education', *Polygraph*, 21. Available here: http://www.eurozine.com/articles/2010-07-01-power-en.html.

[17] Rancière, *The Ignorant Schoolmaster*, p. 31.

[18] Ibid., pp. 66–67.

[19] Lave and Wenger, 'Practice, person, social world'.

[20] Rancière, J. (1981), *La Nuit des prolétaires: Archives du rêve ouvrier*. Paris: Hachette; English edition, Rancière, J. (1989), *The Nights of Labour: The Worker's Dream in Nineteenth Century France*. Philadelphia: Temple University Press.

[21] Rancière, J. (2003), *Le Destin des Images*. Paris: La Fabrique éditions; English edition Rancière, J. (2007), *The Future of the Image*. Trans. G. Elliot, New York and London: Verso.

[22] Whiteman, N. (2007), *The Establishment, Maintenance, and Destabilisation of Fandom: A Study of Two Online Communities and an Exploration of Issues Pertaining to Internet Research*. PhD Thesis, Institute of Education, University of London, available here: http://homepage.mac.com/paulcdowling/ioe/studentswork/whiteman.html.

[23] See, for example, Lewis, L., Black, R., Tomlinson, B. (2009), 'Let everyone play: an educational perspective on why fan fiction is, or should be, legal', *International Journal of Learning and Media*, 1 (1), 67–81; Jenkins, H. (2004), 'Why Heather can write', *MIT Technology Review* (accessed on 6 Feb. 2011). http://www.technologyreview.com/Biztech/13473/page1/; Gee, J. P. (2003), *What Video Games have to Teach us about Learning and Literacy*. New York: Palgrave.

[24] Rancière, J. (2005), *La Haine de la démocratie*. Paris: La Fabrique éditions; English edition, Rancière, J. (2006), *Hatred of Democracy*. Trans. S. Corcoran, London: Verso.

[25] Gee, J. P. (2004), *Situated Language and Learning: A Critique of Traditional Schooling*. London: Routledge.

[26] Ibid., p. 87.

[27] Ibid.

[28] Gee's concern is with non-institutionalized sites of education, but my argument here is that he sees gaming websites as educational sites – as sites that can inform approaches to teaching and learning in schools, once schools 'catch up' temporally with what students are apparently already doing in their popular culture. The transformations I discuss in the concept 'community of practice' are not specific to Gee; they are commonly traceable in education literature, which draws on Lave and Wenger's concept with a view to *creating* communities of practice, notably in professional and vocational education. In identifying these transformations, I do not imply that others have misinterpreted Lave and Wenger's work, but rather interpreted it with a view to creating communities of practice that 'improve learning': such interpretations can be justified with respect to Lave and Wenger's work. My examination of the two moves is an attempt to identify how such interpretations can be justified. It should be clear, however, that I read Lave and Wenger's work differently, and place greater emphasis on the process of legitimization.

[29] Aaron Porter made this statement at the 10 November 2010 demonstration, in a speech to the demonstrators. Subsequent reporting of this demonstration suggested that it marked a split between the NUS leadership and many NUS members.

[30] Because I have examined the debate between Bourdieu and Rancière elsewhere, I will not revisit it here. For a discussion of Rancière's argument with Bourdieu's sociology of education, see Pelletier, 'Education, equality and emancipation'; Nordmann, C. (2006), *Bourdieu/Rancière: La politique entre sociologie et philosophie.* Paris: Editions Amsterdam; and Ross, 'Introduction'.

[31] Frandji, D., and Vitale, P. (eds), (2010) *Knowledge, Pedagogy, and Society: International Perspectives on Basil Bernstein's Sociology of Education.* London: Routledge.

[32] Rochex, J. Y. (2010), 'The work of Basil Bernstein: a non-sociologistic and therefore non-deterministic sociology', in D. Frandji and P. Vitale (eds), *Knowledge, Pedagogy, and Society: International Perspectives on Basil Bernstein's Sociology of Education.* London: Routledge.

[33] Rancière, J. (2006) 'Thinking between disciplines: an aesthetics of knowledge', trans. J. Roffe, *Parrhesia*, 1, 1–12, p. 7

[34] Bernstein, B. (1975), *Class, Codes and Control (Vol 3): Towards a Theory of Educational Transmissions.* London: Routledge, p. 62

[35] Ibid., pp. 97–98.

[36] Ibid., p. 97

[37] Ibid., p. 100

[38] I deduce the characteristics of this 'wound' from Bernstein's argument that educational success confers order, identity and meaning, and that the organization of a curriculum should be deemed a failure if it does not give students a sense of time, place and purpose; see Bernstein *Class, Codes and Control*, Chapter 5, p. 100.

[39] Rancière, J. (2009), *Moments Politiques: Interventions 1977–2009.* Paris: La Fabrique editions, p. 223, my translation.

[40] I am thinking here for instance of the Research Assessment Exercise in the UK, by which academics evaluate and rank one another's research 'outputs' from one to five.

[41] Equality and social justice are two terms commonly found in mission statements of the Institute of Education, which is where I teach.

[42] Ross, 'Introduction'.

[43] It is work which Bingham and Biesta explore imaginatively, concretely and at length. I refer readers to this book (Bingham and Biesta, *Jacques Rancière: Education, Truth, Emancipation*) to develop this conclusion further.

Chapter 7

[1] Rancière, J. (2006), *Hatred of Democracy*. Trans. S. Corcoran, London: Verso, p. 41.

[2] Rancière, J. (2005), *La Haine de la démocratie*. Paris: La Fabrique éditions, p. 48.

[3] 'The most racist forms of socialism were, therefore Blanquism of course, and then the Commune, and then anarchism – much more so than social democracy, much more so than the Second International, and much more so than Marxism itself.' Foucault, M. (2003), *Society Must Be Defended: Lectures at the Collège de France 1975–76*. Trans. D. Macey, New York: Picador, p. 262.

[4] Rancière, *Hatred of Democracy*, p. 49. The passage appears in Plato's *Laws*, 690c. See Plato (2005), *Laws*. Trans. T. Saunders, London: Penguin, pp. 93–94.

[5] Rancière, *Hatred of Democracy*, p. 40.

[6] Rancière, J. (1999), *Disagreement: Politics and Philosophy*. Trans. J. Rose. Minneapolis: University of Minnesota Press, pp. 29–30.

[7] Rancière, *Hatred of Democracy*, p. 49.

[8] Rancière, *Disagreement*, p. 16.

[9] In *Disagreement*, Rancière distances himself from Habermas's thought, arguing that Habermas reduces politics to a rational balancing of interests. Habermas 'locks the rational argument of political debate into the same speech situation as the one it seeks to overcome: the simple rationality of a dialogue of interests.' (Ibid., p. 47) This undercuts the dissensus of politics, which seeks to challenge a particular order of interests in the name of equality rather than to operate with it. I do not wish to challenge this point, which is well taken. It operates, however, on a different register from the discussion here. For Rancière, one challenges a police order in the name of equality, and Habermas' thought, by promoting consensus, fails to accomplish that. In the discussion at hand, we are already presupposing equality and asking what happens within the context of that presupposition. In other words, we are asking about the internal dynamics of the subjectification (in Rancière's sense of the term) that is the challenge to the police order in the name of equality.

[10] Lance, M. (2005), 'Fetishizing process', *Social Anarchism*, 38.

[11] Rawls, J. (2001), *Justice as Fairness: A Restatement*. E. Kelly (ed.), Cambridge, Mass.: Harvard University Press, p. 16.

[12] May, T., Noys, B., and Newman, S. (2008), 'Democracy, anarchism and radical politics today: an interview with Jacques Rancière'. Trans. J. Lechte, *Anarchist Studies*, 16 (2), 173–186, 173.

[13] Rancière, J. (1995), *On the Shore of Politics*. Trans. L. Heron, London: Verso, p. 61.

[14] I discuss the issues raised in this paragraph in more depth in May, T. (2010), *Contemporary Movements and the Thought of Jacques Rancière: Equality in Action*. Edinburgh: Edinburgh University Press, Chapter 5.

[15] See May, T. (2008), *The Political Thought of Jacques Rancière: Creating Equality*. Edinburgh: Edinburgh University Press, Chapter 3.

[16] For a discussion of this distinction, see Peter Kropotkin's seminal article from the 1910 *Encyclopaedia Britannica* 'Anarchism'. Kropotkin, P. (1995), 'Anarchism', from the *Encyclopaedia Britannica*', in M. Shatz (ed.), *The Conquest of Bread and Other Writings*. Cambridge: Cambridge University Press, pp. 236–241.

[17] Crowder, G. (1991), *Classical Anarchism: The Political Thought of Godwin, Proudhon, Bakunin, and Kropotkin*. Oxford: Clarendon Press, p. 4.

[18] Ward, C. (1988), *Anarchy in Action*. London: Freedom Press, p. 136.

[19] Ibid. p. 71.

[20] Ibid. p. 29.

[21] One vivid account of this is provided by Dave Eggers; see Eggers, D. (2009), *Zeitoun*. San Francisco: McSweeney's. Also, the film *Trouble the Water* provides first-person evidence of the mutual aid that arose during Katrina, as well as documenting (like *Zeitoun*) the resistance of governmental organizations to assist in that aid, and in fact to stifle it.

[22] Ward, *Anarchy in Action*, pp. 71–72.

[23] Rancière, *On the Shores of Politics*, p. 48.

[24] Rancière, *Disagreement*, p. 17.

[25] Rancière, *Disagreement*, p. 33.

Chapter 8

[1] Rancière, J. (2003), 'Comment and responses', *Theory and Event*, 6 (4), paragraph 10.

[2] Rancière, J. (1999), *Disagreement: Politics and Philosophy*. Trans. J. Rose. Minneapolis: University of Minnesota Press, p. 30; Originally published as Rancière, J. (1995), *La Mésentente: Politique et Philosophie*. Paris: Galilée.

[3] Rancière, *Disagreement*, p. 28.

[4] Foucault, M. (2007), *Security, Territory, Population: Lectures at the Collège de France 1977–1978*. M. Senellart (ed.), trans. G. Burchell, New York: Palgrave Macmillan, pp. 311–361.

[5] Rancière, *Disagreement*, p. 29.

[6] Ibid., pp. 39–40.

[7] Ibid., p. 35.

[8] Ibid., p. 30.

[9] Ibid., p. 35.

[10] May, T. (2008) *The Political Thought of Jacques Rancière: Creating Equality*. Philadelphia, PA: University of Pennsylvania Press, p. 40.

[11] Ibid., p. 29.

[12] Chambers, S. A. (2010), 'Police and oligarchy', in J. P. Deranty (ed.), *Jacques Rancière: Key Concepts*. Durham: Acumen, pp. 57–68, p. 62.

[13] Rancière, *Disagreement*, p. 31.

[14] Panagia, D. (2001) 'Ceci n'est pas un argument: an introduction to the ten theses', *Theory and Event*, 5 (3), paragraph 1.

[15] Rancière, *Disagreement*, p. 50.

[16] Rancière, J. (2003), 'Comment and responses', *Theory and Event*, 6 (4), paragraph 20.

[17] Rancière, *Disagreement*, p. 49.

[18] Deleuze, G. and Foucault, M. (1972). 'Les intellectuels et le pouvoir,' *L'Arc 49: Gilles Deleuze*, 3–10. Reprinted in Foucault, *Dits et écrits 1954–1988*, t. II, Paris: Gallimard 1994; and in Deleuze, *L'Île Désert et Autres Textes, Textes et Entretiens 1953–1974*, edited by David Lapoujade. Paris: Éditions de Minuit, 2002.

[19] Rawls, J. (2001), *Justice as Fairness: A Restatement*. E. Kelly (ed.), Cambridge, Mass.: Harvard University Press.

[20] Ibid., p. 4.

[21] Ibid., p. 5.

[22] Foucault, M. (1997), *Essential Works of Foucault 1954–1984, Volume 1: Ethics: Subjectivity and Truth*. P. Rabinow (ed.), trans. R. Hurley et al., New York: New Press, p. 315.

[23] Derrida, J. (2001), *On Cosmopolitanism and Forgiveness*. Trans M. Dooley and M. Hughes, London and New York: Routledge, pp. 22–23.

[24] Deleuze, G. and Guattari, F. (1994), *What is Philosophy?* Trans. H. Tomlinson and G. Burchell, New York: Columbia University Press, pp. 99–100.

[25] Rancière, J. (2001), 'Ten theses on politics', trans. D. Panagia and R. Bowlby, *Theory and Event*, 5 (3), Thesis 7.

[26] Rancière, *Disagreement*, p. 99.

[27] Ibid.

[28] Ibid., p. 100.

[29] Ibid., p. 101.

[30] Ibid.

[31] Rawls, J. (2005), 'The idea of public reason revisited: (1997)', in J. Rawls, *Political Liberalism* (expanded edn). New York: Columbia University Press, pp. 440–490, p. 450.

[32] Patton, P. (2010), *Deleuzian Concepts: Philosophy, Colonization, Politics*. Stanford: Stanford University Press, pp. 154–159.

[33] Derrida, J. (2005), *Rogues: Two Essays on Reason*. Trans. P. A. Brault and M. Naas, Stanford: Stanford University Press, p. 86.

[34] Rancière, J. (2006), *Hatred of Democracy*. Trans. S. Corcoran, London: Verso, p. 55; originally published as Rancière, J. (2005), *La Haine de la démocratie*. Paris: La Fabrique éditions.

[35] Rancière, *Hatred of Democracy*, p. 56.

[36] Ibid., p. 62.

[37] Deleuze, G. (1995), *Negotiations 1972–1990*. Trans. M. Joughin, New York: Columbia University Press, p. 172.

[38] Rancière, *Disagreement*, pp. 31–32.

[39] May, T. (2010), 'Wrong, disagreement, subjectification', in J. P. Deranty (ed.), *Jacques Rancière: Key Concepts*. Durham: Acumen, p. 70.

[40] Rancière, *Disagreement*, p. 34.

[41] May, 'Wrong, disagreement, subjectification', p. 76.

[42] May, 'Wrong, disagreement, subjectification', p.76.

[43] Rancière, *Disagreement*, p. 102.

[44] Ibid., pp. 101–102.

[45] Rancière, *Hatred of Democracy*, p. 73.

[46] Rancière, *Disagreement*, p. 113.

[47] Rancière, *Hatred of Democracy*, p. 78.

[48] Foucault, M. (2008) *The Birth of Biopolitics: Lectures at the Collège de France 1978–1979*. M. Senellart (ed.), trans. G. Burchell, New York: Palgrave Macmillan, p. 84.

[49] Rancière, *Disagreement*, p. 102.

[50] Ibid., p. 105.

[51] Ibid., p. 111.

[52] Ibid.

[53] Ibid., pp. 111–112.

[54] Ibid., p. 116.

[55] Ibid.

[56] Ibid., p. 118.

Chapter 9

[1] Rancière, J. (2003), 'Comment and responses', *Theory and Event*, 6 (4), paragraph 10.

[2] Arendt, H. (1994), *Essays in Understanding: 1930–1955*. J. Kohn (ed.), New York: Harcourt, Brace & Co, p. 2.

[3] Ibid., p. 202.

[4] Ibid., pp. 432–433

[5] Canovan, M. (1992), *Hannah Arendt: A Reinterpretation of Her Political Thought*. Cambridge: Cambridge University Press, p. 255.

[6] Arendt, H. (2004), *The Origins of Totalitarianism*. New York: Schocken Books; first published in 1951.

[7] Arendt, H. (1958), *The Human Condition*. Chicago: Chicago University Press.

[8] Cited in May, T. (2008), *The Political Thought of Jacques Rancière: Creating Equality*. Edinburgh: Edinburgh University Press, p. 78.

[9] See Deranty, J. P. (2010), 'Introduction: a journey in equality', in J. P. Deranty (ed.), *Jacques Rancière: Key Concepts*. Durham: Acumen, p. 4.

[10] Badiou, A. (2009), 'The lessons of Jacques Rancière: knowledge and power after the storm', in G. Rockhill and P. Watts (eds), *Jacques Rancière: History, Politics, Aesthetics*. Durham: Duke University Press.

[11] Rancière, J. (1981), *La Nuit des Prolétaires: Archives du rêve ouvrier.* Paris: Hachette; English translation, Rancière, J. (1989), *The Nights of Labour: The Workers Dream in Nineteenth Century France.* Philadelphia: Temple University Press.

[12] Rancière, J. (1995), *La Mésentente: Politique et Philosophie.* Paris: Galilée; English translation, Rancière, J. (1999), *Disagreement: Politics and Philosophy.* Trans. J. Rose. Minneapolis: University of Minnesota Press.

[13] For example, Ingram, J. D. (2006), 'The subject of the politics of recognition: Hannah Arendt and Jacques Rancière', in G. Bertram, R. Celikates, C. Laudou, D. Lauer (eds), *Socialité et reconnaissance. Grammaires de l 'humain.* Paris: L'Harmattan; Ingram, J. D. (2008), 'What is a "Right to Have Rights"? Three images of the politics of human rights', *American Political Science Review*, 102 (4), 401–416.

[14] Rancière, J. (2003), *The Philosopher and His Poor.* Trans. J. Drury, C. Oyster, A. Parker (ed.), Durham: Duke University Press, p. xxviii.

[15] Arendt, H. (2005), *The Promise of Politics.* J. Kohn (ed.), New York: Schocken Books, p. 27.

[16] Parekh, B. (1981), *Hannah Arendt and the Search for a New Political Philosophy.* London: Macmillan, Chapter 1.

[17] Arendt, *Essays in Understanding*, p. 429.

[18] Parekh, *Hannah Arendt*, pp. 61–62.

[19] Arendt, *Essays in Understanding*, p. 443.

[20] Parekh, *Hannah Arendt*, p. 69.

[21] Arendt, *Essays in Understanding*, p. 430.

[22] See Parekh, *Hannah Arendt*, pp. 72–75.

[23] Hinchman, L. P. and Hinchman, S. K. (1984), 'In Heidegger's shadow: Arendt's phenomenological humanism', *The Review of Politics*, 46 (2), 183–211, 196–197.

[24] See Dietz, M. (2000), 'Arendt and the Holocaust', in D. Villa (ed.), *The Cambridge Companion to Hannah Arendt.* Cambridge: Cambridge University Press.

[25] Arendt, *The Promise of Politics*, p. 35.

[26] Canovan, *Hannah Arendt*, p. 258.

[27] Arendt, *The Promise of Politics*, p. 19.

[28] Ibid., p. 14.

[29] Ibid., p. 14.

[30] Ibid., p. 14.

[31] Ibid., p. 6.

[32] Ibid., pp. 11–12.

[33] Ibid., p. 11.

[34] See Markell, P. (2006), 'The rule of the people: Arendt, archê, and democracy', *American Political Science Review*, 100 (1), pp. 1–14.

[35] Arendt, *The Promise of Politics*, pp. 52, 91.

[36] Arendt, *The Human Condition*, p. 223, citing *The Statesman.*

[37] Arendt, *The Promise of Politics*, p. 83.

[38] Arendt, *The Human Condition*, p. 228.

[39] Rancière, J. (2010), *Dissensus: On Politics and Aesthetics.* Trans. S. Corcoran (ed.), London: Continuum, p. 66.

[40] See Schaap, A. (2011), 'Enacting the "right to have rights": Jacques Rancière's critique of Hannah Arendt', *European Journal of Political Theory*, 10 (1): pp. 22–45;

Gündo du, A. (forthcoming), 'Aporias of human rights: Arendt and the "Perplexities of Rights of Man"', *European Journal of Political Theory*.

[41] Rancière, *Dissensus*, p. 64; see Whyte 2009.

[42] Rancière, *Dissensus*, pp. 66–67, my emphasis.

[43] Rancière, *Disagreement*, p. 63.

[44] Arendt, *Essays in Understanding*, p. 430.

[45] Rancière, *Dissensus*, p. 40; Rancière, *Disagreement*, p. 6.

[46] Rancière, 'Comment and responses', pp. 10, 11.

[47] Rancière, 'Comment and responses', p. 12.

[48] Rancière, *Disagreement*, p. 63.

[49] Ibid., p. 63.

[50] Ibid., p. 64.

[51] Ibid., pp. 64–65.

[52] Arsenjuk, L. (2007), 'On Jacques Rancière', *Eurozine*, 1 March, (accessed 20 May 2011), http://www.eurozine.com/articles/2007-03-01-arsenjuk-en.html.

[53] Rancière, *Disagreement*, p. 67.

[54] Arendt, *The Human Condition*, p. 211; see Villa, D. R. (1996), *Arendt and Heidegger: The Fate of the Political*. Princeton: Princeton University Press, pp. 89–90.

[55] Arendt, *The Human Condition*, pp. 189, 222; Markell, 'The rule of the people'; Balibar, E. (2007), '(De)Constructing the human as human institution: a reflection on the coherence of Hannah Arendt's practical philosophy', *Social Research*, 74 (3), 727–738.

[56] Arendt, *The Human Condition*, pp. 198–199; Janover, M. (2011), 'Politics and worldliness in the thought of Hannah Arendt', in A. Yeatman, P. Hansen, M. Zolkos, C. Barbour (eds), *Action and Appearance: Ethics and the Politics of Writing in Hannah Arendt*. London: Continuum.

[57] Rancière's, *Disagreement*, p. 65.

[58] Ingram, 'The subject of the politics of recognition', p. 236.

[59] Rancière, *Disagreement*, p. 70.

[60] Ibid., p. 70.

[61] Ibid., p. 74.

[62] Arsenjuk, 'On Jacques Rancière'.

[63] Rancière, *Disagreement*, p. 75.

[64] Arendt, H. (1990), *On Revolution*. Harmondsworth: Penguin, p. 275.

[65] See Villa, D. R. (1996), *Arendt and Heidegger*, Chapter 1.

[66] Arendt, *On Revolution*, p. 279; see also Arendt, *The Human Condition*, pp. 27–28.

[67] Rancière, J. (2006), *Hatred of Democracy*. Trans. S. Corcoran, London: Verso, pp. 52–53.

[68] Ibid., p. 43.

[69] Ibid., p. 46

[70] Arendt, *The Human Condition*, p. 32; Arendt, *On Revolution*, pp. 30–31; see Balibar, '(De)Constructing the human'.

[71] Rancière, *Dissensus*, p. 29.

[72] Ibid., p. 29.

[73] Ibid., p. 30.

[74] See Rancière, *Hatred of Democracy*, pp. 38–39.

[75] Ibid., p. 48.

[76] Ingram, 'The subject of the politics of recognition', p. 236.

[77] Rancière, *Dissensus*, p. 42.

[78] Ibid., pp. 28, 58; see also Rancière, *Hatred of Democracy*, p. 23.

[79] Rancière, J. and Panagia, D. (2000), 'Dissenting words: a conversation with Jacques Rancière', *Diacritics* 30 (2): 113–26, p. 119.

[80] Rancière, *Dissensus*, p. 42.

[81] Ibid., p. 42.

[82] Rancière, *Disagreement*, p. 64.

[83] Rancière, *Dissensus*, p. 41.

[84] Rancière, *Hatred of Democracy*, p. 35; Rancière, *Disagreement*, p. 22.

[85] Rancière, *Dissensus*, p. 63.

[86] Arendt, *The Human Condition*, p. 46.

[87] Ibid., p. 208.

[88] Arendt, *On Revolution*, p. 64.

[89] Rancière, *Dissensus*, p. 43; Rancière, *Disagreement*, p. 91.

[90] Rancière, *Dissensus*, p. 39.

[91] Ibid., p. 28.

[92] Ibid., p. 58.

[ ] Ibid., p. 54.

[94] Ibid., p. 40; see also McClure, K. M. (2003), 'Disconnections, connections, and questions: reflections on Jacques Rancière's "Ten theses on politics"', *Theory and Event*, 6 (4); and Rancière, 'Comment and responses'.

[95] Rancière, *Dissensus*, p. 28.

[96] Rancière, *Hatred of Democracy*, p. 23, and in this volume.

[97] Rancière, *Disagreement*, p. 126.

[98] Rancière, *Dissensus*, pp. 72–75.

[99] Arendt, *The Origins of Totalitarianism*, p. 289.

[100] See Schaap, 'Enacting the "right to have rights".

[101] Parekh, B. (1979), 'Hannah Arendt's critique of Marx', in M. Hill (ed.), *Hannah Arendt: The Recovery of the Public World*. New York: St Martin's Press; Pitkin 1981; Bernstein, R. J. (1986), 'Rethinking the social and the political', in *Philosophical Profiles: Essays in a Pragmatic Mode*. Cambridge: Polity Press.

[102] Honig, B. (1993), *Political Theory and the Displacement of Politics*. Ithaca: Cornell University Press, p. 204.

[103] Schaap, A. (2010), 'The politics of need', in A. Schaap, D. Celermajer and V. Karalis (eds), *Power, Judgment and Political Evil: In Conversation with Hannah Arendt*. Farnham: Ashgate.

[104] Ingram, 'The subject of the politics of recognition', p. 236.

[105] Ibid., p. 239.

[106] Deranty, J. P. (2003), 'Rancière and contemporary political ontology', *Theory and Event*, 6 (4).

[107] See Rancière, *Disagreement*, pp. 55–56.

[108] See Dikeç, M. (forthcoming), 'Politics is sublime', *Environment and Planning D: Society and Space*.

[109] Rancière, *Disagreement*, p. 61.

[110] Ibid., pp. 137–138.

[111] Deranty, 'Rancière and contemporary political ontology'.

[112] Rancière, *Disagreement*, pp. 55–56.

[113] Ibid., p. 35.

[114] Marchart, O. (2007), *Post-Foundational Political Thought: Political Difference in Nancy, Lefort, Badiou and Laclau.* Edinburgh: Edinburgh University Press, pp. 11–12.

[115] Rancière, *Dissensus*, p. 53.

[116] Rancière, *Disagreement*, p. 27.

[117] Rancière, *Disagreement*, p. 139.

[118] Rancière, *Dissensus*, p. 70.

[119] Rancière, *Disagreement*, p. 9.

[120] Janover, M., 'Politics and worldliness in the thought of Hannah Arendt', in A. Yeatman, P. Hansen, M. Zolkos, and C. Barbour (eds) *Action and Appearance: Ethics and the Politics of Writing in Hannah Arendt.* London: Continuum.

[121] Balibar, '(De)Constructing the human'.

[122] For example, Arendt, *The Human Condition*, pp. 198–199.

[123] Ingram, 'The subject of the politics of recognition'.

[124] Deranty, J. P. and Renault, E. (2009), 'Democratic agon: striving for distinction or struggle against domination and injustice?', in A. Schaap (ed.) *Law and Agonistic Politics.* Farnham: Ashgate.

[125] Rancière, *Disagreement*, p. 33.

[126] Rancière, *Dissensus*, p. 30.

[127] Deranty and Renault, 'Democratic agon'; Frank, J. (2010), *Constituent Moments: Enacting the People in Postrevolutionary America* Durham: Duke University Press, Chapter 2; Christodoulidis, E. and Schaap, A. (forthcoming) 'Arendt's constitutional question', in C. McCorkindale and M. Goldini (eds), *Hannah Arendt and the Law.* Portland: Hart.

[128] Arendt, *The Human Condition*, p. 180.

[129] Cf. Badiou, A. (2005), 'Against Political Philosophy', in *Metapolitics.* London: Verso, p. 21f.

[130] Rancière, *Disagreement*, p. 18.

[131] Ingram, 'The subject of the politics of recognition', p. 244.

[132] Arendt, *The Human Condition*, p. 179.

[133] Ibid., p. 176.

[134] Rancière, *Disagreement*, p. 36.

[135] McNay, L. (2010), 'Feminism and post-identity politics: the problem of agency', *Constellations*, 17 (4): pp. 512–525.

[136] Rancière, *Disagreement*, p. 39.

[137] Ibid., p. xii.

Chapter 10

[1] Rancière, J. (1996), 'Le concept de critique et la critique de l'économie politique des *Manuscrits* de 1844 au *Capital*', in L. Althusser, E. Balibar, R. Establet, P. Macherey and J. Rancière, *Lire le Capital* (new edn). Paris: PUF, pp. 82–199.

[2] It might even be justified to examine even a step before this one, since the Althusserian point of view replaced a former Sartrian/humanist interpretation of Marx that could also have played a role in the general evolution of Rancière's thought.

See Rancière's contribution to this volume in which he discusses the Sartrian influence.

[3] See Rancière, J., notably 'Le concept de critique'.

[4] See Rancière, J. (1974), 'On the theory of ideology (the politics of Althusser)', *Radical Philosophy*, 7 (2), 2–15.

[5] Rancière, J. (1976), 'How to use *Lire le capital*', *Economy and Society*, 5 (3), 377–384. Also republished in Rattansi, A. (ed.) (1989), *Ideology, Method and Marx*. London, Routledge, pp. 181–189.

[6] Rancière, J. (1974), *La Leçon d'Althusser*. Paris: Gallimard.

[7] Rancière's contributions are collected in Rancière, J. (2003), *Les Scènes du peuple*. Paris: Horlieu.

[8] See Rancière, J. (2003), *The Philosopher and his Poor*. Trans. A. Parker, C. Oster and J. Dury, Philadelphia: Temple University Press. Originally published as Rancière, J. (1983), *Le Philosophe et ses Pauvres*. Paris: Fayard.

[9] See Rancière, J. (1999), *Disagreement: Politics and Philosophy*. Trans. J. Rose. Minneapolis: University of Minnesota Press. Originally published as Rancière, J. (1995), *La Mésentente: Politique et philosophie*. Paris: Galilée.

[10] Althusser, L. (2005), *For Marx* (new edn). Trans. B. Brewster, London: Verso.

[11] There are indeed some original aspects of Rancière''s reading of the manuscripts of 1844, such as the interpretation of the role of the critique of abstraction, and the tensions between the Kantianism of the first manuscript and the Hegelianism of the third.

[12] Marx, K. (1981), *Capital: A Critique of Political Economy* (*Vol. 3*). Trans. D. Fernbach, London: Penguin Books, Chapter 48, pp. 953–971.

[13] One could remark, for example, that the interpretation of the Parisian manuscripts as a critique of political economy is controversial (Marx is mainly taking notes on the political economy that he only discovers), or that the problematic of fetishism differs in its logic and functions from that of the sources of income. An even more obvious objection relates to the fact that the critique of political economy is reduced to the critique of a discourse, and the critique of the reality to which it is essentially linked (that is, capitalist society) simply disappears.

[14] Intended for the third edition of *Lire le capital*, it was rejected by some of the co-authors and published in *Les Temps Modernes* instead in November 1973. Rancière, J. (1973), 'Mode d'emploi pour une ré-édition de *Lire le capital*', *Les Temps Modernes*, 328, 788–807.

[15] Rancière, 'How to use *Lire le capital*', p. 378.

[16] Rancière speaks of 'a game of breaks, shifts and substitution, in which the exterior of the text never appears except as its unthought, which is always the thought of another text', ibid., p. 377.

[17] Ibid., p. 378.

[18] Ibid.

[19] Ibid., p. 379.

[20] Ibid.

[21] Ibid., p. 382.

[22] Ibid., p. 379.

[23] Ibid., p. 380.

[24] Ibid., p. 379.

[25] Rancière, *La Leçon d'Althusser*, p. 9. Translations mine.

[26] Ibid., p. 10.

[27] Rancière was part of the Gauche Prolétarienne, the main Maoist organization, where he was doing political work with those members of the party that were introduced in factories south of Paris.

[28] The following quotes from 'The theory of ideology' refer to this French edition as the *Radical Philosophy* edition is even harder to get hold of.

[29] Particularly important for this transition is the strike and the social appropriation of the clock-manufacturing plant LIP, near Besançon, in 1973. Whereas the Maoist strategy targeted the unemployed, the unskilled and immigrant workers, the most radical social struggle of the post-1968s was conducted by white skilled workers. The Gauche Prolétarienne drew this conclusion by self-dissolution. The LIP example plays an important role in *Althusser's Lesson*. And the fact that one of the LIP strikers' mottos was: 'economy for human beings' ('l'économie au service de l'homme') obviously influences the new discussion about humanism and revolution.

[30] In Althusser, L. (1976), *Essays in Self-Criticism*. New York: Schocken Books.

[31] Rancière, *La Leçon d'Althusser*, pp. 228–229.

[32] Ibid., p. 273.

[33] Althusser, L. (1971), 'Ideology and ideological state apparatuses (notes towards an investigation)', in L. Althusser, *Lenin and Philosophy, and Other Essays*. Trans. B. Brewster, London: New Left Books, pp. 127–188.

[34] Rancière, *La Leçon d'Althusser*, pp. 232–236.

[35] Ibid., p. 238.

[36] Ibid., pp. 264–268.

[37] Ibid., pp. 249–250.

[38] Ibid., pp. 253–256.

[39] Ibid., p. 255.

[40] At the time, Foucault was supporting some of the struggles of the Gauche Prolétarienne to which Rancière was associated.

[41] 'Without revolutionary theory, no revolutionary action ... We now have to draw the conclusion from what the cultural revolution and the ideological revolt of students have reminded us: namely, that, severed from revolutionary practice, all revolutionary theory transforms into its opposite', Rancière, *La Leçon d'Althusser*, p. 277.

[42] Ibid., pp. 49–50; 53–54; 181–189.

[43] Ibid., pp. 86–87; 118–120; 142.

[44] Ibid., p. 35.

[45] Ibid., pp. 34–37.

[46] Ibid., pp. 24–26.

[47] Ibid., pp. 29–32.

[48] Ibid., p. 51.

[49] Ibid., pp. 119–121.

[50] Ibid., p. 42.

[51] Ibid., p. 40.

[52] Ibid., p. 96.

[53] Ibid., pp. 144–145.

[54] 'The education of the individuals necessary to the reproduction of bourgeois relations occurs less through the game of illusions produced by texts and juridical practice, than through the practical and discursive effects of a whole set of disciplines: workshop, factory, school disciplines, and so on', ibid., p. 178.

[55] Rancière, *La Leçon d'Althusser*, p.178, 188, with the same quote from *Capital*.

[56] Ibid., p. 251.

[57] Ibid.

[58] Ibid., p. 41.

[59] Ibid., p. 12.

[60] Ibid., p. 225.

[61] Rancière's postface to Rancière, J., and Faure, A. (eds) (2007), *La Parole ouvrière*. Paris : La Fabrique éditions, p. 338.

[62] Rancière et al., *La Parole ouvrière*, p. 337.

[63] Rancière, *La Leçon d'Althusser*, pp. 168–172.

[64] Ibid., p. 169.

[65] Ibid., pp. 153–154.

[66] Ibid.

[67] Ibid., p. 176.

[68] Rancière, *Les Scènes du peuple*, p. 316.

[69] Ibid., pp. 298–300.

[70] What is at stake is plainly stated in this comment on *The Civil War in France*: 'the convergence in 1871 of Marx's thought with the thought and practice of the Parisian leaders of the workers' movement is more than just a conversion of Marxism, as though it had suddenly been awakened by the thought from below. In order to join ranks with the proletarian government, Marx's political thinking and the "apolitical" thinking of the Parisian internationals both had to transform themselves ... There is never a pure discourse of proletarian power, nor a pure discourse of its lack of power; neither a consciousness from below which would be self-sufficient nor a pure science that could be imported into it. The strength of Marx's thought – but also its untenable aspect perhaps – might well reside in his effort hold together all these contradictions', ibid., pp. 319–320..

[71] Ibid., p. 325.

[72] Rancière, *The Philosopher and his Poor*, pp. 68–91.

[73] Ibid., p. 209.

[74] Ibid., pp. 73–74.

[75] Ibid., p. 75.

[76] Ibid., pp. 83–90. See also the recent article, Rancière, J. (2009), 'Des communistes sans communisme', in J. Rancière, *Moments Politiques: Interventions 1977–2009*. Paris: La Fabrique éditions, pp. 217–232.

[77] Obviously Rancière had earlier developed plenty of arguments against such a reading. It is surely true that the bourgeoisie is presented as a revolutionary class in the *Communist Manifesto*, but the historical writings of Marx (that are now mentioned in a very selective way) prove that he renounced this idea after 1848, and it is difficult to forget that Marx wrote in the 'Status' of the International, in 1864, that 'the emancipation of the worker will be made by the workers'.

[78] Rancière, *The Philosopher and his Poor*, pp. 112–125.

[79] Ibid., p. 93.
[80] Rancière, J. (2008), 'Les mésaventures de la pensée critique', in J. Rancière, *Le Spectateur émancipé*. Paris: La Fabrique éditions
[81] Rancière, *The Philosopher and his Poor*, pp. 93–100.
[82] Rancière, *Disagreement*, pp. 91–92.
[83] Ibid., p. 92.
[84] Ibid., pp. 82–83.
[85] Ibid., pp. 84–85.
[86] Ibid., pp. 86–87.

Chapter 11

[1] A useful synthesis showing how the different dimensions of work are articulated in Marx is provided by Emmanuel Renault, in Renault, E. (2011), 'Comment Marx se réfère-t-il au travail et à la domination?', *Actuel Marx*, 49, 15–31.
[2] Braverman, H. (1974), *Labour and Monopoly Capitalism: The Degradation of Work in the Twentieth Century*. New York: Monthly Review Press.
[3] Althusser, L., Balibar, E., Establet, R., Macherey, P. and Rancière, J. (1996), *Lire le Capital* (new edn). Paris: PUF, p. 155.
[4] Ibid., p. 109.
[5] Ibid., p. 184.
[6] An excellent summary of the historical situation and how it impacted on theoretical endeavours at the time can be found in Alain Badiou's intervention at the Cerisy colloquium on Rancière. See Badiou, A. (2009), 'The lessons of Jacques Rancière: knowledge and power after the storm', in G. Rockhill and P. Watts (eds), *Jacques Rancière: History, Politics, Aesthetics*. Durham: Duke University Press, pp. 30–54. See also the excellent introduction by Donald Reid, to the English translation of Rancière, J. (1989), *The Nights of Labour: The Workers Dream in Nineteenth Century France*. Philadelphia: Temple University Press, pp. xv–xxxvii.
[7] Rancière, J. (1974), *La Leçon d'Althusser*. Paris: Gallimard, p. 40. Translations my own.
[8] Rancière, J., and Faure, A. (eds) (2007), *La Parole ouvrière*. Paris, La Fabrique éditions, p. 19.
[9] Rancière, *La Leçon d'Althusser*, p. 154.
[10] In Rancière, *La Parole ouvrière*; and Rancière, J. (1983), *Le Philosophe plébéien Louis-Gabriel Gauny*. Paris: Presses Universitaires de Vincennes.
[11] See the excellent presentation of the project by Kristin Ross, in Ross, K. (2002), *May '68 and its Afterlives*. Chicago: Chicago University Press.
[12] Rancière, *La Leçon d'Althusser*, p. 154.
[13] Rancière, *La Parole ouvrière*, p. 10.
[14] See in particular the first series of texts in Rancière, *La Parole ouvrière*, pp. 28–108. See, for instance, this typical statement, establishing the continuity between the 1789 and the 1830 revolutions: 'We only overthrew the yoke of noble aristocracy to fall under the domination of financial aristocracy. We chased away the tyrants with parchments only to throw ourselves in the arms of millionaire despots …

Beware of the impetuous élan of a nation who, rather than staying within the boundaries of moderation, could indulge in terrible excesses if you force it to once again resort to imposing force by shouting out loud: FREEDOM, FREEDOM!', Colin, A. (1831), 'Le cri du people,' as cited in Rancière, J. (2007), *La Parole ouvrière*, p. 43.

[15] Ibid., p. 18.

[16] Rancière, *La Parole ouvrière*, p. 17. See Rancière, J. (1983), 'The myth of the artisan: critical reflections on a category of social history', *International Labour and Working Class History*, 24, 1–16. This post-*Nights of Labour* article assumes the dichotomy between work as status and work as *métier* but also provides a prime example of Rancière's in-depth knowledge of the reality of proletarian work in the nineteenth century.

[17] The split between the two sides is well documented in Rancière, 'The myth of the artisan'.

[18] Rancière, J. (1989), *The Nights of Labour: The Workers Dream in Nineteenth Century France*. Philadelphia: Temple University Press, p.11. See also the Introduction to Rancière, J. (2003), *Les Scènes du peuple*. Paris: Horlieu, pp. 7–18; or the postface to Rancière, *La Parole ouvrière*, pp. 332–342.

[19] Rancière, *The Nights of Labour*, p. 15. Translation slightly altered and words added for clarity.

[20] Ibid., p. 31.

[21] Ibid.

[22] Ibid., p. 20.

[23] Ibid., p. 28.

[24] Ibid., p. 45. Translation altered.

[25] Rancière, *La Parole ouvrière*, p. 153 ; Rancière, *The Nights of Labour*, pp. 45–49.

[26] Rancière, *The Nights of Labour*, p. 58. See also Rancière, 'The myth of the artisan', pp. 4–6.

[27] Rancière, *The Nights of Labour*, pp. 49–68.

[28] See, for instance, Rancière, J. (1999), *Disagreement: Politics and Philosophy*. Trans. J. Rose. Minneapolis: University of Minnesota Press, p. 41; or Rancière, J. (2004), 'Who is the subject of the rights of man', *South Atlantic Quarterly*, 103 (2–3), 297–310, pp. 303–304.

[29] To take another example in a different field, see my presentation of the 'regimes of the arts', as attempting to define historically changing structural conditions of aesthetic judgement and practice, and as defining at the same time historically determined modes of free creation, in Deranty, J. P. (ed.) (2010), *Jacques Rancière: Key Concepts*. Durham: Acumen, pp. 116–130.

[30] A similar study, comparing *The Nights of Labour* and the later texts would reveal similar interesting overlaps in relation to the aesthetic or the pedagogical. See Rancière, *The Nights of Labour*, pp. 51–52, where the figure of Jacotot appears for the first time. The 'erring letter' and 'mute speech' theorized in *La Parole muette*, the book where the parameters of Rancière's aesthetics are put in place, seem to grow organically from the study of the wandering proletarians in the first part of *La Nuit*. See Rancière, J. (1998), *La Parole muette. Essai sur les contradictions de la littérature*. Paris: Hachette Littératures; Rancière, J. (1981), *La Nuit des prolétaires: Archives du rêve ouvrier*. Paris: Hachette.

[31] Rancière, *Disagreement*, p. 7. Translation altered.

[32] Ibid., p. 9. See also, for another explicit reference to work as principle of domination/emancipation, pp. 38–39, and pp. 52–53.

[33] Ibid., p. 23.

[34] Ibid., pp. 23–25. The ironic opposition between the long forgotten workers' demands and the prestigious German philosopher is Rancière's own performative way of claiming the quality of speaking beings.

[35] Ibid., pp. 82–87.

[36] Ibid., pp. 118–121.

[37] See Paul Patton's contribution in this volume.

[38] See Andrew Schaap's contribution in this volume.

Chapter 12

[1] See, in particular, the texts by Grignon at the time of the taylor's strike of 1833, which led to the creation of the 'Atelier National'. Rancière, J., and Faure, A. (eds) (2007), *La Parole ouvrière*. Paris, La Fabrique éditions, pp. 55–63; and Rancière, J. (1989) *The Nights of Labour: The Workers Dream in Nineteenth Century France*. Philadelphia: Temple University Press, pp. 50–60. All footnotes by the translator.

[2] Rancière, J. (1999), *Disagreement: Politics and Philosophy*. Trans. J. Rose. Minneapolis: University of Minnesota Press, pp. 23–26.

[3] Rancière, J. (1974), *La Leçon d'Althusser*. Paris: Gallimard, Chapter 4, pp. 155–203.

[4] Rancière, *La Parole ouvrière*, pp. 284–295.

[5] Rancière, *Disagreement*, pp. 81–94.

[6] Rancière, *The Nights of Labour*, pp. 77–98. Also referred to in Rancière, J. (2010), 'The aesthetic heterotopia,' *Philosophy Today*, 54, 15–25, (the Gauny reference is at pp. 19–20).

[7] Rancière, J. (2003), *The Philosopher and His Poor*. Trans. J. Drury, C. Oyster, A. Parker (ed.), Durham: Duke University Press, p. 208.

[8] Kant, I. (1987), *Critique of Judgement*. Trans. W. Pluhar, Indianapolis, IN: Hackett, §2.

[9] Ibid., §5.

[10] See, for instance, letter 23, in Schiller, F. (2004), *On the Aesthetic Education of Man*. Trans. R. Snell. Mineola, New York: Dover Publications.

[11] Rancière, *The Philosopher and His Poor*, p. 200.

[12] Sartre, J. P. (1988), '*What is Literature?' and Other Essays*. Cambridge, Mass.: Harvard University Press, pp. 109–131.

Bibliography

Aelian (1866) *Claudii Aeliani Varia Historia* Vol. II. R. Hercher (ed.). Leipzig: Teubner.

Althusser, L. (1971) 'Ideology and ideological state apparatuses (notes towards an investigation)', *Lenin and Philosophy, and Other Essays*. Trans. B. Brewster. London: New Left Books.

— (1976) *Essays in Self-Criticism*. New York: Schocken Books.

— (2005) *For Marx* (new edn). Trans. B. Brewster. London: Verso.

Althusser, L., Balibar, E., Establet, R., Macherey, P., and Rancière, J. (1996) *Lire le Capital* (new edn.). Paris: PUF.

Arendt, H. (1958) *The Human Condition*. Chicago: Chicago University Press.

— (1990) *On Revolution*. Harmondsworth: Penguin.

— (1994) *Essays in Understanding: 1930–1955*. J. Kohn (ed.). New York: Harcourt, Brace & Co.

— (2004) *The Origins of Totalitarianism*. New York: Schocken Books.

— (2005) *The Promise of Politics*. J. Kohn (ed.). New York: Schocken Books.

Aristotle, (1965) 'Poetics', in R. Kassel (ed.), *Aristotlis de Arte Poetica Liber*. Oxford: Clarendon.

Arsenjuk, L. (2007) 'On Jacques Rancière', *Eurozine*, 1 March, (accessed 20/5/2011), http://www.eurozine.com/articles/2007-03-01-arsenjuk-en.html.

Badiou, A. (2005) *Metapolitics*. Trans. J. Barker. London and New York: Verso.

— (2009) 'The lessons of Jacques Rancière: knowledge and power after the storm', in G. Rockhill and P. Watts (eds), *Jacques Rancière: History, Politics, Aesthetics*. Durham: Duke University Press.

Balibar, E. (2007) '(De)Constructing the human as human institution: a reflection on the coherence of Hannah Arendt's practical philosophy', *Social Research*, 74 (3), pp. 727–38.

Barthes, R. (1977) 'The third meaning: research notes on some Eisenstein stills', in S. Heath, (ed. and trans.), *Image Music Text*. New York: Hill and Wang.

— (1995) *Michelet*. Paris: Seuil.

Bazin, A. (1967) 'The ontology of the photographic image', *What is Cinema?* Vol. 1. Trans. H. Gray. Berkeley: University of California Press.

Benjamin, W. (1972) 'A short history of photography', *Screen*, 13 (Spring), pp. 5–26.

Bernabé, B. (ed.) (1987) *Poetae et Epici Graeci. Testimonia et Fragmenta. Pars I*. Leipzig: Teubner.

Bernstein, B. (1975) *Class, Codes and Control (Vol 3): Towards a Theory of Educational Transmissions*. London: Routledge.

Bernstein, J. M. (1997) 'Against voluptuous bodies: of satiation without happiness', *New Left Review I*, 225.

Bernstein, R. J. (1986) *Philosophical Profiles: Essays in a Pragmatic Mode*. Cambridge: Polity Press.

Bingham, C. and Biesta, G. (2010) *Jacques Rancière: Education, Truth, Emancipation*. London: Continuum.

Bois, Y. A. and Krauss, R. E. (1997) *Formless: A User's Guide*. New York: Zone Books.

Bourriaud, N. (2009) 'Precarious constructions: answer to Jacques Rancière on art and politics,' *Open*, 17, pp. 20–40.

Bratu Hansen, M. (1997) 'Introduction', in S. Kracauer (ed.), *Theory of Film: The Redemption of Physical Reality*. Princeton: Princeton University Press.

Braudel, F. (1949) *La Méditerranée et le monde méditerranéen à l'époque de Philippe II*. Paris: Colin.

— (1958) 'Histoire et sciences sociales: la longue durée', *Annales E.S.C.*, 13 (4), pp. 725–53.

— (1969) *Ecrits sur l'Histoire*. Paris: Flammarion.

— (1976) *The Mediterranean and the Mediterranean World in the Age of Philip II*. Vols. *I–II*. Trans. S. Reynolds. New York: Harper & Row.

Braverman, H. (1974) *Labour and Monopoly Capitalism: The Degradation of Work In the Twentieth Century*. New York: Monthly Review Press.

Canovan, M. (1992) *Hannah Arendt: A Reinterpretation of Her Political Thought*. Cambridge: Cambridge University Press.

Cavell, S. (1971) *The World Viewed*. Cambridge, MA: Harvard University Press.

— (1979) *The World Viewed, Enlarged Edition*. Cambridge, MA: Harvard University Press.

Chambers, S. A. (2010) 'Police and oligarchy', in J. P. Deranty (ed.), *Jacques Rancière: Key Concepts*. Durham: Acumen.

Christodoulidis, E. and Schaap, A. (forthcoming) 'Arendt's constitutional question', in C. McCorkindale and M. Goldini (eds), *Hannah Arendt and the Law*. Portland: Hart.

Cicero, (1928) *De Republica. De Legibus [On the Republic. On the Laws]*. Trans. C. W. Keyes. Cambridge, MA and London: Harvard University Press.

Collingwood, R. G. (1994) *The Idea of History: With Lectures 1926–1928* (revised edn.). W. J. Van Der Dussen (ed.), Oxford: Oxford University Press.

Confucius, (2003) *Analects, with Selections from Traditional Commentaries*. Trans. E. Slingerland, Indianapolis: Hackett.

Crowder, G. (1991) *Classical Anarchism: The Political Thought of Godwin, Proudhon, Bakunin, and Kropotkin*. Oxford: Clarendon Press.

Debord, G. (1958) 'Théorie de la dérive', *Internationale situationniste*, 2, December.

— (2006) 'Theory of the derive', in K. Knabb (ed. and trans.), *Situationist International Anthology* (revised edn.). Berkeley: Bureau of Public Secrets.

Deleuze, G. (1995) *Negotiations 1972–1990*. Trans. M. Joughin. New York: Columbia University Press.

— (2003) *Deux Régimes de fous. Textes et entretiens 1975–1995*. D. Lapoujade (ed.). Paris: Éditions de Minuit.

— (2004) *Desert Islands and Other Texts 1953–1974*. D. Lapoujade (ed.), Trans. M. Taormina. New York: Semiotext(e).

Deleuze, G. and Foucault, M. (1972) 'Les Intellectuels et le pouvoir', *L'Arc 49: Deleuze*, Paris, pp. 3–10.

Deleuze, G. and Guattari, F. (1994) *What is Philosophy?* Trans. H. Tomlinson and G. Burchell. New York: Columbia University Press.

Deranty, J. P. (2003) 'Rancière and contemporary political ontology', *Theory and Event*, 6 (4).

Deranty, J. P. (ed.) (2010) *Jacques Rancière: Key Concepts*. Durham: Acumen.

Deranty, J. P. and Renault, E. (2009) 'Democratic agon: striving for distinction or struggle against domination and injustice?', in A. Schaap (ed.), *Law and Agonistic Politics*. Farnham: Ashgate.

Derrida, J. (2001) *On Cosmopolitanism and Forgiveness*. Trans M. Dooley and M. Hughes, London and New York: Routledge.

— (2005) *Rogues: Two Essays on Reason*. Trans. P. A. Brault and M. Naas, Stanford: Stanford University Press.

Derry, J. (2004) 'The unity of intellect and will: Vygotsky and Spinoza', *Educational Review*, 56 (2), pp. 113–120.

Dietz, M. (2000) 'Arendt and the Holocaust', in D. Villa (ed.), *The Cambridge Companion to Hannah Arendt*. Cambridge: Cambridge University Press.

Dikeç, M. (forthcoming) 'Politics is sublime', *Environment and Planning D: Society and Space*.

Eggers, D. (2009) *Zeitoun*. San Francisco: McSweeney's.

Febvre, L. (1943) 'Parole, matière première de l'histoire', *Annales d'Histoire sociale*, 15.

Foucault, M. (1988) *Politics Philosophy Culture: Interviews and Other Writings 1977–1984*. L. D. Kritzmann (ed.), Trans. A. Sheridan et al. London: Routledge.

— (1990) *The History of Sexuality: An Introduction Vol. 1*. Trans. R. Hurley. New York: Vintage Books.

— (1997) *Essential Works of Foucault 1954–1984, Volume 1: Ethics: Subjectivity and Truth*. P. Rabinow (ed.), Trans. R. Hurley et al. New York: New Press.

— (2003) *Society Must Be Defended: Lectures at the Collège de France 1975–1976*. Trans. D. Macey. New York: Picador.

— (2007) *Security, Territory, Population: Lectures at the Collège de France 1977–1978*. M. Senellart (ed.), Trans. G. Burchell. New York: Palgrave Macmillan.

— (2008) *The Birth of Biopolitics: Lectures at the Collège de France 1978–1979*. M. Senellart (ed.), Trans. G. Burchell. New York: Palgrave Macmillan.

Frandji, D. and Vitale, P. (eds) (2010) *Knowledge, Pedagogy, and Society: International Perspectives on Basil Bernstein's Sociology of Education*. London: Routledge.

Frank, J. (2010) *Constituent Moments: Enacting the People in Postrevolutionary America* Durham: Duke University Press.

Gee, J. P. (2003) *What Video Games Have to Teach Us About Learning and Literacy*. New York: Palgrave.

— (2004) *Situated Language and Learning: A Critique of Traditional Schooling*. London: Routledge.

Godard, J. L. (1988–1998) *Histoire(s) du Cinema*. Gaumont.

— (1956) 'Montage, mon beau souci', *Cahiers du Cinéma*, 65, pp. 30–31.

— (1986) 'Montage my fine care,' in T. Milne (ed.), *Godard on Godard*. Trans. T. Milne. Cambridge, MA: Da Capo Press, pp. 39–41.

Godard, J. L. and Ishaghpour, Y. (2005) *Cinema: The Archaeology of Film and the Memory of a Century*. Trans. J. Howe. Oxford and New York: Berg.

Goncourt, E. and Goncourt, J. (1981) *French Eighteenth-Century Painters*. Trans. R. Ironside, Oxford: Phaidon.

Gündoğdu, A. (forthcoming) 'Aporias of human rights: Arendt and the "Perplexities of Rights of Man"', *European Journal of Political Theory*.

Heath, S. (1975) 'Film and system: terms of analysis Part I', *Screen*, 16 (1), pp. 7–77.

Hecataeus. (1954) *Hecatei Milesii Fragmenta*. G. Nenci (ed.), Firenze: La Nuova Italia.

Hedges, I. (1993) 'Jean-Luc Godard's *Hail Mary*: Cinema's "Virgin Birth"', in C. Warren and M. Locke (eds), *Jean-Luc Godard's Hail Mary: Women and the Sacred in Film*. Carbondale and Edwardsville: Southern Illinois University Press.

Hegel, G. W. F. (1993) *Introductory Lectures on Aesthetics*. Trans B. Bosanquet and M. Inwood (eds). London: Penguin.

— (1998) *Aesthetics: Lectures on Fine Art Vol. 1*. Trans. T. M. Knox. Oxford: Clarendon Press.

Heidegger, M. (1981) *Nietzsche: Volume 1, 'The Will to Power as Art'*. Trans D. Farrell Krell. London: Routledge.

Henrich, D. (1992) *Aesthetic Judgement and the Moral Image of the World: Studies in Kant*. Stanford, CA: Stanford University Press.

Hinchman, L. P. and Hinchman, S.K. (1984) 'In Heidegger's shadow: Arendt's phenomenological humanism', *The Review of Politics*, 46(2), pp. 183–211.

Honig, B. (1993) *Political Theory and the Displacement of Politics*. Ithaca: Cornell University Press.

Hunt, L. (2007) *Inventing Human Rights*. New York: Norton.

Huret, J. (1994) 'Interview with Stéphane Mallarmé (1891)', in H. Dorra (ed.), *Symbolist Art Theories: A Critical Anthology*. Berkeley: University of California Press.

Ingram, J. D. (2006) 'The subject of the politics of recognition: Hannah Arendt and Jacques Rancière', in G. Bertram, R. Celikates, C. Laudou, and D. Lauer (eds), *Socialité et reconnaissance. Grammaires de l'humain.* Paris: L'Harmattan.

— (2008) 'What is a "Right to Have Rights"? Three images of the politics of human rights', *American Political Science Review*, 102(4), pp. 401–416.

Jacoby, F. (1956) 'Hekataios,' in F. Jacoby, *Griechische Historiker.* Stuttgart: Alfred Druckenmüller Verlag.

Jakobson, R. (1980) 'Two aspects of language and two types of aphasic disturbances', in R. Jakobson and M. Halle (eds), *Fundamentals of Language.* The Hague: Mouton.

Janover, M. (2011) 'Politics and worldliness in the thought of Hannah Arendt', in A. Yeatman, P. Hansen, M. Zolkos, and C. Barbour (eds) *Action and Appearance: Ethics and the Politics of Writing in Hannah Arendt.* London: Continuum.

Jenkins, H. (2004) 'Why Heather can write', *MIT Technology Review.* http://www.technologyreview.com/Biztech/13473/page1/.

Jonas, H. (1984) *The Imperative of Responsibility: In Search of an Ethics for the Technological Age.* Trans. H. Jonas with D. Herr. Chicago: The University of Chicago Press.

Kant, I. (1987) *Critique of Judgement.* Trans. W. Pluhar. Indianapolis, IN: Hackett.

Kantorowicz, E.H. (1997) *The King's Two Bodies: A Study in Medieval Political Theology.* Princeton: Princeton University Press.

Kracauer, S. (1997) *Theory of Film: The Redemption of Physical Reality.* Princeton: Princeton University Press.

Kropotkin, P. (1995) '"Anarchism", from the Encyclopaedia Britannica', in M. Shatz (ed.), *The Conquest of Bread and Other Writings.* Cambridge: Cambridge University Press.

Lacan, J. (1979) *The Four Fundamental Concepts of Psycho-Analysis.* J. A. Miller (ed.), Trans. A. Sheridan. Harmondsworth: Penguin Books.

Lachaud, Y. (1997) 'Les pauvres et leur philosophie', *Critique*, 601–02, pp. 421–445.

Lance, M. (2005) 'Fetishizing Process', *Social Anarchism*, 38.

Lave, J. and Wenger, E. (1991) *Situated Learning: Legitimate Peripheral Participation.* Cambridge: Cambridge University Press.

— (1996) 'Practice, person, social world', In H. Daniels (ed.), *An introduction to Vygotsky.* London: Routledge.

Le Roy Ladurie, E. (1975) *Montaillou, Village Occitan: De 1294 à 1324.* Paris: Gallimard.

Lewis, L., Black, R., and Tomlinson, B. (2009) 'Let everyone play: an educational perspective on why fan fiction is, or should be, legal', *International Journal of Learning and Media*, 1 (1), pp. 67–81.

Lunts, L. (1998) 'In the Desert [V pustyne]', *The Serapion Brothers. Anthology.* Moscow: Shkola-Press.

Malraux, A. (c.1949) *Psychologie de l'art: La Monnaie de l'absolu.* Paris: Albert Skira.

Marchart, O. (2007) *Post-Foundational Political Thought: Political Difference in Nancy, Lefort, Badiou and Laclau.* Edinburgh: Edinburgh University Press.

Markell, P. (2006) 'The rule of the people: Arendt, archê, and democracy', *American Political Science Review*, 100 (1), pp. 1–14.

Marrati, P. (2008) 'A lost everyday: Deleuze and Cavell on Hollywood', *Gilles Deleuze: Cinema and Philosophy.* Trans. A. Hartz. Baltimore: The Johns Hopkins University Press.

Marx, K. (1981) *Capital: A Critique of Political Economy Vol. 3.* Trans. D. Fernbach. London: Penguin Books.

May, T. (2008) *The Political Thought of Jacques Rancière: Creating Equality.* Edinburgh: Edinburgh University Press; Philadelphia, PA: University of Pennsylvania Press.

— (2010) 'Wrong, disagreement, subjectification', in J. P. Deranty (ed.), *Jacques Rancière: Key Concepts.* Durham: Acumen.

— (2010) *Contemporary Movements and the Thought of Jacques Rancière: Equality in Action.* Edinburgh: Edinburgh University Press.

May, T., Noys, B., and Newman, S. (2008) 'Democracy, anarchism and radical politics today: an interview with Jacques Rancière', Trans. J. Lechte, *Anarchist Studies*, 16 (2), pp. 173–186.

McClure, K. M. (2003) 'Disconnections, connections, and questions: reflections on Jacques Rancière's "Ten Theses on Politics"', *Theory and Event*, 6 (4).

McNay, L. (2010) 'Feminism and post-identity politics: the problem of agency', *Constellations*, 17 (4), pp. 512–525.

Mecchia, G. (2010) 'Philosophy and its poor: Rancière's critique of philosophy', in J. P. Deranty (ed.), *Jacques Rancière: Key Concepts*. London: Acumen.

Michelet, J. (1967) *History of the French Revolution*. in G. Wright (ed.), Trans. C. Cocks. Chicago: The University of Chicago Press.

— (1984) *Mother Death. The Journal of Jules Michelet, 1815–1850*. Trans. E. K. Kaplan (ed.). Amherst: The University of Massachusetts Press.

Nikulin, D. (2008) 'Memory and history', *Idealistic Studies*, 38 (1/2), pp. 75–90.

Nora, P. (ed.) (1996) *Realms of Memory: Rethinking the French Past, Volume 1, Conflicts and Divisions*. Trans. A. Goldhammer, L. D. Kritzman (ed.). New York: Columbia University Press.

— (1997) *Realms of Memory: The Construction of the French Past, Volume 2, Traditions*. Trans. A. Goldhammer, L. D. Kritzman (ed.). New York: Columbia University Press.

— (1998) *Realms of Memory: The Construction of the French Past, Volume 3, Symbols*. Trans. A. Goldhammer, L. D. Kritzman (ed.). New York: Columbia University Press.

Nordmann, C. (2006) *Bourdieu/Rancière: La Politique entre sociologie et philosophie*. Paris: Editions Amsterdam.

Panagia, D. (2001) 'Ceci n'est pas un argument: an introduction to the ten theses', *Theory and Event*, 5 (3).

Parekh, B. (1979) 'Hannah Arendt's critique of Marx', in M. Hill (ed.), *Hannah Arendt: The Recovery of the Public World*. New York: St Martin's Press.

— (1981) *Hannah Arendt and the Search for a New Political Philosophy*. London: Macmillan.

Pasquier, R. (2004) 'Politiques de la lecture', *Labyrinthes*, 17 (1), pp. 33–63.

Patton, P. (2010) *Deleuzian Concepts: Philosophy, Colonization, Politics*. Stanford: Stanford University Press.

Pelletier, C. (2009) 'Education, equality and emancipation: Rancière's critique of Bourdieu and the question of performativity', *Discourse: Studies in the Cultural Politics of Education*, 30 (2), pp. 137–150.

—(2009) 'Rancière and the poetics of the social sciences', *International Journal of Research & Method in Education*, 32 (3), pp. 267–284.

Perkins, V. F. (1993) *Film as Film: Understanding and Judging Movies*. New York: De Capo Press.

Pitkin, H. (1981) 'Justice: on relating public and private,' *Political Theory*, 9 (3), pp. 327–352.

Plato (2005) *Laws*. Trans. T. Saunders. London: Penguin.

— (2005) *Phaedrus*. Trans. C. Rowe. London: Penguin.

Power, N. (2009) 'Axiomatic equality: Rancière and the politics of contemporary education', *Polygraph*, 21.

Propp, V. (1968) *Morphology of the Folk Tale*. L.A. Wagner (ed.), Trans. L. Scott. Austin: University of Texas Press.

Proust, M. (1932) *Remembrance of Things Past: Volume Two*. Trans. by C.K. Scott Moncrieff. New York: Random House.

Rancière, J. (1973) 'Mode d'emploi pour une réédition de Lire le Capital', *Les Temps Modernes*, 328, pp. 788–807.

— (1974) 'On the theory of ideology (the politics of Althusser)', *Radical Philosophy*, 7 (2), pp. 2–15.

— (1974) *La Leçon d'Althusser*. Paris: Gallimard.

— (1976) 'How to use "Lire le Capital"', *Economy and Society*, 5 (3), pp. 377–384.

— (1981) *La Nuit des prolétaires. Archives du rêve ouvrier*. Paris: Hachette.

— (1983) *Le Philosophe plébéien Louis-Gabriel Gauny.* Paris: Presses Universitaires de Vincennes.

— (1983) 'The myth of the artisan: critical reflections on a category of social history', *International Labour and Working Class History*, 24, pp. 1–16.

— (1983) *Le Philosophe et ses pauvres.* Paris: Fayard.

— (1987) *Le Maître ignorant: Cinq Leçons sur l'émancipation intellectuelle.* Paris: Fayard.

— (1989) *The Nights of Labour: The Workers Dream in Nineteenth Century France.* Philadelphia: Temple University Press.

— (1991) *The Ignorant Schoolmaster: Five Lessons in Intellectual Emancipation.* Trans. K. Ross. Stanford: Stanford University Press.

— (1992) *Les Noms de l'histoire: Essai de poétique du savoir.* Paris: Seuil.

— (1994) *The Names of History. On the Poetics of Knowledge.* Trans. H. Melehy, Minneapolis: University of Minnesota Press.

— (1995) *La Mésentente:Politique et philosophie.* Paris: Galilée.

— (1995) *On the Shores of Politics.* Trans. L. Heron. London: Verso.

— (1996) 'Le concept de critique et la critique de l'économie politique des *Manuscrits* de 1844 au *Capital*', in L. Althusser, E. Balibar, R. Establet, P. Macherey, and J. Rancière (eds), *Lire le Capital* (new edn.). Paris: PUF.

— (1998) *La Parole muette. Essai sur les contradictions de la littérature.* Paris: Hachette Littératures.

— (1999) *Disagreement: Politics and Philosophy.* Trans. J. Rose. Minneapolis: University of Minnesota Press.

— (2000) *Le Partage du sensible: Esthétique et politique.* Paris: La Fabrique Éditions.

— (2001) *L'Inconscient esthétique.* Paris: Galilée.

—(2001) 'Ten theses on politics', Trans. D. Panagia and R. Bowlby, *Theory and Event,* 5 (3).

— (2002) 'The aesthetic revolution and its outcomes: emplotments of autonomy and heteronomy', *New Left Review*, 14 (March/April), pp. 133–151.

— (2003) *Les Scènes du peuple.* Paris: Horlieu.

— (2003) *Le Destin des images.* Paris: La Fabrique Éditions.

— (2003) *The Philosopher and His Poor.* Trans. J. Drury, C. Oyster, and A. Parker (eds). Durham: Duke University Press.

— (2003) 'Comment and responses', *Theory and Event*, 6 (4).

— (2004) 'The politics of literature', *SubStance,* 33 (1), pp. 10–24.

— (2004) *The Flesh of Words: The Politics of Writing.* Trans. C. Mandell. Stanford: Stanford University Press.

— (2004) 'Aesthetics, inaesthetics, anti-aesthetics', in P. Hallward (ed.), *Think Again: Alain Badiou and the Future of Philosophy.* London: Continuum.

— (2004) *The Politics of Aesthetics: The Distribution of the Sensible.* Trans. G. Rockhill. New York: Continuum.

— (2004) 'Who is the subject of the rights of man?', *South Atlantic Quarterly*, 103 (2–3), pp. 297–310.

— (2005) 'Literary misunderstanding', *Paragraph*, 28 (2), pp. 91–103.

— (2005) 'L'héritage difficile de Michel Foucault', *Chroniques des temps consensuels.* Paris: Éditions du Seuil.

— (2005) *La Haine de la démocratie.* Paris: La Fabrique Éditions.

— (2006) *Hatred of Democracy.* Trans. S. Corcoran. London: Verso.

— (2006) *Film Fables.* Trans. E. Battista. Oxford: Berg.

— (2006) 'Thinking between disciplines: an aesthetics of knowledge', Trans. J. Roffe, *Parrhesia*, 1, pp. 1–12.

— (2007) *The Future of the Image.* Trans. G. Elliot. New York and London: Verso.

— (2007) *Politique de la littérature.* Paris: Galilée.

— (2008) 'Why Emma Bovary had to be killed', *Critical Inquiry,* 34 (2), pp. 233–248.

— (2008) 'Les mésaventures de la pensée critique', *Le Spectateur émancipé*. Paris: La Fabrique Éditions.

— (2009) *Moments Politiques: Interventions 1977–2009*. Paris: La Fabrique Éditions.

— (2009) *Aesthetics and its Discontents*. Trans. S. Corcoran. Malden, MA: Polity.

— (2009) 'Des communistes sans communisme', *Moments Politiques: Interventions 1977–2009*. Paris: La Fabrique Éditions.

— (2010) 'The aesthetic heterotopia,' *Philosophy Today*, 54, pp. 15–25.

— (2010) *Dissensus: On Politics and Aesthetics*. Trans. S. Corcoran (ed.). London: Continuum.

— (2011) *The Politics of Literature*. Cambridge: Polity Press.

Rancière, J. and Faure, A. (eds) (2007) *La Parole ouvrière*. Paris, La Fabrique Éditions.

Rancière, J. and Hallward, P. (2003) 'Politics and aesthetics: an interview', *Angelaki*, 8 (2), pp. 191–211.

Rancière, J. and Panagia, D. (2000) 'Dissenting words: a conversation with Jacques Rancière', *Diacritics*, 30 (2), pp. 113–126.

Rattansi, A. (ed.) (1989) *Ideology, Method and Marx*. London, Routledge.

Rawls, J. (2001) *Justice as Fairness: A Restatement*. E. Kelly (ed.). Cambridge, MA: Harvard University Press.

— (2005) 'The idea of public reason revisited: (1997),' in J. Rawls (ed.). *Political Liberalism* (expanded edn.). New York: Columbia University Press.

Renault, E. (2011) 'Comment Marx se réfère-t-il au travail et à la domination?', *Actuel Marx*, 49, pp. 15–31.

Rochex, J. Y. (2010) 'The work of Basil Bernstein: a non-sociologistic and therefore non-deterministic sociology', in D. Frandji and P. Vitale (eds), *Knowledge, Pedagogy, and Society: International Perspectives on Basil Bernstein's Sociology of Education*. London: Routledge.

Rosenbaum, J. (2009) 'Trailer for Godard's Histoire(s) du Cinéma', (accessed 17/02/2011) http://www.jonathanrosenbaum.com/?p = 15760 (revised January 2009). Originally published (1997) in *Trafic*, 21, Printemps.

Ross, A. (2007) 'The aesthetic anomaly: art, politics and criticism in recent European philosophy (from Adorno to Rancière)', *Theory@buffalo*, 11, pp. 97–121.

Ross, A. (2009) 'The aesthetic fable: cinema in Jacques Rancière's "Aesthetic Politics"', *SubStance*, 38 (1), pp. 128–151.

Ross, K. (1991) 'Introduction', in J. Rancière (ed.), *The Ignorant Schoolmaster: Five Lessons in Intellectual Emancipation*. Stanford: Stanford University Press.

Ross, K. (2002) *May'68 and its Afterlives*. Chicago: Chicago University Press.

Sartre, J. P. (1988) *What is Literature? and Other Essays*. Cambridge, MA: Harvard University Press.

Schaap, A. (2010) 'The politics of need', in A. Schaap, D. Celermajer, and V. Karalis (eds), *Power, Judgment and Political Evil: In Conversation with Hannah Arendt*. Farnham: Ashgate.

Schaap, A. (2011) 'Enacting the "right to have rights": Jacques Rancière's critique of Hannah Arendt', *European Journal of Political Theory*, 10 (1): pp. 22–45.

Schiller, F. (2004) *On the Aesthetic Education of Man*. Trans. R. Snell, Mineola, NY: Dover Publications.

Scholles, R. (1974) *Structuralism in Literature: An Introduction*. New Haven and London: Yale University Press.

Sontag, S. (2001) 'A century of cinema', in S. Sontag (ed.), *Where the Stress Falls: Essays*. New York: Farrar, Straus and Giroux.

Tacitus. (1931) *Histories, Books 4–5. Annals, Books 1–3*. Trans. C. H. Moore and J. Jackson, Cambridge. MA and London: Harvard University Press.

Taminiaux, J. (1997) *The Thracian Maid and the Professional Thinker: Arendt and Heidegger*. Trans. M. Gendre. Albany: State University of New York Press.

Tchir, T. (2011) 'Daimon appearances and the Heideggerian influence in Arendt's account of political action', in A. Yeatman, P. Hansen, M. Zolkos, and C. Barbour (eds), *Action and Appearance: Ethics and the Politics of Writing in Hannah Arendt*. London: Continuum.

Thompson, K. (1999) 'The concept of cinematic excess', in L. Braudy and M. Cohen (eds), *Film Theory and Criticism: Introductory Readings* (fifth edn.). New York: Oxford University Press.

Todorov, T. (1981) 'Les catégories du récit litteraire', *L'Analyse structurale du récit*. Paris: Seuil.

Vermeren, P. (2008) 'Equality and democracy', *Diogenes*, 55 (4), pp. 55–68.

Villa, D. R. (1996) *Arendt and Heidegger: The Fate of the Political*. Princeton: Princeton University Press.

Ward, C. (1988) *Anarchy in Action*. London: Freedom Press.

West, M. L. (ed.) (2003) *Greek Epic Fragments. From the Seventh to the Fifth Centuries B.C.* Trans. M. L. West. Cambridge, MA: Harvard University Press.

White, H. (1994) 'Foreword', in J. Rancière (ed.), Trans. H. Melehy, *The Names of History. On the Poetics of Knowledge*. Minneapolis: University of Minnesota Press.

Whiteman, N. (2007) *The Establishment, Maintenance, and Destabilisation of Fandom: A Study of Two Online Communities and an Exploration of Issues Pertaining to Internet Research*. PhD Thesis, Institute of Education, University of London, http://homepage.mac.com/paulcdowling/ioe/studentswork/whiteman.html.

Whyte, J. (2009) 'Particular rights and absolute wrongs: Giorgio Agamben on life and politics', *Law and Critique*, 20, pp. 147–161.

Wolin, S. (1990) 'Hannah Arendt: democracy and the political', in R. Garner (ed.), *The Realm of Humanitas: Responses to the Writings of Hannah Arendt*. New York: Peter Lang.

Wollen, P. (1999) 'Godard and counter cinema: *vent d'est*', in L. Braudy and M. Cohen (eds), *Film Theory and Criticism: Introductory Readings* (fifth edn.). New York: Oxford University Press.

Wood, M. (1989) *America in the Movies*. New York: Columbia University Press.

Index